A DISCIPLESHIP Journey

A GUIDE FOR MAKING DISCIPLES THAT MAKE DISCIPLE-MAKERS

DAVID BUEHRING

HIGHERLIFE
DEVELOPMENT SERVICES, INC

Oviedo, Florida

A Discipleship Journey
A Guide for Making Disciples That Make Disciple-Makers
Copyright © 2004 by David K. Buehring

Published by: HigherLife Publishing
                400 Fontana Circle
                Building 1 – Suite 105
                Oviedo, Florida 32765
                (407) 563-4806
                www.ahigherlife.com

Printed in the United States of America
ISBN 13: 978-1-935245-53-7
ISBN 10: 1-935245-53-8

Third Edition

Cover and Book Design: Corrie Commisso
For additional copies, visit www.lionshare.org

*Dedicated to those who have set their heart to
obey the disciple-making mandate of Jesus. May you
be renewed by His Presence and empowered by His
Spirit to fulfill this mission where He has appointed
you to serve.*

Table of Contents

Acknowledgements

I am deeply humbled and extremely grateful for the many people that Jesus has brought into my life on my own discipleship journey. In reality, this book is simply a compiling of the deposits of numerous godly leaders, teachers, disciple-makers, mentors, coaches, challengers, encouragers and friends that have impacted my life. Without their investment in me, what you hold in your hands would not be possible. I honor each of them in my heart.

From Lutheran pastors in my early years, to Youth With A Mission leaders and teachers in my late-teens to mid-twenties, to Messenger Associates that I've walked with for years and older godly spiritual fathers – I will always be very thankful for those who have pushed me closer to the heart of God and have taught me His ways. Among them are men like Loren Cunningham, Winkie Pratney, Steve Fry and John Dawson, just to name a few. There are those, too, at the University of the Nations and Regent University who challenged me to become a student of God's Word – people like Ron & Judy Smith. And, of course, there are the authors, many of whom I have never had the privilege of meeting, who have shaped me through their lives and the words they have written (see the bibliography in the back if you want to taste of their lives as well).

There have also been many teammates, staff and friends along the way that Jesus has used to model His character and to speak into my life. From dear YWAM friends in Kona and around the world, to the flocks of Valley Christian Fellowship, The Grace Community, Belmont Church and Grace Chapel that I have served with, to the Messenger Fellowship community of leaders that has become my 'tribe' and to the many I have encountered along the way while leading the Lionshare Leadership Group. My life has been forever marked because of your influence.

Dad and Mom, thank you for pointing me to Jesus and giving me a good start on my journey. Tom, thanks for your love and friendship – you are a friend that sticks closer than a brother.

Ryan and Malia – you are the best! You have taught me more about God and His ways than any one on earth through the privilege of being your Dad. I love you and am proud of you, and my greatest anticipation in life is watching what God will do in and through you in the days ahead to change the world.

Cheryl, what an absolute gift you are to me. I could not have made it here without your love, companionship, support and prayers. You, more than any other, have unselfishly sacrificed to help me learn many of God's ways penned here. I appreciate you listening to my heart, standing with me in my dreams and faithfully walking beside me day-by-day – it continues to mean more to me than you will ever know. I love you.

I want to extend special thanks to several others who helped me in the creating of this resource. Much applause goes to Elizabeth DeBeasi and Vicki Campbell for their tireless work in the developmental process, and to Corrie Commisso for her layout and design. Many thanks to Steve Berger and Matt Dolan for helping me make the video component of this resource a reality. I am also very grateful for David Welday and his team at Higher Life for their work and counsel in developing our new 'disciple-making starter kit'. I couldn't have done it without all of your help.

Finally, I am eternally grateful to the Lord Jesus. I am well aware (as are those who know me) that apart from Him I can do absolutely nothing of any consequence. In Him I can continue to learn to love well, obey well, serve well and finish well. By His grace – and for His glory – that is my aim.

David Buehring

How To Effectively Use **A Discipleship Journey**

'Making Disciples That Make Disciple-Makers'

A *Discipleship Journey (ADJ)* has been created in such a way that you can use it in multiple kinds of settings with various groupings of people (leaders, small groups, men, women, youth, young adults, etc.). The primary way it is used is as a one-year discipleship journey, utilizing the 12-15 minute video teachings – four for each of the 12 chapters – over a period of 48 weeks. The video teachings work side-by-side with the assigned study/reflection portions below. If you would like to purchase the video component or additional books visit www.lionshare.org.

One suggested method of walking through this series is within a small group, providing you with an opportunity to share the experience of learning and growing together. This approach begins with each person committing to be in the Scriptures and in their ADJ manual for 60-90 minutes each week working on the assigned pages, along with reflecting on one of attributes of God's character from the back of the manual. When the small group participants gather, they take the first 20-30 minutes to share what they've learned and are applying in their lives. They then view the next 12-15 minute video in the series, discussing together for 15-20 minutes what they've just heard. The group then closes in prayer by praying for each other to fully embrace and engage the obedience and application points highlighted to them by the Holy Spirit through the Scriptures and the ADJ material. The process then starts over and is repeated over the period of 48 weeks. The focus is always obeying God through life application. The aim is making disciples so each participant can become an effective disciple-maker, repeating the process with those God has brought in to their lives.

A Discipleship Journey Week-by-Week

CHAPTER 1
KNOWING GOD

 ## A VIEW FROM THE SHORE

"This is what the Lord says: 'Let not the wise man boast of his wisdom or the strong man boast of his strength or the rich man boast of his riches, but let him who boasts boast about this: that he understands and knows me, that I am the Lord, who exercises kindness, justice and righteousness on the earth, for in these I delight,' declares the Lord."

Jeremiah 9:23, 24

Who is God and what is He really like? I'm not talking about the image of God that we conjure up in our minds or that the devil has tried to establish in our thinking. I'm referring to who He really is. God has chosen to reveal Himself to us in ways we can understand and relate to. He so wants us to know Him that He went as far as sending Jesus to Earth so we would experience Him—God as man, One who has walked among us. And Jesus tells us, "Anyone who has seen Me has seen the Father" (Jn. 14:9).

Scripture paints an indelible portrait of God, illustrating what He's like. Through the names and titles attributed to Him, He reveals His nature, personality and character. In the book of Revelation, alone, we see God on full display. He is the Alpha and Omega (the beginning and the end), the One who was and is and is to come, the Living One, the One who holds the keys to death and hell. He is revealed as the Lord God Almighty, the Lamb of God, the King of Kings and the Lord of Lords, the One who sits upon the throne, the Ruler of the kings of the Earth, the One the nations worship. He is holy (set-apart) and worthy to receive honor, glory and praise. And that's only a sampling of the attributes found in this one book of the Bible. Imagine how much more we can know Him as we gaze through all 66 books!

I believe that from the beginning of our lives the devil tries to distort the character of God to prevent us from knowing our Creator. Strategically harassing us with lies and accusations that play on the hurts of our hearts, or taunting us with our own sinful choices, Satan lodges a dark and distorted image of God in our hearts and minds—an image that doesn't remotely resemble the God revealed to us in Scripture. Because sin has entered the world, this is true to some degree for all of us.

Think for a moment. What factors have shaped your impression of God? Could a difficult relationship have tainted your perception of His character? Maybe you experienced a negative event through which the devil has lied to you about who God is. Perhaps your background includes other religious philosophies or worldviews that superimpose false beliefs upon God's true nature. Maybe your view of God was shaped through an empty church life, lacking in fruit and void of love.

In this chapter, you will have an opportunity to see God for who He really is according to the scriptures. To further help, in the back of the book you'll find 52 reflections on God's character—one for each week of the year. Pause now as you begin and ask God to reveal Himself to you in this chapter.

1

SETTING SAIL

God invites us to know Him personally, not merely to know *of* or *about* Him. He desires to draw us into a real relationship, a relationship as personal and tangible as the most enduring we've experienced in life. He desires for us to have first-hand knowledge of Him, <u>not to settle on the second-hand hearsay of others. He calls us to know Him for ourselves.</u>

Many men and women in Scripture knew God intimately. They pursued God with a passion that allowed Him to reveal Himself to them. Abraham was called a friend of God (Jam. 2:23), Moses spoke to Him face-to-face (Ex. 33:7-11), David's one desire was to gaze upon His beauty (Ps. 27:4). Mary just wanted to sit at Jesus' feet (Lk. 10:38-42), and Paul was willing to forsake everything to know Him (Phil. 3:7-14).

God In Relationship

Throughout Scripture vivid accounts of people who experienced God in a significant relationship speak to our lives and reveal what it means to *know* God. Consider these few examples:

Adam & Eve – Gen. 2 & 3
- God created them and breathed life into them.
- He allowed Adam to team with him in the naming of the animals.
- He met their needs: Adam's for a suitable helper, their need to be clothed.
- God communed with them. They recognized the sound of Him walking in the garden.

Enoch – Gen. 5:24; Heb. 11:5
- The Bible tells us that Enoch walked with God.

Abraham & Sarah
- Abraham knew God's calling on his life and God's intention to bless him (Gen. 12:1-3).
- God made a covenant with Abraham and revealed Himself to him (Gen. 15,17).
- God visited Abraham & Sarah (Gen. 18:1-15).

THOUGHTS & NOTES

- The mere fact that Adam & Eve could recognize God being with them blows my mind.
- Also makes me sad that others dont want to have a relationship with Him. ☺

- Abraham encountered God in the place of prayer (Gen. 18:16-33).
- Abraham experienced God in the place of obedience (Gen. 22:1-19).
- God called him His friend (2 Chr. 20:7; Is. 41:8; Jam. 2:23).

Moses
- God met Moses at the burning bush where He reveals His character, His name and His call to him (Ex. 3,4).
- God revealed His power to Moses the first of many times (Ex. 4:1-9).
- Moses found favor with God (Ex. 32:7-14).
- Moses spoke face-to-face with God as a man speaks to his friend (Ex. 33:7-11).
- Moses desired to know God's ways so that he might know Him (Ex. 33:13; Ps. 103:7).
- When Moses asked God to show him His glory, God revealed Himself to Moses by passing by him while declaring His character (Ex. 33:18-34,7).

David
- David was a man after God's own heart (1 Sam. 13:14, Acts 13:22,36).
- His single greatest desire was to know God (Ps .27:4). *This is what mine should be.
- David's songs (Psalms) reveal much about what he knew about the character of God (Ps. 145).
- Because David knew God he did great exploits for God (1 Sam. 17).

Jesus
- Jesus spoke with God as His Father, and encouraged us to do the same (Mt. 6:9-13).
- He spent time alone with the Father in prayer (Mt. 14:23; Lk. 6:12-16. 22:39-44).
- Jesus knew His Father's heart and will (Jn. 5:19,20, 12: 49,50).
- Jesus desired to bring the Father glory (Jn. 17:4, 5).
- Jesus desired His disciples to know God as intimately as He does (Jn. 17:23-26).

God invites us to know Him personally, not merely to know of or about Him.

The main thing about Christianity is not the work we do, but the relationship we maintain and the atmosphere produced by that relationship. That is all God asks us to look after, and it is the one thing that is being continually assailed.

Oswald Chambers, 1874-1917, Scottish Preacher

Martha & Mary

- They ministered to Jesus personally in their home (Lk. 10:38-42).
- Mary sat at the feet of Jesus learning from Him (Lk. 10:38-42).
- They experienced Jesus as the resurrection and the life at the raising of their brother, Lazarus (Jn .11:1-44).

Paul

- Jesus revealed Himself to Saul (Paul) on the road to Damascus while he was on the way to persecute the church (Acts 9:1-19).
- Paul's greatest desire was to know Jesus better (Phil. 3:7-14).
- Paul's mission and prayer was that people would know Jesus better (Eph. 1:17).

Knowing God In Scripture

God's Attributes

God reveals Himself in the Scriptures through His names, titles and attributes. As you read through the Bible, note each time you come across an expression of God's character. Pay close attention to the context of each reference as it may provide further insights into that trait of God. For example, when you read through the book of John, note references such as:

- He is the *Word*, the *Lamb of God* and a *Teacher* (John 1)
- He is the *God of Miracles* and the *Cleanser of the Temple* (John 2).
- He is a *Good Shepherd*, a *Father* and Jesus is revealed as *God's Son* (John 10).
- He is the *True Vine*, the *Gardener*, and the *Counselor* (John 15).

God's Ways

Insights into God's heart, mind and attitudes reveal His ways and His principles for living in His Kingdom, which is another way to get to know Him. We must consider that God's ways are not our ways, nor are they the ways of the world (Is. 55:8,9). Moses desired to know God's ways so that He could know God better (Ex. 33:13). David cried out for God to show him His ways (Ps. 25:4,5). Here are some examples of the Ways of God:

- If you want to really live you must first die to yourself (Lk. 9:23-25).
- When you walk in humility you will experience the grace of God (Jam. 4:6).
- To walk in wisdom you must first walk in the Fear of the Lord (Prov. 9:10).
- To become great in God's Kingdom you must become the greatest servant (Mt. 20:25-28).

THOUGHTS & NOTES

God's Works

God's acts and behavior display who He is and what He is like.

- The parting of the Red Sea for His people displays His power, protection and a commitment to His promises (Ex.14, 15).
- David's defeat of Goliath demonstrates God's ability to accomplish much through those who are willing to be used by Him for His purposes (1 Sam. 17).
- The story of Job lets us in on what transactions often occur in the spiritual realm around us and how God displays His glory through them (Job).
- The way Jesus handled the situation of the woman caught in adultery shows us the extent of God's forgiveness (Jn. 8:1-11).

God's Words

What God says provides us with opportunities to know and understand Him better. *true.*

- "Let us make man in our own image, in our likeness..." reveals God's heart and plan in creating man. The "us" also unveils the Trinity to us in creation (Gen. 1:26).
- "Honor your father and mother...You shall not murder. You shall not commit adultery. You shall not steal..." demonstrate God's desire for healthy relationships (Ex. 20:12-15).
- "I am the way, the truth and the life. No one comes to the Father except through me..." shows us the only way to relate to God is through the Person of Jesus Christ (Jn. 14:6).
- "It is more blessed to give than to receive..." reveals God's heart towards giving (Acts 20:35).

God reveals Himself in the Scriptures through His names, titles and attributes.

We are at this moment as close to God as we really choose to be.
True, there are times when we would like to know a deeper intimacy,
but when it comes to the point, we are not prepared to pay the price involved.

J. Oswald Sanders, 1902-1992, New Zealand Theologian and Missionary Leader

Experiencing God In Your Life

Just as we would invest in our earthly relationships and spend significant time with the people we love, respect and admire, we are invited to invest in our relationship with Jesus. God desires to meet with us to convey the realness of His Person and Presence. We can know Him intimately and personally.

Seek God

Those who seek Him with their whole hearts will find Him (Jer. 29:13). When you spend time in the scriptures and live in relationship with God, pay close attention to how He reveals more of His character and ways to you.

Love God

Express your love for God in worship. Use what you are learning about His character to declare your adoration of Him to Him. Use the book of Psalms as a worship songbook from which to bring Him thanksgiving, praise and worship. (Mt. 22:37,38).

Pray to God

Bring before Him the things He has laid upon your heart to pray for. As you do, He may give you specifics on how He wants you to pray. This allows you to team with God in advancing His Kingdom (Jn. 15:7,8).

Wait on God

Build time into your life to quietly wait on God and allow Him to speak to your heart. Learning to listen to His voice is essential for following Jesus (Ps. 37:7; Jn. 10:27).

Obey God

One of the greatest ways you can know and experience God is by walking daily in obedience to Him. As God leads and guides you, obey Him completely. Cultivate a heart that delights to obey Him (Jn. 14:23). *I can see in myself I am beginning to form that :)*

One of the greatest ways you can know and experience God is by walking daily in obedience to him.

OBEDIENCE

THOUGHTS & NOTES

I need to become more comfortable praising God openly in private & in public.

I want to hear God speak to me.

Trust God

There are times during our walk with God that we are not seeing the fruit or results that we would like to see. This doesn't mean that God's not working. We must simply trust Him with the circumstances of our lives, even when we don't understand (Prov. 3:5,6).

Fear God

At all times, we must walk in reverence and awe of who God is, remembering it is He who made us, we are the work of His hands. Knowing His character and ways allows us to walk humbly before Him, keeping our relationship with Him in proper perspective (Prov. 9:10; Is. 64:8).

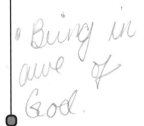
• Being in awe of God.

Hindrances To Knowing God

Sometimes we grow distant from good friends. Our paths diverge for other interests and we lose sight of a relationship that had once been important to us. The same can happen in our relationship to God. Though He never removes Himself from us, we can lose sight of Him because of the distractions of this world. Here are a few of the factors that threaten to hinder our relationship with God.

Distortion

False views of what God is really like can keep us from touching His heart. Make sure you allow the scriptures to renew your heart and mind according to who He really is.

Apathy

Riches, material possessions and being overfed spiritually without giving to others can make one apathetic towards God and His purposes. This doesn't mean that wealth and material goods are evil. It does mean that we must consider the things that God has blessed us with as something He has given us to bless others and to use for the advancement of His Kingdom.

Independence

It's easy to start relying on our wisdom and experiences, subtly withdrawing from relying on God's truth and counsel. The whole essence of our walk with Him is living in complete dependence upon his character and presence in our lives.

• the goal is to not become independent without God.

Sin

This refers to our sinful choices as well as being sinned against. We must guard our hearts from sin, bitterness and resentment, as these eat away at the foundation of our friendship with God.

★ • Forgive myself for past mistakes.

The greatest competitor of devotion to Jesus is service for Him. The one aim of the call of God is the satisfaction of God, not a call to do something for Him.

Oswald Chambers, 1874-1917, Scottish Preacher

Busyness

If the devil can't persuade you to sin, he'll attempt to busy you into distraction. Beware of times in your life when you've become so busy you can't seem to afford time alone with Jesus.

Pride

When it becomes all about us, instead of about Jesus, watch out. Beware of success' trappings. God will not share His glory with another.

Idolatry

Have you placed anything in your life above Jesus? How about your possessions or activities? Where do your relationships stand, including your relationship with your spouse and children? Has ministry risen above the One in whose name you minister? Stop, and look at what your life says about your heart. *— get priorities in check.*

deeper waters

*The Nature of God**

God's nature is multifaceted. The following qualities are intrinsic to who He is.

God is Living – Dt. 5:26; Rev. 1:18

Throughout the Old and New Testament God is declared to be living and alive. *God is alive.*

- "As the Lord lives" was an Old Testament expression used as an oath (1 Sam. 14:39,45).
- Peter's declaration about Jesus stated that He was "the Christ...the son of the living God" (Mt. 16:16).
- Believers are referred to as the "temple of the living God" (2 Cor. 6:16). *I am a temple of God + I need to represent Him well.*
- Angels bear "the seal of the living God" (Rev. 7:2).

This truth serves in contrast to worshiping an idol or graven image, which is lifeless. *= Include Him in all parts of my life.*

THOUGHTS & NOTES
○ Always make time for Jesus.

* I would like to acknowledge Dr. J. Rodman Williams, a professor at Regent University's School of Divinity in Virginia Beach, VA, whose lectures and mat rials on God, the World and Redemption have helped shape my understanding of the nature of God, the Trinity, and the character of God. I have gleane from his material on these subjects and it is used here with his expressed permission.

- Because He is the living God, He is able to give life, renew life and bring it back from the dead (Jn. 11:17-44).
- He is the One who gives eternal life (Jn. 3:15, 16,36).
- God is contemporaneous, meaning that He has not just been alive in the past, but is intensely alive at this very moment.

(ETERNAL)

God is Spirit – Jn. 4:24

God is incorporeal, meaning that He has no body and is not made of blood, flesh and bones. His reality is entirely spiritual.

- He does not have the bodily visibility of man (1 Tim. 1:17).
- Since His being is formless, He may be seen through His own self-revelation in Scripture.
- To behold God is impossible in man's present state. It would be to his own destruction (Ex. 33:20).
- When Jesus came to Earth, He came in bodily form and had a body like our own in every way (1 Jn. 1:1-4) and in the end we shall see His face (Rev. 22:4).

God is dynamic. As Spirit, He is unbound, free and uncoerced.

- He knows no limits of any kind. He is totally free to express Himself and do as He wills. His being is utter spontaneity (2 Cor. 3:17).
- There are no boundaries or limitations of any kind within Him. He is not bound by internal struggle or driven by inner needs.
- He is not bound by His creation or its laws and structures. He moves freely within His created order and can move beyond it, acting in ways that surpass what He has revealed to man.
- He cannot be held ransom by man. He is not compelled by obligation, but acts according to His supreme will.
- God's actions are not arbitrary, based on whim. His will rises from His character, which is perfect holiness, justice, love, wisdom, etc.

God is dynamic. As Spirit, He is unbound, free and uncoerced.

I believe there is nothing lovelier, deeper, more sympathetic, and more perfect than the Savior; there is in the world only one figure of absolute beauty: Christ.

Fyodor Dostoyevsky, 1821-1881, Russian Novelist, Journalist, Short-Story Writer

God is Personal
God purposefully reveals who He is in the scriptures.
- He desires for us to know Him.
- Because He is personal, Scripture employs many names, titles and attributes to depict what one name cannot.

We see His personal relationships with people.
- Throughout Scripture God speaks to people and people to Him (Ex. 33:11; Acts 9:1-19).
- He enters into covenants with others (Gen. 9:8-17; Gen. 17:7,8; 2 Sam. 7:11-16).
- God communicates His essence to people through the use of anthropomorphic pictures—that is, He depicts Himself as one with personal traits like laughter, anger, sorrow; or with physical attributes, as One possessing eyes, arms, hands, etc. (Ps. 2; Is. 40:10-12).

He offers us a portrait of Himself in the person of Jesus (Mt. 1:23; Jn. 14:9).
- Jesus came to earth as a human being—at once, fully God and fully man (Jn. 1:1-14; 1 Jn. 1:1-4).
- He was born (Lk. 2:7) and experienced childhood (Lk. 2:40,52).
- He had a mind (Lk. 2:52), a soul (Jn. 12:27), and emotions (Jn. 11:35; Heb. 5:8,9).
- He became tired (Jn. 4:6), hungry, and thirsty (Mt. 4:11; Jn. 19:28).
- People viewed Jesus as a man (Mt. 13:55,56; Mk. 6:3).

God is Infinite
- He transcends space (1 Ki. 8:27; Job 11:7-9).
- God is unconfined, unlimited, and unbounded, while human beings are restrained by space.
- God is Most High, exalted above everything human, earthly and heavenly.

God is Eternal
- He transcends time (Ps. 90:4; 2 Pet. 3:8).
- God transcends and overarches time, while our years are limited.
- He is the everlasting God who has no beginning, no middle, no end. He beholds the end from the beginning (Rev. 4:8).
- God has no progression of days, years, decades, centuries. God is.

THOUGHTS & NOTES

God is Unchanging

- God transcends His creation.
- God's nature and character is unchanging (Mal. 3:6).
- God is without fluctuation. He is constant and stable in all that He is.
- When the Bible refers to God "changing His mind", this emphasizes God's response to man and man's behavior. This "change of mind" is not really a change in God at all but rather a bringing to bear of some other aspect of His character and being based on man's response to Him (Ex. 32:14; Num. 23:19; Jonah 3:1-10).

God is Omnipotent

- God is all-powerful.
- God's power is attested to throughout Scriptures (Ex. 15:6; Rom. 1:16; Eph. 1:19).
- He is God Almighty. No task is beyond His capability to accomplish (Gen. 18:14; Jer. 32:17; Mt. 19:26).
- He is the God of miracles, performing the extraordinary and the supernatural (Ex. 14:21-31; 1 Ki. 18:16-40; Mt. 8:1-9:38; Lk. 1:26-38).
- Because God can do all things doesn't mean that He does all things. His power is tethered to His character, which is love, kindness, wisdom, justice, etc.
- Any philosophy that sees God as possessing limited power is completely unbiblical (Ps. 62:11).

God is Omniscient

- God is all-knowing.
- God is perfect in knowledge, His understanding is complete and beyond measure (1 Jn. 3:20; Job 37:16; Ps. 147:5).
- God's knowledge is not acquired in the same manner as ours is. As the Author and Creator of all things, He possesses no need for anyone to teach Him (Is. 40:13,14).
- He knows every aspect of His creation—from atoms to persons to galaxies.
- He foreknows what is yet to happen (Ps. 139:4,16; Is. 42:9). He knows all things—every event in history, human life, and the future. He sees each moment with equal clarity. His foreknowledge is not so much a foreknowing as it is knowledge unlimited by time.

More often than not, all of these concepts are difficult to wrap my mind around.

Whence comes this idea that if what we are doing is fun, it can't be God's will?
The God who made giraffes, a baby's fingernails, a puppy's tail, a crooknecked squash, the
bobwhite's call, and a young girl's giggle, has a sense of humor.
Make no mistake about that.

Catherine Marshall, 1914-1983, American Writer

- God knows every aspect of our existence. He knows every thought and feeling (Ez. 11:5; Jer. 17:9, 10). He knows our words before they are formed on our tongues (Ps. 139:4; Mt. 12:36,37). Jesus stressed the importance of living our lives with the constant recognition of God's personal knowledge of us. He is aware of our needs and attends to the smallest details of our lives, even how many hairs we have on our heads (Mt. 6:32, 10:30).
- Because God is all-knowing it challenges us to live righteously as all our ways are constantly before Him (Ps. 119:168).
- God's omniscience is also a tremendous comfort to us as He knows what is in our hearts (Ps. 139).

God is Omnipresent
- God is everywhere.
- God is simultaneously present in the entire Universe. He is not spatially bound or distributed throughout creation—He is completely and equally present in all places at once (Jer. 23:24).
- God is immediately present to you and me (Acts 17:27,28).
- We cannot flee from God's presence (Ps. 139:7-12).
- Though a person may be far from God it doesn't mean God is far from them.
- God is uniquely present in the lives of believers through the indwelling of the Holy Spirit (Jn. 14:17).

God is Providential
- God's overseeing care and guardianship of His creation.
- God is intimately concerned with His creation and actively involved with it.
- Providence refers to God's preservation of His Creation. In Him all things are held together (Col. 1:17; Heb. 1:3) He put everything from atoms to stars in place. He created our hearts to beat and causes our oxygen-rich blood to course through our veins. It is by His providence that we are kept alive and provided for (Mt. 6:25-34).
- God's providence not only supports our physical needs, but it also preserves us from unseen dangers. His hand withholds threat to our health and unseen spiritual attacks.
- His providence illustrates His involvement with Creation. It was God who breathed life into man (Gen. 2:7), and He continues to intervene in the affairs of mankind.

THOUGHTS & NOTES

- God led Israel with a pillar of cloud by day and a pillar of fire by night. He also provided them with the Ten Commandments (Ex. 13:21, 22, 20:1-17).
- God came to earth in the person of Jesus—Immanuel, "God with us" (Mt. 1:23).
- He told the disciples that He would be with them always (Mt. 28:20).
- The disciples declared that He is not far from each of us (Acts 17:27,28).
- God's Providence includes His direction for Creation. From the very beginning God has led man toward His divine purposes, and not even the pride or selfishness of man's heart can hinder what He ordains. He is the Lord of History and His purpose is for all nations and peoples to know Him (Acts 17:24-27). This doesn't deny man's freedom—God employs all to establish His will, even the sinful deeds of man. God fully accomplishes His purposes in spite of the evil deeds of man. (Acts 2:23,24).

The Trinity

The Trinity

Christianity holds to the belief in one God and one God alone. This oneness cannot be affirmed too strongly. The affirmation of God's oneness is seen in the phrase, "The Lord our God is one Lord"—a phrase that became known as the *Shema*, which was recited daily by the people of Israel (Deut.6:4). Jesus reaffirmed this truth in the New Testament (Mk. 12:29). The word *Trinity* is never used in the Bible, however, the truth of the Trinity is evidenced throughout scripture (Gen. 1:26, 3:22; Lk. 3:21,22; Mt. 28:19).

God in Three Persons—Father, Son and Holy Spirit

- Each is a Person (Lk. 3:21, 22).
- We see the truth of the Trinity as early as the book of Genesis, with the use of the plural voice (Gen. 1:26, 3:22, 11:7).
- We witness the Trinity at the baptism of Jesus, and again, when Jesus commissions His disciples (Mt. 3:16,17; Mt. 28:19).
- Each Person within the Trinity is God: Father (Is. 64:8; Mt. 6:9); Son (Jesus) (Jn. 1:1,14,18; Heb. 1:8); and Holy Spirit (Acts 5:3,4).

Let your religion be less of a theory and more of a love affair.

Gilbert K. Chesterton, 1874-1936, British Writer

Our hearts were made for You, O Lord, and they are restless until they rest in you.

St. Augustine of Hippo, 354-430, Church Father

One God in Three Persons

- All the Persons of the Trinity, or Godhead, are God.
- The Father is totally God, the Son is totally God, and the Holy Spirit is totally God.
- Each Person of the Trinity contains the whole of the Godhead and is the one undivided God.
- There are no works of the Father that are not also the Son, etc.
- They have the same attributes—whatever is said of one is true for all.
- There is a supernatural union of three Divine Persons. Each is to be worshiped and honored as God.
- Each is to be worshiped as possessing all the same attribute—in worshiping one the others are being worshiped as well.

The Persons of the Trinity are Distinct

- The three Persons of the Trinity eternally exist and remain eternally distinct. They are not figures of speech, titles or expressions for various ways that God is revealed.
- The "three-ness" does not deny the "oneness."
- Some of the acts of the Godhead throughout Scripture help to define their distinctness.
    - The Father is the fountain and source of creation.
    - The Son (Jesus) became the Incarnation of God in human flesh.
    - The Holy Spirit was sent upon people by the Father and the Son.

The Mystery of the Trinity

- The human mind cannot fully comprehend the Trinity, yet it stands as scriptural truth upon which the foundation of the Christian faith rises.
- This truth must be embraced through faith. It is Spirit-revealed.

The human mind cannot fully comprehend the Trinity, yet it stands as scriptural truth upon which the foundation of the Christian faith rises.

THOUGHTS & NOTES

The Character of God

God's character is displayed in how He chooses to relate to His creation. Though the traits that comprise His character are many, a few foundational qualities depict who He is.

God is Holy

- Holiness is at the core of His character. It means "set-apart" (Is. 6:3).
- He is awesome and majestic (Ex. 3:5, 6; Rev. 1:12-17).
- His holy Presence produces a profound reverence and awe within His creation (Eccl. 12:13,14; Is. 8:13; Mt. 10:28).
- He is pure, without corruption of any unclean thing (Hab. 1:13).
- He is completely righteous (Ps. 119:137, 145:17).
- He is just, rendering to each person according to His work, and compassionate toward the abused and downtrodden (Ps. 89:14, 97:2, 103:6, 140:12).

God is Love – 1Jn. 4:8

- God sent Jesus to demonstrate His love (Jn. 3:16; Rom. 5:8).
- The love of God is active and self-giving, regardless of its recipient's attitude. It is unfathomable, yet it is lavished upon us without end (Jer. 31:3; Eph. 3:17-19; 1Jn. 3:1).
- God's love is expressed in His:
    - Lovingkindness (Ex. 34:6,7; Ps. 136).
    - Grace (Ex. 33:19; Eph. 2:1-10).
    - Mercy (Eph. 2:4; Ps. 119:156).
    - Goodness (Ps. 118:1).
    - Forgiveness (Eph. 1:7)

God of Truth

- God possesses perfect integrity, without shading of truth, without understatement or overstatement (Num. 23:19; 2Tim. 2:13).
- God is dependable and His Word is sure (Ps. 145:13).
- God is faithful (Ex. 34:6,7; Lam. 3:21-23).

The Scotch catechism says that man's chief end is 'to glorify God and enjoy Him forever.' But we shall then know that these are the same thing. Fully to enjoy is to glorify. In commanding us to glorify Him, God is inviting us to enjoy Him.

C.S. Lewis, 1898-1963, English Intellectual Giant, Writer

Reflections on the Character of God

You will find 52 names, titles and attributes of God in the back of this book for you to reflect upon. Contemplating God's names is one way to use Scripture to renew your mind in relation to who He is and what He's really like. I recommend that you take one attribute per week and record your thoughts and insights. Enjoy a year of intimate reflection. Once you have finished the 52, you'll find an additional 170 or so to inspire you in your journey toward knowing God more .

The Hebrew Names of God

One of the ways to get to know God is by contemplating His Names. The following is a list of some of His Hebrew names, with their meanings and where they are found in Scripture.

Elohim
- This is the name that introduces God in the beginning of the Bible (Gen. 1:1).
- *El* means God and is connected to God's power, might, glory and authority. *Ohim* speaks of plurality, and gives us the first picture of the Trinity. The name Elohim is connected to God's mighty acts.

Jehovah
- This is His name of relationship and covenant.
- God introduced Himself to man in the garden as Jehovah the *Lord God* (Gen. 2:7).

Jehovah El-Shaddai
- Almighty God—The God of might, bounty and blessing.
- God revealed Himself to Abraham as El-Shaddai when He promised Him a son (Gen. 17:1,2).

THOUGHTS & NOTES

Adonai

- This name, translated *Lord* or *Master*, refers to God's ownership and rule over our lives.
- Abraham referred to God as Adonai when God told him what was about to happen to Sodom and Gommorah (Gen. 18:3).

Jehovah-Jireh

- The Lord my Provider.
- This name was revealed when God spared Isaac and provided a ram for Abraham to sacrifice (Gen. 22:14).
- This name foreshadows God's provision of His Son for our redemption and salvation.

Jehovah-Rapha

- The Lord my Healer.
- It was when Israel came to Marah that God made a covenant of healing with His people (Ex. 15:22-26).

Jehovah-Nissi

- The Lord my Banner, or covering, protection and victory.
- This name was revealed when Moses lifted up the rod of victory, in the place of prayer, during a battle against the Amalekites (Ex. 17:15).

Jehovah-M'kadesh

- The Lord my Sanctifier. He is the One who sets us apart for service and makes us wholly belonging to the Him.
- The Lord said He would be the sanctifier of Israel if they would walk in obedience to Him (Ex. 31:13).

Contemplating God's names is one way
to use Scripture to renew your mind
in relation to who He is and what He's really like.

We would be still and know that you are God. We stand in awe of You.
Your awesome holiness, majestic splendor, blazing glory, limitless power
and unquestionable sovereignty. We worship You for Your flawless character,
Your infinite knowledge and wisdom, Your absolute justice, unswerving faithfulness, unend-
ing mercy. We bow our hearts and bend our knees before
Your dazzling beauty, Your fascinating personality, Your incomprehensible humility, Your
unsearchable understanding and Your unfathomable love.

Our greatest need is to have a far greater revelation of what You are really like.

Joy Dawson, New Zealand Bible Teacher

Jehovah-Shalom
- The Lord my Peace.
- This is the name Gideon gave to the altar he built to commemorate the angel of the Lord who commissioned him as a warrior to free Israel from the Midianites, assuring him that he would not die because he had seen the angel (Jud. 6:23,24).

Jehovah-Tsidkenu
- The Lord my Righteousness.
- God told Jeremiah to prophesy that a righteous branch of David would come to save Judah, and that Israel would dwell in safety. This is a picture of Jesus, our righteousness. Only through Him can we live rightly before the Lord (Jer. 23:6).

Jehovah-Rohi
- The Lord my Shepherd.
- David declared, "The Lord is my shepherd." This speaks of leadership, as well as intimacy (Ps. 23:1).

Jehovah-Shammah
- The Lord is there.
- This name refers to the restored and beautified city where God will make His dwelling with His people forever (Ez. 48:35).

God's character is displayed in how He chooses to relate to His creation.

THOUGHTS & NOTES ———————————

_____

_____

_____

_____

CASTING THE NET

What are the images that you carry around in your heart and mind about God and what He's like? How did they get there? Do these images align with Scripture? What images contradict Scripture?

• Nature: sunset, trees, the different seasons.
• Hearing others talk about God. My favorite saying is God is like the wind - you can't see Him, but you can feel Him.
• Yes they align with Scripture.

• My goal is to be able to hear what God is saying.

What names, titles or attributes of God mean the most to you in your life today?

• Adonai
• Jehovah - Rapha

Nobody ever got anything from God on the grounds that he deserved it. Having fallen, man deserves only punishment and death. So if God answers prayer it's because God is good. From His goodness, His lovingkindness, His good-natured benevolence, God does it! That's the source of everything.

A.W. Tozer, 1897-1963, American Pastor and Writer

How can you know and experience God more personally? How can you develop your relationship with God? What do you need to give more attention to?

- Meditating on God
- Spending more 1 on 1 time w/ Him
- Reading & investing more of my time in the Bible, waiting and listening.
- PATIENCE.

What spoke to you most about the nature of God?

- He is forgiving and has mercy on His people.

Take a look at the back of this book and begin your journey of reflection by choosing an aspect of God that you would like to know more fully. Write down your insights.

- God as a Father figure

pg. 266

THOUGHTS & NOTES

CATCH OF THE DAY

Chapter Summary

- God desires for us to know Him, and the devil will do everything he can to hinder that from happening, particularly by disfiguring God in our hearts and minds.
- We can be more intentional in knowing God by pursuing Him and remaining aware of the areas that can hinder our pursuit.
- God reveals Himself to us through His names, titles and attributes, His ways, His works and His words in Scripture.
- God invites us to know His nature and character. We can see Him more clearly as we reflect on His names, titles and attributes.

What are the two or three things the Holy Spirit spoke most clearly to you through this chapter, and how will you respond to Him?

? I dont know how to differniate what
· God is saying vs. what I'm saying.
·I feel like my mind is cloudy...
·I feel distracted.

CHAPTER 2
A CALL TO DISCIPLESHIP

A VIEW FROM THE SHORE

"If anyone would come after Me, he must deny himself and take up his cross
and follow me. For whoever wants to save his life will lose it,
but whoever loses his life for me and for the gospel will save it.
What good is it for a man to gain the whole world, yet forfeit his soul?"

Mark 8:34-36

We find the above verse written in three of the four gospels, emphasizing the seriousness of the Lord's call to discipleship. In Matthew, the passage is preceded by the account of Peter's revelation of Jesus as the Christ, and it's followed by the rebuke Peter receives for allowing Satan to influence the things of God. Both experiences—the recognition and confession of Jesus as the Son of God, and refusing Satan access to his heart and mind—were only the start of what it would mean to be Jesus' disciple. Indeed, if anyone would come after Him, it would cost more—it would require their very lives. Of the twelve original disciples, ten would eventually die for their Messiah and the proclamation of His good news (gospel).

A disciple is someone who places himself under another's tutelage to learn his way of life and to carry his cause. The disciple-student learns from his master-teacher by listening, watching and participating together with him in the events of daily living. The student is shaped by the teacher's influence and gleans from his expertise and experiences. Disciples are instructed, corrected, encouraged and coached along in a discipleship journey. In short, the disciple-student becomes a lot like the master-teacher, in life and in purpose. This is what Jesus

had in mind when He called men and women to follow Him in discipleship. He called them to become like Him and to disciple others to so the same.

A disciple of Jesus is not merely someone who believes Jesus is real, or regularly attends church activities. Becoming baptized doesn't make a person a disciple, nor does tithing or simply being good. These things are important, but Jesus gave us a higher criterion for what it means to be His disciple. In the above scripture, He said a disciple denies himself, takes up his cross, and follows after Him, giving his or her life to Christ and the gospel.

To grow as a disciple requires a willing and teachable heart, not to mention a radical commitment to obey Jesus. It takes the support of other people who are further along in their walk with God. To get the most from this book, find another person or group of people you can walk with as you work through these chapters. As these relationships develop, invite them to speak into your life. Remember that discipleship is born from relationship, first with Jesus, then with others. We are all to place ourselves under the tutelage of Jesus, and it is His desire that we help each other mature in our lives as disciples. Who are the people in your life discipling you, and who are you discipling?

SETTING SAIL

To those who would hear and believe, Jesus has called them to join Him in the purposes of His Father. Discipleship is a lifestyle, not merely church membership. It requires *discipline*, hence the term, which is obviously built from the same root used in *discipleship*. We are cautioned to count the cost of our commitment, for it is not an idle or passive vow we make. The call to discipleship essentially is a call to become trainers. In taking up the call we, ourselves, must be trained so we can train others.

The Conditions of Discipleship

When Jesus spoke to the multitudes, He cautioned them, saying, "Enter through the narrow gate." He said, "Wide is the gate and broad is the road that leads to destruction, and many enter through it. But small is the gate and narrow the road that leads to life and only a few find it." (Mt. 7:13-14). At that very moment, as Jesus spoke, the Master Discipler identified the ground upon which He stood and the uncommon path He traversed. To follow Him meant diverging from the road commonly traveled. The disciple's journey would not resemble the life he or she had previously known. It was also marked by key conditions.

Repentance – Mt. 4:17-22; Acts 2:38, 26:20; 2 Cor. 7:10
Repentance is a turning around, a turning from sin towards God and His ways. Repentance is a heart change that comes in response to a revelation of God's grace and mercy, the depth and consequences of our sin and selfishness, and the need for Jesus in our lives. It leads to confession of sin and includes making things right with those whom we have sinned against, and asking forgiveness from God and others. Repentance reflects the willingness of the heart to let Jesus be Lord—to allow Him charge over our lives.

Faith in Jesus – Mk. 1:15; Rom. 10:9,10; Eph. 2:8,9; Heb. 11:6
Faith, or believing, is not mere credence, but an active trust and reliance on Jesus for everything, from our salvation to our daily needs. We no longer look to ourselves for answers or follow our own lead, but we place our lives in His hands.

THOUGHTS & NOTES

CHAPTER 2 — A CALL TO DISCIPLESHIP

Loving Jesus – Mt. 10:37-39; Mk. 12:28-31
Disciples love Jesus above everything and everyone. Their foremost thoughts and affections, motivations, desires, actions and commitments all support an uncompromising love for God, bringing Him glory and honor.

Denying Self and Taking Up the Cross– Mt. 16:24; Mk. 8:34; Lk. 9:23
Self-denial, from a biblical point of view, yields to the desires of the Holy Spirit rather than to the desires of the flesh. The Bible teaches us that the flesh and the Spirit are in conflict with each other (Gal. 5:16-26). This does not mean that we can't enjoy God-given things in life. It simply means that we live in pursuit of the Holy Spirit's desires rather than being driven by what we want to do. The Cross modeled death for us, and beckons us to die to our rights to our talents, resources, family and friends, use of our time, career, reputation, future. We surrender all rights to His service.

Following Jesus – Mt. 4:18-22; Mk. 10:17-31; Lk. 5:27-32; Jn. 21:15-25
Following Jesus means forsaking all else. The call of the disciple requires us to leave everything behind in order to free ourselves to serve Jesus. Discipleship places our lives completely under His Lordship and allows Him reign as the Master of our lives. When we commit to discipleship, we commit to follow where He leads (Mt. 28:20).

The Cost of Discipleship

When a teacher of the law approached Jesus, saying that he would follow Him wherever He led, Jesus presented the man with a vivid picture of what that commitment would entail. Jesus said to him, "Foxes have holes and birds of the air have nests, but the Son of Man has no place to lay his head" (Mt 8:19-21). Imagine, the King of Kings without even a modest place to call home. Are you prepared to follow where He leads? Have you considered the cost?

A Difference in Standards – 2 Cor. 5:17; Eph. 4:17-21
Disciples of Jesus live by the absolutes, truths and values revealed in Scripture, not according to the standards of the world around them.

Disciples love Jesus above everything and everyone.

Lord, I give up all my own plans and purposes, all my own desires and hopes, and accept Thy will for my life. I give myself, my life, my all utterly to Thee to be Thine forever. Fill me and seal me with Thy Holy Spirit. Use me as Thou wilt. Send me where Thou wilt. Work out Thy whole will in my life at any cost, now and forever.

Betty Scott Stam, 1906-1934, American Missionary to China, Martyr

A Despising by Society – Mt. 5:10-12; Jn. 15:19-20; 2 Tim. 3:12

Because disciples of Jesus live for God, those who don't will not understand. They may reject you or become angry because you don't fit in to their crowd or the world's system any more. The same reaction may even come from lukewarm, backslidden Christians.

A Discipline of Self – Gal. 5:22-23; Eph. 4:27; 1 Cor. 9:24-27

The disciple of Jesus allows the Holy Spirit into their lives to tighten up areas where they have been lax or let themselves go. They choose not to give any edge to the devil.

A Battle to Engage – Jn. 10:10; Eph. 6:10-18; 2 Tim. 2:1-4

When we become Christians, the enemy of our soul, the devil, will do everything he can to steal, kill and destroy our walk with Jesus. The good news is that Jesus has overcome the devil, so we can too (1 Jn. 3:8, 4:4).

A Life Laid Down – Jn. 12:23-26, 13:1-17, 15:13; Rev. 12:11

Following Jesus is others-centered. It requires laying down our rights and desires to follow Jesus wherever he leads us and to give of ourselves on behalf of others.

A Sticking to the Task – Rom. 5:1-5; Phil. 3:12-14; 2 Tim. 4:7-8; Heb. 12:1-3

Disciples of Jesus have been called to the most awesome assignment in the world—to know God and to make Him known to the world. The disciple's journey will have ups and downs, but as we cling to Jesus, the author and finisher of our faith, we will finish well.

The Characteristics of Disciples

Observations from the Book of I John

When we love Jesus, we see the truth He brings and we are changed. With a heart to follow Him, we are presented with choices in our thoughts, actions, and attitudes. Answering the call of discipleship, however, requires that we become like the One who disciples us. A disciple of Christ surrenders his or her choices for the perfect and holy will of the Father.

* Disciples testify to and proclaim the reality of Jesus (1 Jn. 1:1-4).
* Disciples walk in the light (1 Jn. 1:5-10).
* Disciples obey Jesus (1 Jn. 2:3-5).
* Disciples live like Jesus (1 Jn. 2:5-6).
* Disciples don't love the world (1 Jn. 2:15-17).
* Disciples don't practice sin (1 Jn. 3:8-10, 5:18).

THOUGHTS & NOTES

- Disciples love other people (1 Jn. 3:14-18, 4:7-21).
- Disciples are of the Spirit (1 Jn. 4:1-6, 13).
- Disciples aren't driven by fear (1 Jn. 4:18).
- Disciples overcome the world, the flesh and the devil (1 Jn. 2:15-17, 3:8, 5:1-5, 5:18).
- Disciples pray according to God's will (1 Jn. 5:13-15).
- Disciples keep themselves from idols (1 Jn. 5:21).

The Disciple's Cause

Disciples of Jesus desire to see all nations worship Him. They carry a vision in their hearts described in the book of Revelation where every tribe, language, people and nation worships before the throne of God. This passion permeates all that they do. Disciples view everything through this vision. Their choices arise from viewing their entire lives through the grid of the Great Commission (Mt. 28:18-20).

Preach the Good News to All Creation – Mk. 16:15-20
The message of the gospel of grace will advance only if disciples of Jesus obey His command to make sure that everyone has the opportunity to hear the gospel. Paul, the apostle, decided where he would minister next according to where the need existed (Acts 13-28; Rom. 10:14,15, 15:20).

Serve as Ambassadors of Reconciliation – 2 Cor. 5:17-21
God has given us the ministry and message of reconciliation. The lives of disciples are given to reconciling man to God, and as an overflow, people to people. This includes the reconciling of families, races and generations.

Make Disciples of All Nations – Mt. 28:18-20
God created every tribe, language, people and nation to express His character and glory in the Earth. He desires them to gather at His throne in heaven (Rev. 5:9-14, 7:9-12). His disciples recognize that leading people to a new faith in Jesus is just the beginning of their journey as believers. Disciples pass on what has been passed to them—they commit to disciple new believers in truths from God's Word and to mentor them in God's ways.

Give God Glory – Jn. 17:4; 1 Cor. 10:31
Jesus brought the Father glory by completing what He had been given to do on Earth. As disciples of Jesus, we follow His lead. Our lives purpose to bring God glory. We want Jesus lifted up, not ourselves.

If Jesus Christ be God and died for me, then no sacrifice can be too great for me to make for Him.

C.T. Studd, 1860-1931, British Cricket Player and Missionary to China, India, Africa

The price is high. God does not want partnership with us, but ownership of us!

Leonard Ravenhill, 1907-1994, English Evangelist and Revivalist

DEEPER WATERS

Disciples of Jesus stand out because they reflect God's light in a dark world. They display the character of the one true God, drawing the world to their Savior. Disciples commit themselves to following Jesus and to walking in His ways. Through this devotion, they bring glory to God.

The following seven qualities reside at the core of the disciple's life. These areas need continuous cultivation and development within the deepest places of a disciple's heart. These qualities rightly align one to God's ways and purposes, while also providing a fortress of defense against the fiery darts of the devil. They are keys to walking in unity with other believers, and they reflect, in attitude, the very heart of Jesus, giving unbelievers the opportunity to experience Him through our lives.

Love

Choosing the Highest Good for God, Others, and Yourself
Foundations of Love
- God is love (1 Jn. 4:16).
- We can love because He has first loved us (1 Jn. 4:19).
- Disciples love Jesus above everyone and everything else (Mt. 22:37-38; Jn. 21:15-17).
- We are to love our neighbors as ourselves (Mt. 22:39).
- Love is the distinguishing mark for the world to know that we are disciples of Jesus (Jn. 13:34-35).
- Jesus commanded His disciples to love one another, which means it's possible (Jn. 15:12).
- Love is expressed in its greatest way when we lay down our lives (and agendas) for others (Jn. 15:13).
- We are to love our enemies (Mt. 5:44).
- The love of Jesus compels us to reach the lost (2 Cor. 5:11-21).

Love is the distinguishing mark for the world to know that we are disciples of Jesus.

THOUGHTS & NOTES

Qualities of Love – 1 Cor. 13:1-8

- No matter who we are, or what we believe, or how God can use us, without love we are nothing (vv. 1-3).
- Love is patient. It is longsuffering, not easily irritable or quick to flash a temper (v.4).
- Love is kind. It thinks more highly of others; recognizes and creatively meets the needs of others (v. 4).
- Love does not envy. It appreciates what others have without entertaining jealousy (v. 4).
- Love does not boast. It does not draw attention to oneself or seek to contrive a favorable impression (v. 4).
- Love is not proud. It is not self-centered; it recognizes that life doesn't revolve around oneself (v. 4).
- Love is not rude. It honors others at all times (v. 5).
- Love is not self-seeking. It is not primarily concerned with self-gratification, but with seeking the comfort and welfare of others (v. 5).
- Love is not easily angered. It lays down one's own life for others. When one's will is crossed, they do not become emotionally charged. Love is not overly-sensitive or quick to take on feelings of rejection or hurt (v. 5).
- Love keeps no record of wrongs. It does not rehearse wrongs that have been forgiven (v. 5).
- Love does not delight in evil, but rejoices with the truth. It mourns sinfulness, taking no pleasure in another's failure. It despises deceit and deception. Love seeks, receives and celebrates truth at all times and at all costs (v. 6).
- Love always protects. It doesn't expose the sin and weaknesses of others, but covers (v. 7).
- Love always trusts. It believes in a person's worth and integrity (v. 7).
- Love always hopes. It persists through dark times. Love never gives up because God is love (v. 7).
- Love always perseveres. It continues to love even when there is not love in return (v. 7).
- Love never fails. It is still there when everyone and everything else is gone (v. 8).

Disciples of Jesus stand out because they reflect God's light in a dark world. They display the character of the one true God, drawing the world to their Savior.

Be faithful in the little practices of love which will build in you the life of holiness and make you Christlike.

Mother Teresa of Calcutta, 1910-1997, Missionary to the Poor

Christian love, either towards God or towards man, is an affair of the will.

C.S. Lewis, 1898-1963, English Intellectual Giant, Writer

Forgiveness

Releasing Others from Wrongs Suffered

Injury, especially emotional injury, tempts us to cling to the wrong-doings of others. We want to believe that our forgiveness depends on the debt we're owed and our perpetrator's willingness to compensate for the pain he or she has caused. Scripture, however, teaches us about true forgiveness.

- Jesus died for our sins that we might know His forgiveness (Col. 1:13-14).
- God forgives our sins (Ps. 103:2-5; 1 Jn. 1:9).
- As far as the east is from the west, so far He has removed our sins from us (Ps. 103:12).
- Because we have been forgiven, we are able to forgive others (Mt. 18:21-35).
- We are to forgive those who have sinned against us (Mt. 6:9-15).
- We are to forgive others just as Jesus has forgiven us (Eph. 4:32; Col. 3:13).
- We are to forgive people for repeated offenses (Mt .18:21-22).
- Just as Jesus forgave the man on the cross, we forgive those who bring hurt to our lives (Lk. 23:32-43).

Humility

Willing to be Known for Who We Really Are

The Apostle Paul reflected on Jesus' earthly life, reminding us that though He was in "very nature God, [Jesus] did not consider equality with God something to be grasped." On the contrary, Jesus "made himself nothing" (Phil. 2:5-11). He assumed the appearance of man, never speaking up on His own behalf and never taking the privileges due Him. Though He was King, He chose to be born in a stable and to live the entirety of His earthly life without demanding the comforts of a palace, or gold, or fine linens.

- Jesus is our model of humility (Phil. 2:5-11; Mt. 11:28-30).
- Humility is what the Lord requires of us (Mic .6:9).
- The Lord esteems the humble (Is. 66:2).
- God opposes the proud and gives grace to the humble (Jam. 4:6).
- We are to be completely humble (Eph. 4:2-3; Col. 3:12).
- We are to humble ourselves. Because God values humility so much, if we refuse to humble ourselves, He will use other people and life circumstances to humble us (1 Pet. 5:5-6).
- We are to walk in humility before all people (Tit. 3:1-2).
- A little child gives us a picture of what humility should look like (Mt. 18:4).
- God raises the humble up at the right time (Jam. 4:10; 1 Pet. 5:5-6).

THOUGHTS & NOTES

Fruits of a Humble Life
- The humble acknowledge when they are wrong and others are right.
  The humble are teachable and correctable.
- The humble actively promote others, even when they are like-gifted, because their humility provides them with a true security in who they are.
- The humble submit under God's delegated authorities.
- The humble exude a genuineness and honesty. They are approachable and appropriately vulnerable and transparent.
- The humble have become comfortable "going low" before God and man.
- Their willingness to be known for who they really are also includes areas of giftedness and strengths, therefore moving in humility lets them find their right place on the team in the kingdom, while also recognizing and making room so everybody else finds their place as well.
- Where humility is, unity follows. It is impossible to cultivate division where people eagerly humble themselves. Conversely, a lack of unity points to a lack of humility, and a lack of humility eventually destroys the bonds of unity.
- God manifests His presence to people and communities that are saturated in humility (2Chr. 7:14, 34:27).

Brokenness

Complete Yieldedness and Dependence Upon God

God often uses people and life circumstances to bring us to the end of ourselves, leaving us completely yielded and dependent on Him. Like a wild stallion that must be broken to channel its beauty and strength into productivity and fruitfulness, so it is with disciples of Jesus with whom He intends to use for His glory.
- Jesus modeled brokenness in the Garden of Gethsemane when He yielded His will to do His Father's will (Mt.26:36-46; Lk.22:40-46).
- Jesus said that apart from Him we can do nothing (Jn.15:5).
- God requires a breaking of our wills and a dependence on Him so that we can participate in the objectives of His kingdom purposes.
- God does not despise the broken (Ps.51:17).
- God loves it when we depend on Him completely. He will orchestrate things in our lives, from His perfect love for us, to develop within us a brokenness and reliance on Him (see the story of Joseph in Gen. 37-50).
- When you recognize that God is taking you to a deeper place of brokenness, yield to Him. Take every opportunity to yield your will to His will and depend on Him to lead you.

Let this be thy whole endeavor, this thy prayer, this thy desire — that thou mayest be stripped of all selfishness, and with entire simplicity follow Jesus only.

Thomas à. Kempis, 1380-1471, German Mystic and Author

Obedience

Doing What Jesus Has Asked Me to Do
Obedience Modeled
- Jesus was obedient to His Father, even to the point of death on the cross (Phil. 2:5-11).
- Jesus learned obedience, which means we can too (Heb. 5:7-10).
- The disciples were obedient to Jesus in the book of Acts. Below are a few examples.
    - Jesus told them to wait, so they did (Lk. 24:49/Acts 1:12-14).
    - He told them to preach the gospel, so they did (Mk. 16:15/Acts 2:14-41, 8:5-8).
    - He told them to lay hands on the sick, so they did (Mk. 16:17-20/Acts 3:1-10).

Obedience Defined
- As disciples, we must obey God above all else (Acts 5:29).
- Obedience is an expression of our love for God (Jn. 14:15,21,24).
- Our obedience to God demonstrates His Lordship in our lives (Gen .22:1-14).
- Obedience brings blessing (Dt. 28:1-14).
- Disobedience has consequences (Dt. 28:15-68). Delayed obedience is disobedience. It is better to obey right away. As an example of this truth see the story of the prophet Jonah (Jonah 1-4).
- Disciples of Jesus walk in obedience to God's revealed truth in Scripture and to the leading of the Holy Spirit in their lives, as demonstrated throughout the book of Acts.
- The Holy Spirit will never lead us to do anything that is contrary to God's character or what is revealed in the Scriptures. We can recognize His leading because it will always agree with who God is and the truth of His Word (Acts 5:29).

Servanthood

Laying My Life Down for Others
Servanthood Modeled
- Jesus came as a servant (Mt. 20:28; Phil. 2:5-11).
- Jesus demonstrated servanthood by washing his disciples feet (Jn. 13:1-17).

Servanthood Defined
A servant relinquishes his rights so that he may better serve God and others (Phil. 2:5-7). The heart of a servant desires to be available to God for His purposes, which include serving others. A servant's attitude is one of open and upward palms, willing to allow the Lord to take from him, as well as to give to him (1 Cor. 9:24-27).

THOUGHTS & NOTES

- Servants surrender their rights to their family.
- Servants surrender their rights to marriage.
- Servants surrender their rights to singleness when they marry.
- Servants surrender their rights to their friends.
- Servants surrender their rights to their freedom.
- Servants surrender their rights to their finances and possessions.
- Servants surrender their rights to popularity and reputation.
- Servants surrender their rights to their time.
- Servants surrender their rights to food, shelter, sleep and comfort.
- Servants surrender their rights to their position, rank or place of importance.
- Servants surrender their rights to their nationality or denomination.
- Servants surrender their rights to their gifts and ministry.
- Servants surrender their rights to their opinions and the right to be right.
- Servants surrender their rights to their future.

- Surrendering one's rights does not mean that one does not take responsibility for the people and things in their lives. The purpose of the servant relinquishing their rights is for the sake of being available to God to serve Him and others more effectively, not to become irresponsible.
- Whatever rights we don't relinquish to God can subtly drive our lives, even to the point of mastering us (1 Cor. 6:12, 9:24-27).
- Evidence of not relinquishing our rights may include reactions of anger, self-pity, or attempts to control.

Servants Walk in Humility – Phil. 2:8
- Servants don't do things for man's applause or approval, but for their Father's in heaven.
- Servants don't seek to be noticed, but are willing to serve in the hidden places.
- Servants are willing to serve no matter how messy the job.
- Servants don't seek positions of leadership to exercise power over people, but rather to serve others.

Servants Walk in Obedience – Phil. 2:8
- The evidence of a servant's love for their Master is obedience.
- Servants walk in a godly way, with a godly attitude, always under authority.
- Servants are obedient to God even when they don't fully understand what He is doing. They trust His character and ways.
- Servants are obedient to God even when it goes against what the world says to do.

Just as a servant knows that he must first obey his master in all things, so the surrender to an implicit and unquestionable obedience must become the essential characteristic of our lives.

Andrew Murray, 1828-1917, South African Pastor, Missionary and Writer

I know the power obedience has of making things easy which seem impossible.

Teresa of Avila, 1515-1582, Reformer and Contemplative

Servants Serve All People

- Servants serve anyone God calls them to serve.
- Servants serve regardless of someone's background or nationality.
- Servants serve regardless of someone's looks, attitudes or actions.
- Servants serve regardless of how they "feel" about others or how others feel about them. Servants serve regardless of how others treat them.

Servants Die To Self And Live for God and Others

- Servants die to self-will to do God's will.
- Servants die to self-pleasing in order to please God.
- Servants die to self-confidence (relying alone on one's self) to put their full trust in God.
- Servants die to their opinions to embrace God's ways.

Dying to Self

When you are forgotten, neglected or purposely set aside, and you don't sting and hurt with the insult or the oversight, but you keep your heart right before God, glad to be counted as worthy to suffer for Jesus — *that is dying to self.*

When your good is evil spoken of, when your wishes are crossed, your advice disregarded, your opinions ridiculed, and you refuse to let anger rise in your heart or even defend yourself – *that is dying to self.*

When you lovingly and patiently bear any disorder, irregularity, unpunctuality or any annoyance, and when you stand face-to-face with waste, foolishness, extravagance and spiritual insensitivity, and endure it as Jesus did — *that is dying to self.*

When you are content with any food, clothing, climate, culture – and any interruption by the will of God — *that is dying to self.*

When you never care to refer to yourself in conversation or to record your own good works or itch after commendations; when you truly love to be unknown — *that is dying to self.*

When you can see someone else prosper and have their needs met and can honestly rejoice with them from your heart, and feel no envy, nor question God while your own needs are far greater — *that is dying to self.*

THOUGHTS & NOTES

When you can receive rebuke and correction from one of less stature than yourself and can humbly submit inwardly as well as outwardly, finding no places of rebellion or resentment rising up within your heart — *that is dying to self.*

Are you dead yet? In these days, the Holy Spirit desires to bring us to the cross that we might become more like Jesus (Phil. 3:10).

— Anonymous

Fear of the Lord

Reverencing and Referencing God in All You Do

God is love, and perfect love casts out fear (1 Jn. 4:18). This we know from Scripture. When we love perfectly, we trust, and our trust dispels the threats that fear brings. Have you ever wondered, then, what God means when He says that we should *fear* Him? To *fear the Lord* does not mean to be scared of Him, or to entertain doubts of a life that He sovereignly controls. Rather, it refers to a deep sense of awe and reverence, to an internal bowing of our spirit in recognition of who He really is.

Promises to Those Who Fear the Lord

The Scriptures state many promises for those who fear God. They include:
- Fruitfulness (Ex. 1:17-21)
- Keeping us from sin (Ex. 20:20)
- Blessings on us and our children (Dt. 5:29)
- Prolonged days (Pr. 9:10-11)
- Guidance (Ps. 25:12)
- The confiding of God (Ps. 25:14)
- Angelic protection/deliverance (Ps. 34:7)
- Provision for needs (Ps. 34:9)
- Wisdom (Ps. 111:10; Pr. 9:10)

To fear the Lord does not mean to be scared of Him... Rather, it refers to a deep sense of awe and reverence, to an internal bowing of our spirit in recognition of who He really is.

It is only the fear of God that can deliver us from the fear of man.

John Witherspoon, 1723-1794, Preacher, President of Princeton University

**Resolved, never to do anything which I should be afraid to do
if it were the last hour of my life.**

Jonathan Edwards, 1703-1758, American Preacher and Theologian

- Earned respect (Neh. 5:9)
- Blessing related to family life (Ps. 128)
- Companionship (Ps. 119:63)
- Wealth, honor and life (Pr. 22:4)
- Fulfilled desires (Ps. 145:19)
- Abundant goodness (Ps. 31:19)
- Preservation of life (Pr. 19:23)
- Honor for women (Pr. 31:30)
- A heritage (Ps. 61:5)
- Blessings from God (Ps. 112:1-10)

The Fear of the Lord is taking God seriously
- It is standing in deep respect and awe of who God is (Is. 40:12-31).
- It is the recognition that God is the Supreme Authority in the universe (Ps. 33:8-9).
- Moses encountered God and the ground became holy (Ex. 3:1-6).
- Isaiah saw a vision of heaven where God was holy and it caused him to become undone (Is. 6:1-8).
- Our obedience to God is directly related to how much we fear the Lord (Gen. 22:1-14).
- When we see God for who He really is, which moves us to take Him seriously, it becomes a ridiculous thought to disobey God.
- God wants to bring us to the place where *what He tells us to do* is not nearly as important as *Who tells us to do it*. The commands pale in the glory of a majestic Commander.

The Fear of the Lord is the hatred of evil – Pr. 8:13, 16:6
- God has absolutely no tolerance for sin (Gen. 6:6-7; Gen. 19-20; Lev. 19:2).
- The degree to which we fear the Lord is the same degree to which we hate sin.
- We are only as holy as our thought lives are holy (Ps .19:14, 51:6; Phil .4:8).
- We are to have the Fear of the Lord on our tongues (Ps. 34:11-14; Mt. 12:36; Jam. 3:1-12).
- We are to have the Fear of the Lord in the way we relate to others (Jam. 4:11-12).
- We are to walk in the Fear of the Lord in the way we relate to those in authority (Num. 12:9-10; 1Sam. 24:1-7; 2Ki. 2:23-24; Ps. 105:15).

The Fear of the Lord Leads to Seeking God in Everything
- Those who fear God reference Him in their daily lives, in everything they do (Ps.25:14).
- Those who fear God avoid the sin of presumption—they avoid doing things without referencing God (Ps.19:13).

THOUGHTS & NOTES

The Fear of Man

To serve God, one must place no other gods before Him. Being concerned more for man's reactions than God's reactions indicates a greater respect for man than for God. Rather than a righteous Fear of God, this represents an unholy fear of man. The fear of man is present when we determine what we will or won't do based on anything other than God's truth and His leading in our lives.

- The fear of man brings a snare (Pr. 29:25).
- The fear of man leads to people pleasing.
- The fear of man hinders our obedience to Jesus.

CASTING THE NET

Have you become Jesus' disciple yet? If not, consider the conditions and cost of discipleship, and then commit yourself now to becoming a sincere and wholly-devoted disciple of the Lord.

_____

_____

_____

_____

_____

_____

_____

He is no fool who gives what he cannot keep to gain what he cannot lose.

Jim Elliot, 1927-1956,, American Missionary to Ecuador, Martyr

What characteristics of a disciple do you see evident in your life? Are there areas where you need to grow?

_____

_____

_____

_____

_____

_____

_____

_____

_____

Have you committed yourself to the Lord's causes in discipleship? Where do you stand today?

_____

_____

_____

_____

_____

_____

_____

_____

_____

_____

THOUGHTS & NOTES ———

_____

_____

_____

_____

Examine yourself before the Lord in the areas of love, forgiveness, humility and brokenness. What did the Holy Spirit speak most loudly to you in reference to these areas?

_____

_____

_____

_____

_____

_____

_____

_____

What about the other three areas—obedience, servanthood, and the Fear of the Lord? Where do you stand in these areas, and where do you need to grow?

_____

_____

_____

_____

_____

_____

_____

_____

_____

_____

Character is always lost when a high ideal is sacrificed on the altar of conformity and popularity.

Charles Spurgeon, 1834-1892, English Preacher and Author

CaTCH OF THE Day

Chapter Summary

- Scripture identifies the biblical conditions of being a disciple of Jesus, and tells us that it is important to consider, or count, the costs.
- Although each of us is unique, common biblical characteristics identify those who have chosen to live as a disciple of Jesus.
- We have been called to a cause as Jesus' disciples, with a purpose of bringing glory to God by knowing Him and making Him known to others.
- For one's spiritual health and development, and for his or her life to affect a broad and lasting impact, it is essential to walk in love, forgiveness, humility, brokenness, obedience, servanthood and the Fear of the Lord.

What are the two or three things the Holy Spirit spoke most clearly to you through this chapter, and how will you respond to Him?

_____

_____

_____

_____

_____

_____

_____

_____

_____

_____

THOUGHTS & NOTES

_____

_____

_____

_____

A VIEW FROM THE SHORE

"For it is by grace you have been saved, through faith—and this not from yourselves, it is the gift of God—not by works, so that no one can boast."

Ephesians 2:8-9

God's grace is woven throughout Scripture, ever present from generation to generation, beginning with the inception of time. In Genesis 3 , He pursued Adam and Eve, despite their sin. He came to them when they hid in shame and fear. Disciplining their rebellion, He removed them from the garden. Still, He extended grace to them, giving them garments to cover their nakedness.

When we study the lives of our Old Testament heroes, such as Abraham, Moses, David, Esther and Daniel, we see God's grace displayed. It finds expression in God's love and kindness. Sometimes we see it as His intervention on man's behalf. Grace often empowers man to overcome his sin or difficulties. Grace is frequently bestowed as a divine enablement to walk in obedience and accomplish God's will on the Earth.

The grace of God is seen more vividly in the New Testament. Jesus came "full of grace and truth" (Jn. 1:14-17). In a Nazarean synagogue, He declared that He came "to preach good news to the poor, proclaim freedom for prisoners, recovery of sight for the blind, release the oppressed and proclaim the year of the Lord's favor" (Lk. 4:14-21). Everything He did—feeding the multitudes, healing the sick, ministering to the poor, teaching on the Kingdom of heaven, delivering the demon-possessed, raising the dead—revealed God's favor and desire to act on man's behalf. The ultimate expression of God's grace was His Son's death on the Cross—a demonstration unparalleled, save for His resurrection from the dead. Jesus won for us something we could never gain on our own. He who was without sin died so that sin might be destroyed—that we might be reconciled to an eternal love-relationship with a heavenly Father (2 Cor 5: 17-28). By grace, we are children and heirs of God (Rom. 8:15-17; Jn. 3:1).

Grace is an overflow of who God is. We have not received it through anything we have done. It is a showering of God upon us, a free gift unlike anything else we will ever receive. Grace changes hearts, leads us to relationship with Jesus, empowers us to resist fear and temptation, and to do the will of God. Grace produces repentance and instills faith in thanksgiving to God.

In this chapter, we will examine grace more closely. We will consider the blessings of grace in our lives, discover God's father heart for us, and learn how His grace brings about a heart change within us and empowers us to live Godly lives that result in walking in obedience to Him.

SETTING SAIL

In the book of Acts, the message of the grace of Jesus continued to spread. It permeated the lives and ministries of His disciples, and was at the core of their gospel message. The disciples knew it provided their means of salvation, as Peter testified at the famed Jerusalem Council when he stated that, "We believe it is through the grace of our Lord Jesus that we are saved" (Acts 15:11). Acts tells us that God confirmed their declaration of His grace through demonstrations of signs and wonders (Acts 14:3). Grace so richly permeated their lives that it became the evidence by which believers in Christ were recognized (Acts 11:23). The young church was urged to continue in the grace of God, which promised to build them up (Acts 20:32, 13:43). As they were sent out to preach the gospel, they were commended to grace (Acts 14:26, 15:40).

In each of Paul's thirteen epistles, or letters, he greets his brothers and sisters in the Lord with a blessing of grace, reaffirming that same blessing as he says goodbye. Paul knew the power of grace to sustain even a persecuted church. In the book of Romans, we find over one fourth of the eighty-plus times that Paul mentions grace in his writings. These references weave through the tapestry of his discourse in which he grounds his Roman audience in the truths of God's foundation of grace.

Paul Preaches the Grace of God

Ephesians 2:1-10
In the Apostle Paul's letter to the Ephesian Church, we find one of the most complete teachings on God's grace. Let's take a little closer look at grace through this passage.

.
Our Desperate Condition (2:1-3)
* We were dead in our transgressions and sin.
* We followed the ways of the world.
* We followed the ruler of the kingdom of the air.
* We were disobedient.
* We gratified the cravings of our sinful nature following its desires and thoughts.
* We were objects of God's wrath.

THOUGHTS & NOTES

God Responds to Our Need (2:4-7)
- Out of His great love for us.
- God bestows grace because He is rich in mercy.
- He made us alive—even when we were dead in our transgressions.
- It is by grace we are saved.
- God raised us up with Christ.
- God has seated us with Jesus in the heavenly realms.
- God wants to show the incomparable riches of His grace and His kindness to us in Christ Jesus in the coming ages.

Saved by Grace (2:8-10)
- It is by grace we have been saved.
- It is through faith.
- Salvation is not from ourselves.
- Salvation is the gift of God.
- We cannot earn salvation through works.
- We cannot boast in our salvation.
- We are God's workmanship created in Christ Jesus for good works.
- God has prepared good works in advance for us to do.

Spiritual Blessings of Grace

Ephesians 1:3-14
Grace provides for us right relationship with God and all that we need to live holy in Him.

Who we are "In Christ"
- We are blessed in the heavenly realms with every spiritual blessing in Christ (Eph. 1:3).
- We have been chosen before the creation of the world to be holy and blameless (Eph. 1:4).
- We have been adopted (accepted) in love by God (Eph. 1:4-5).
- We have become sons/children of God (Eph. 1:5).
- We have been freely given His glorious grace (Eph. 1:6).
- We have been redeemed (Eph. 1:7).
- We have been forgiven of our sins (Eph. 1:7).
- We have been lavished with the riches of His grace (Eph. 1:7-8).

Few souls understand what God would accomplish in them if they were
to abandon themselves unreservedly to Him and if they were to allow
His grace to mold them accordingly.

Ignatius, 50-117, Bishop of Antioch

- We know the mystery of His will – to bring all things in heaven and earth together under Jesus (Eph. 1:10).
- We have been chosen for the praise of His glory (Eph. 1:11).
- We have been included in Christ (Eph. 1:13).
- We have been marked with a seal, the Holy Spirit (Eph. 1:13).
- We have a guaranteed inheritance (Eph. 1:13-14).

Jesus, Our Grace Giver

Scripture affirms gifts freely given to us as a result of God's grace. Some of these gifts are listed below. Review them periodically to remind yourself of what Jesus has done for you, and to remember the special position you have in Christ.

- Jesus has tasted death for us so that we no longer have to be afraid it (Heb. 2:9).
- Jesus bore our sins on the cross for us so that we might die to sins and live for righteousness, and that by His wounds we are healed (1 Pet. 2:21-24).
- Jesus has become the Shepherd and Overseer of our souls (1 Pet. 2:24-25).
- Jesus has reconciled us to God (2 Cor. 5:17-20).
- Jesus not only tasted death for us, but He actually became sin for us (2 Cor. 5:21).
- Jesus has made us ambassadors with the ministry and message of reconciliation (2 Cor. 5:18-20).
- Jesus has freed us from the power and grip of sin and condemnation (Rom. 8:1-4).

Grace changes hearts, leads us to relationship with Jesus, empowers us to resist fear and temptation, and to do the will of God.

THOUGHTS & NOTES

- Jesus has delivered us from Satan's power (Col. 2:13-15; 1Jn .3:8)
- Jesus has provided us with eternal life (Jn. 3:16).
- Jesus is building us together to become a dwelling in which He lives by His Spirit (Eph. 2:22).
- Jesus has made us children of God (Gal. 4:4-7).
- Jesus has brought us near (Eph. 2:12-13).
- Jesus has made us fellow citizens with God's people and members of His household (Eph. 2:19).
- Jesus has made us heirs (Rom. 8:15-17).
- Jesus has given us authority over the devil (Lk. 10:19).

deeper waters

The Christian message is "the gospel of the grace of God" (Acts 20:24). God sent His Son to redeem a fallen world as an expression of His extravagant and amazing grace. As we encounter grace, it allows us to know the love of God, the changing of our hearts, and the power necessary to live godly lives and to walk in obedience to Jesus. Let's define the grace of God and take a deeper look at how it affects our lives.

God's Action on Man's Behalf

As Ephesians 2 reminds us, every one of us was "dead in our sins... and followed the ways of the world." The "ruler of the kingdom of the air" affected each of our lives. No matter how *good* we may have been, our past included "gratifying the cravings of our sinful nature." In Scripture, we see a reflection of our heart. Though our sinful nature is depicted accurately, it is written— "But God..." In other words, God stepped in. He took initiative and expressed His kindness toward us.

Grace is God stepping in to our circumstances to intervene on our behalf. While we are undeserving, God treats us as though we are.

Repentance and faith don't save us; rather, they are a proper heart response to God's expression of grace.

Trust the past to God's mercy, the present to God's love and the future to God's providence.

St. Augustine of Hippo, 354-430, Church Father

- God is the one who takes the ungodly and makes them right before Him (Rom. 4:5).
- Jesus died for us when we were powerless (Rom. 5:6).
- While we were still sinners, God demonstrated His love towards us by dying for us (Rom. 5:8).
- All of us have sinned and fall short of God's glory, but are freely made right with God by His grace (Rom. 3:23-24).
- Jesus attended a party at Matthew's home to be with sinners (Mt. 9:9-13).
- Jesus took action on behalf of a woman caught in the middle of sin (Jn. 8:1-11).
- In the story of Zacchaeus we are told that Jesus came to seek and save what was lost (Lk. 19:1-10).
- In the Parable of the Lost Sheep, he leaves the ninety-nine and goes after the one lost sheep until it is found (Lk. 15:1-7).
- In the parable of the Lost Coin, a woman searches the house until she finds it, and then she throws a party for her friends and neighbors to rejoice with her when she does (Lk. 15:8-10).
- In the parable of the Prodigal Son, the father watches and waits for his son to return. When he does return, the father is filled with compassion and runs to meet him, throwing his arms around him and kissing him. His son then receives a special robe and a ring, and they celebrate his homecoming with feasting (Lk. 15:11-32).

A Proper Response to God's Grace
The Bible teaches that we are saved by grace, and not by works (Eph. 2:8-9). Repentance and faith don't save us; rather, they are a proper heart response to God's expression of grace toward us. *Thankfulness*, rooted in the same Greek word as grace, is also a natural overflow of an encounter with the grace of God.

God's Undeserved Love & Favor Towards Man

One of the most important facets of grace is God's undeserved love and favor. God desires for people to know and experience His love for them. He loves and accepts us, and His attitude towards us is one of favor. Did you know that God looks at you with eyes of favor? To get a taste of the gracious love and favor of God, consider these passages from the Psalms.

- "For surely, O Lord, you bless the righteous; you surround them with your *favor* as a shield" (Ps. 5:12).
- "Show the wonder of your great *love*...keep me as the apple of your eye" (Ps. 17:7-8).

THOUGHTS & NOTES

- "For your *love* is ever before me and I walk continually in your truth" (Ps. 26:3).
- "For His anger lasts only a moment, but His *favor* lasts a lifetime" (Ps. 30:5).
- "Your *love*, O Lord, reaches to the heavens...how priceless is your unfailing *love*... continue your *love* to those who know you" (Ps. 36:5,7,10).
- "May your *love* and your truth always protect me" (Ps. 40:11).
- "Within your temple, O God, we meditate on your unfailing *love*" (Ps. 48:9).
- "Have mercy on me, O God, according to your unfailing *love*" (Ps. 51:1).
- "Because your *love* is better than life, my lips will glorify you" (Ps. 63:3).
- "Answer me, O Lord, out of the goodness of your *love*" (Ps. 69:16).
- "The Lord bestows *favor* and honor; no good thing does He withhold from those whose walk is blameless" (Ps. 84:11).
- "Who redeems your life from the pit and crowns you with *love* and compassion (Ps. 103:4).
- "Consider the great *love* of the Lord" (Ps. 107:43).
- "Preserve my life according to your *love*" (Ps. 119:88).
- "Let the morning bring me word of your unfailing *love*, for I have put my trust in you" (Ps. 143:8).

God as Friend of the Broken-Hearted

All of us have suffered rejection, some more deeply than others. We live in a sinful world—we have sinned, and we have been sinned against. Even those with great influence in our lives, such as our parents and family members, authority figures, and peers have hurt us at one time or another. Perhaps these painful experiences have caused us to live with insecurity and in fear of failure and more rejection. Sometimes the pain causes us to build walls within our personalities to keep people away so we won't suffer further hurt.

Wounded by rejection and attempting to compensate for the pain, we often gravitate towards things that are pleasurable to us. One approach to fill our love deficit is through lust, which is an abnormally strong desire to selfishly use or have something. This could include lust for such things as food, alcohol, drugs, power, pornography or sex. Or, we may try to fill our void of love through pride, by performing for people's acceptance. This may look like striving to be superior to others in academics, on the job, in sports, through various talents, or even in ministry. All of these attempts eventually will fail to meet the deep void of love within our hearts.

Instead, we need to turn to Jesus in the midst of pain. Suffering more pain and rejection than anyone, He understands completely (Is. 53:3). He desires to reveal His love, to comfort us, and to heal us of rejection's pain (Ps. 34:18, 147:3). He loves us and accepts us even when we feel like we have been rejected by everyone (Ps. 27:10). He also knows the right people to send our way to express His gracious love and favor towards us.

Though I am not what I ought to be, nor what I wish to be, nor what I hope to be, I can truly say that I am not what I once was...by the grace of God I am what I am.

John Newton, 1725-1807, English clergyman and hymn writer

When rejection comes through those who are supposed to love us most—our parents—a lasting imprint of hurt can mark our lives. Over the years, I have observed that the lack of fathering in a child's life can lead to significant problems as an adult. While both parents play crucial roles in one's emotional development, fathers inherently possess the ability to cast an image of God that reflects their own fathering. The way men live before their children becomes embedded in the souls of young people and affects they way they live their lives.

God as Restorer of Losses

The enemy of our soul, the devil, will do whatever he can to disfigure the character of God in our eyes. Though our parents tried to love us the best they could, Satan attempts to use the wounds our parents suffered at the hands of other people to hinder our own lives. In other words, they rejected and hurt us because they had been rejected and hurt. Hence, the sins of the father are perpetuated from one generation to the next, as Scripture tells us (Ex. 20:4-6, 34:7). To render Satan powerless in our lives and to break the cycle of pain, we must ask God for His grace to forgive those who have hurt us. Because hurt people hurt others and healed people heal others, God's grace will free us to bless anyone who has hurt us, that they might receive God's love and favor through our lives.

God as Father in Heaven

Scripture refers to God as "Everlasting Father" (Is. 9:6) and "a father to the fatherless" (Ps. 68:5). Jesus referred to Him as our "Father in heaven"(Mt .6:9). God desires to 're-parent' us in His love and in His ways. He alone can restore the losses that have impacted our sense of love, acceptance and worth, as well as our sense of belonging and purpose. A look at Psalm 139 reveals God's heart for us as one who knows and loves us completely, is always present, and created us uniquely with a purpose.

The image of God that we carry around in our hearts and minds affects the way we live our daily lives.

THOUGHTS & NOTES

For more on the subject of dealing with hurt and rejection, as well as the healing of the heart, I recommend Dr. Bruce Thompson's book, Walls of My Heart, published by Crown Ministries International.

Our Heavenly Father Knows Us and Loves Us Completely: Psalm 139:1-6
At some point in our lives, most of us question who God is and how connected we are to Him. Is a real relationship possible? We wonder, *How well does He know me and love me?* Scripture tells us that He is our heavenly Father and He loves us perfectly and completely. Let's look more closely at Psalm 139:1-6. Remember, as we look through this passage, that God is not a big one of us—nor is He like our earthly fathers.

- v. 1 – *searched* (Hebrew: means "to dig into"); God has dug deep into us and therefore knows and understands us beyond what we know and understand of ourselves.
- v. 2 – He is aware of the conscious parts of our life: when we sit (passive life) and rise (active life). He knows the subconscious parts: from where our thoughts arise, even before they surface. God knows how we think and what we think about, even how our thoughts form and flow to our minds.
- v. 3 – He is familiar with our choices and habits, our ways of life. God is intimately acquainted with our ways, both inside and out.
- v. 4 – His knowledge of us is thorough. God understands us, He knows our language (what we mean when we talk) and He relates to us and loves us completely.
- vv. 5-6 – He is timeless and infinite—*behind* (our past) and *before* (our future), and His hand upon me (present). His knowledge of us was too wonderful for the Psalmist, David, to comprehend. God knows our past, our present and our future and He has laid His hand on our lives. God knows us better than anyone.

Our Father's Loving Heart
- Our Father in heaven knows everything about us (Mt. 10:29,30).
- He loved us even when we were at our worst (Rom. 5:8).
- He is affectionate towards us and lavishes His love upon us (Dt. 33:12; 1Jn. 3:1).
- He has loved us so much that He has adopted us into His family (Gal. 4:4-7).
- He calls us by name (Jn. 10:3).
- He is our "Abba" Father (Rom. 8:15).
- His love for us will never ever end (Jer. 31:3).
- His love is a giving, self-sacrificial love (He died for us) (Jn. 3:16).
- Our Father in heaven loves us as much as He loves Jesus (Jn. 17:23).

God loves each of us as if there were only one of us.

St. Augustine of Hippo, 354-430, Church Father

Images of God as Father

It was May 28, 1984, and I would never be the same after this day. My wife, Cheryl, was nine months pregnant and ready for birth of our first child. When the time came for her to give birth, I was at her side and had the privilege of seeing our son born into the world.

Cheryl and I were thrilled and thankful to God that he had given us a little boy. Within minutes of his birth, he was whisked away by a nurse who asked me to follow. I walked close to her as we made our way down a hallway in this little hospital in Kealakekua, Hawaii.

We took a right and entered into a little side room where the nurse began to fill the sink with lukewarm water. While doing so, she handed me my freshly born bloody and slimy son, and instructed me to wash him. She gave me a towel and left the room, leaving me alone with my son for the very first time.

I looked at him and studied him—and found that he had my chin! As I began to gently wash him, I spoke tenderly and I experienced feelings I had never felt before. I told him that his name was Ryan David, that I loved him, that I would always love him, and that I would remain committed to him all the days of my life.

As I expressed my love and commitment to my new little boy, he laid before me, peacefully observing this man that he would soon come to know as his father. He didn't have to get cleaned up for me to love him. He didn't have to promise me anything, or perform to gain my love and acceptance. He had already won my heart—and I had given him my unconditional love long before I ever saw him.

I had thoughts and emotions that night unlike anything I had ever experienced. It was wonderful to have a child whom I could love and give myself to. Although I knew I would make many mistakes as I raised him, my heart was steadfast in that I would love him no matter what. Later, it dawned on me—If I could express that kind of deep love and commitment to a child as a finite father, how much more does God, as an infinite heavenly Father, desire for us to know His unconditional love and commitment towards us?

For our heavenly Father, we don't have to get cleaned up, promise anything or perform to gain His heart's attention. His love knows no bounds and His commitment towards us is everlasting. How He longs for us to catch just a glimpse of how much He wants to lavish His love upon us. He knows that once we grasp hold of His amazing love for us, we will never be the same again.

THOUGHTS & NOTES

Our Heavenly Father is Always Present: Psalm 139:7-12
- vv. 7-8 – Two questions are asked here, both dealing with escaping God's presence. The answer is simply that no destination can separate us from God.
- vv. 9-10 – When David writes about the "wings of the dawn," he seems to be imagining riding on the rays of sunlight that shoot across the sky into the heavens as the sun comes up over the horizon each morning. He then imagines settling across the full expanse of the seas to the farthest point from God. No matter where we go, God preceded us and we will find Him as though He had been awaiting our arrival. His hand will be there to guide and hold us.
- vv. 11-12 – Darkness, that which is of ultimate physical limitation, does not obscure His sight. The blackest night cannot conceal our whereabouts. Absolutely nothing can hide us from God's presence. Darkness is as light to God.

Our Father's Present and Attentive Heart:
- He is our everlasting Father (Is. 9:6).
- He is always with us and will never leave or abandon us (Dt. 31:6).
- He keeps us in His hands (Jn. 10:29).
- He is a father to the fatherless (Ps. 68:5).
- When we feel rejected and forsaken, He receives us (Ps. 27:10).
- He is always attentive to us and cares for us (1 Pet. 5:7).
- He knows our needs and provides for us (Mt. 6:8, 25-32).
- He is compassionate and a comforter (2 Cor. 1:3).

Images of God as Father

My precious and beautiful daughter, Malia Joy, was barely five-years-old when it happened. It was something that happens to everyone at some point in their life—but now it had happened to my little girl.

To appreciate the drama of the moment for me, you must first understand something. As a father who loves his daughter, I had done everything I had known to do to keep her safe, both physically and emotionally. I taught her not to run in the street, not to go with strangers, and to hold hands when we were in crowds. I held her often, and told her I loved her over and over and prayed for her. But none of that helped on this particular day when the safe place we created for our daughter was violated—by another five-year-old! Oh, Malia was fine physically, but she encountered something new that day. She discovered what it meant to be rejected and to have a hurting heart.

We have ... unbroken fellowship with Him. A father never sends his child away with the thought that he does not care about his child knowing that he loves him. The father longs to have his child believe that he has the light of his father's countenance upon him all the day - that, if he sends the child away to school, or anywhere that necessity compels, it is with a sense of sacrifice of parental feelings. If it be so with an earthly father, what think you of God?

Andrew Murray, 1828-1917, South African Pastor, Missionary and Writer

I won't forget when she came to me and said, "Daddy, why would someone say that they don't like me and won't play with me?" I took her into my arms to comfort and reassure her, all the while dealing with some emotions of my own! Of course I had compassion for the confused and hurting heart of my daughter, but, surprisingly, I also wanted to get my hands on that five-year-old to let her experience a little hurt of her own! Fortunately, I focused on Malia that day, wanting to be close to her and available to show her how precious she was to me.

God is so much more present to us than I could ever hope to be for my loved ones. I wasn't around when my daughter got hurt—but God was. He is always with us. He knows every time we have been rejected or abandoned. He longs to reveal Himself as a Father to comfort and care for us, more than an earthly father ever could.

Invite God's presence, even now, into those closed-off places of your life, to touch those areas of rejection and to heal the tender places of hurt and injury. He loves you and longs to take your hurting heart into His embrace.

Our Heavenly Father Has Created Us Uniquely with Purpose: Psalm 139:13-18

- vv. 13,14 – David recognized that he was uniquely and wonderfully created by God and is amazed at the complexity of his being, both inside and out. He recognizes from the design of his body that there is someone greater that is regulating even the physical systems of his life. His heart beats by itself. He breathes without deciding to do so. His inner organs function 24 hours a day, without deliberate thought. God has given us physical looks, a personality, abilities and gifts. David is in awe of God's wondrous creation. While still in our mother's womb, God created each of us according to His design as He desired.
- vv. 15-16 – My frame...woven together (Heb. means: embroidered)...unformed body—all speak of God's hand in the formation of our beings. God has uniquely hand-crafted each of us to enable us to fulfill His purposes in and through our lives. Therefore, we must be content in who God has made us to be and never compare ourselves with others.
- vv. 17-18 – precious thoughts... outnumbering the grains of sand—God is constantly thinking an uninterrupted stream of loving thoughts towards us as though no one else exists.

THOUGHTS & NOTES

Our Father's Giving Heart
- He is generous and a giver of gifts (Mt. 7:11).
- When He disciplines us it is out of love and not anger, and to get us back on track (Heb. 12:7-13).
- He doesn't compare us with others, He is impartial (1 Pet. 1:17).
- He gives us the desires of our hearts (Ps. 37:3-5).
- He had made us His heirs (Gal. 4:4-7).
- He is crafting us for His special purposes (Is. 64:8).
- He will lead us (Ps. 139:24).
- He has prepared a special place for us in heaven (Jn. 14:23).

Images of God as Father

When my children were young I always brought home something special for them when I returned from a trip, just to let them know how much I had been thinking of them and missing them. My family waiting at the airport for me had become somewhat of a tradition. Cheryl would bring Ryan and Malia to the gate where they would run to greet me, leap into my arms and smother me with hugs and kisses. When I put them down, their eyes would look into mine with anticipation as they would ask, "Dad, what did you bring us?" At that point, I would pull something from my briefcase—sometimes it was candy, other times it was a toy. One time it was even a cactus from the desert.

Around this time, Ryan and Malia began to express their desire to add an addition to our family—a dog. We talked about this for many weeks and looked through dog books to try to determine what kind we might get. One Sunday afternoon, Cheryl saw an advertisement in the local newspaper about a family who was giving away puppies. After calling and learning that they lived a few blocks from us, Cheryl went to take a look. Returning home, she declared that she had picked out an adorable three-week-old Black Labrador/German Shepherd puppy. I went to see it for myself and found that Cheryl was right—she would be perfect for us. There was one catch, though. The puppy was too young to be given away and wouldn't be ready until the weekend of my next trip. Instead of telling the kids about the dog, Cheryl and I decided to surprise them and bring the pup home as my special gift when I returned from that journey.

The three weeks dragged on as our kids told us daily how they wanted a dog. Everything within us wanted to reveal our secret, but we knew it would spoil a wonderful surprise. Finally the day came. Cheryl had someone stay with the kids so we could pick up the puppy on our way from the airport to surprise them when we walked in the front door. The anticipation was almost unbearable—we could hardly wait to see their expressions.

I am graven on the palms of His hands. I am never out of His mind. All my knowledge of Him depends on His sustained initiative in knowing me. I know Him, because He first knew me, and continues to know me. He knows me as a friend, One who loves me; and there is no moment when His eye is off me, or His attention distracted for me, and no moment, therefore, when His care falters.

J.I. Packer, Theologian and Writer

When we walked in the door, the kids met me with the traditional hugs and kisses, while I concealed the new addition to our family in my hand behind my back. At last, Ryan and Malia popped the question—"Dad, what did you bring us?" This was the moment Cheryl and I had been planning, preparing and waiting for! I moved my hand from behind my back and there was the little black puppy before their wide eyes and squeals of delight. For a minute they wondered if the dog was real or just a toy, and then when it pottied on the floor they knew it was for real! Needless to say joy and laughter abounded in our home on that night as "Lady" became a part of our family.

Just as Cheryl and I anticipated giving something special to our kids, our Father in Heaven has prepared many special things for us. At just the right moment, He will pull His hand from behind His back, so to speak, and reveal His gift. Perhaps He will hold before us something pertaining to our calling. Maybe it will be the person we will eventually marry. Perhaps it is a child, or a healing, or a provision we can't feasibly attain for ourselves. There are myriad desires and longings of our hearts that our heavenly Father wishes to fulfill for us.

Be assured of this—God has prepared wonderful things in advance for me and for you. He knows the best time to give us the things we want or need. He desires to bless you beyond anything you could imagine. You can trust Him completely.

God's Enabling Power

Grace more than saves us. It permeates our beings and sustains us. When we walk in God's grace as power, He is able to live His life through us. This enables us to walk in obedience, becoming more like Him, accomplishing His purposes and bringing Him glory. Let's look at some of the areas of our lives where we are to let grace have its way in and through us.

Power to Change Hearts

God wants us rightly related to Him, so He drops His plumbline of truth next to our hearts to expose hidden things that would prevent us from drawing into His presence (Am. 7:7-9). A plumbline is a standard of measure used to ensure that something is properly aligned. God's plumbline, so to speak, is His heart conveyed to us through the absolutes, values and truth revealed in Scripture. By these, His grace aligns our hearts and transforms our lives.

All of us have measured our perceptions by false plumblines, dropped unknowingly into our lives by parents, authority figures, peers, and the culture we've grown up in. The result of these errant measures is that they've deceived us into believing incomplete or distorted truths, affecting the way we view and relate to God, ourselves, and others. Our entire belief system needs to be rightly aligned to God's plumbline—His absolutes, values and truth.

THOUGHTS & NOTES

Our hearts play an important role in our decisions, actions and relationships.
* It is the wellspring of life (Pr. 4:23).
* As we think in our hearts, so are we (Pr. 23:7).
* As water reflects a man's face, so the heart reflects the man (Pr. 27:19).
* God looks at the heart more than the outward appearance (1 Sam. 16:7).
* The heart is deceitful and desperately sick—who can know it? (Jer. 17:9-10).

What is in your heart is the real you. God will use difficult situations and circumstances, the storms of life, to expose our reactions and reveal what resides in our hearts. Our reactions become windows to our hearts. When we see that something is out of line with God's truth, we can invite God to come and cleanse, heal, forgive and rightly align us to His absolutes, values and truths that are revealed in His Word. The key is yielding to His Spirit—He will do it by His grace. He promises to give us a new heart and a new spirit (Ez. 36:26,27; Heb. 8:10).

Power to Live Godly Lives

* God's grace, as power, enables us to overcome sin and to live godly lives (Titus 2:11-14).
    - Grace teaches us to say no to ungodliness and worldly passion.
    - It teaches us to live self-controlled, upright and godly lives.
    - It is His enabling power to overcome sin (Rom. 6:14).
    - Grace to overcome sin is given to those who recognize their weaknesses and in their time of need call out to Jesus to rescue them (Heb. 4:14-16).
    - God gives grace to the humble and actively opposes any reliance in human ability to overcome sin (Jam. 4:6).
    - To experience God's grace as power to overcome sin, we must realize the truth of what Jesus said, "Apart from me you can do nothing" (Jn. 15:5).
* God's grace as power enables us to minister grace to others through our words (Eph. 4:29).
* God's grace as power enables us to function in our spiritual gifts (Rom. 12:6; 1 Pet. 4:10).
* God's grace as power enables us to grow through trials and difficulties (1 Pet. 5:8).
* God's grace as power can keep us from bitterness (Heb. 12:14-15).
* God's grace as power enables us to deal well with unbelievers (Col. 4:5-6).
* God's grace as power enables us to move in signs and wonders while declaring the gospel of grace (Acts 14:3).

Faith is a living, daring confidence in God's grace, so sure and certain that a man could stake his life on it a thousand times.

Martin Luther, 1483-1546, German Theologian and Reformer

Candidates for Grace

Let's close this chapter by taking a look at those who are candidates for the amazing grace of God.

The Sinner – Rom. 3:23-24; 5:20-21
- Never write off those who don't yet know Jesus as they are prime candidates for God's grace.
- When we sin as believers we are candidates for grace; run to Him and confess your sin and know His cleansing.
- Grace is how God responds to our failures.

The Powerless – Rom. 5:6, 8
- When we feel helpless, out of control, unable to bring about change, or unable to stand, God extends his grace to us.

The Weak – 2 Cor. 12:9, 10
- The grace and power of God is made perfect in our weakness.
- John the Baptist knew that he must decrease so Jesus could increase (Jn. 3:30).
- The weaker we become, the more grace abounds and the more glory God receives.

The Needy – Heb. 4:14-16
- The feeble, frail, desperate and weary.
- When we are in need, we can come confidently to the Throne of Grace knowing that we will receive mercy and grace in our time of need.

The Humble – Jam. 4:5; 1 Pet. 5:5, 6
- Acknowledging our need for God primes us to receive grace.
- Humility attracts the presence of God.
- Are you willing to humble yourself?

THOUGHTS & NOTES

CASTING THE NET

What was your concept of God's grace before studying this chapter? How has it changed?

_____
_____
_____
_____
_____
_____
_____
_____
_____
_____

What spoke to you the most from the portion of this chapter entitled _The Spiritual Blessings of Grace_ and _Jesus, Our Grace Giver?_

_____
_____
_____
_____
_____
_____
_____
_____
_____
_____
_____
_____

_____
_____
_____

Grace is but Glory begun, and Glory is but Grace perfected.

Jonathan Edwards, 1703-1758, American Preacher and Theologian

What has been the image of God that you've carried around inside of you up to this point? How does a fresh understanding of God as your heavenly Father change your impression? Where do you need Him to reveal more of Himself as a Father to you?

_____

_____

_____

_____

_____

_____

_____

_____

_____

_____

_____

_____

_____

_____

_____

_____

_____

_____

THOUGHTS & NOTES

_____

_____

_____

Where do you need to know God's grace as His enabling power in your life? What has His plumbline revealed about your heart? Are there sin issues you need His grace to help you overcome?

_____

_____

_____

_____

_____

_____

_____

_____

How are you a candidate for God's grace today?

_____

_____

_____

_____

_____

_____

_____

_____

_____

_____

_____

_____

You say grace before meals. All right. But I say grace before the concert and the opera, and grace before the play and pantomime, and grace before I open a book, and grace before sketching, painting, swimming, fencing, boxing, walking, playing, dancing and grace before I dip the pen in the ink.

Gilbert K. Chesterton, 1874-1936, British Writer

CATCH OF THE DAY

Chapter Summary

- Jesus Christ came full of grace and truth. Grace is an overflow of who God is.
- The disciples of Jesus, Paul, and the other New Testament writers were impacted by God's grace. It was at the core of their gospel message.
- We have been saved by God's grace. He has acted on our behalf. Our salvation is a gift, and is nothing that we deserve or could have earned through works.
- Grace as God's undeserved love and favor has been extended to us. We have a Father in heaven that looks at us with eyes of favor. We can also know and experience God's grace as power that enables us to live godly lives and walk in obedience to Him.
- We are not only saved by the grace of God, but our lives are to be permeated by it. When we sin, feel powerless, weak, needy, and humble, we are candidates for grace. It is in that place that Jesus will meet us, fill us with His grace, and receive much glory through our lives.

What are the two or three things the Holy Spirit spoke most clearly to you through this chapter, and how will you respond to Him?

_____

_____

_____

_____

_____

_____

_____

THOUGHTS & NOTES ——

A VIEW FROM THE SHORE

"We implore you on Christ's behalf: Be reconciled to God.
God made Him who had no sin to be sin for us, so that in Him
we might become the righteousness of God."

2 Corinthians 5:20-21

The Cross. While it has become the identifying symbol of Christians around the world today, in Jesus' day it was something people did not want to be identified with. The Roman cross was an object of shame.

Crucifixion was a common sight in the first century. People were accustomed to roadways lined with the crucified bodies of criminals, slaves, assassins, and society's rebels. While the Jews did not crucify living persons, they had been known to suspend the bodies of the executed upon a tree to further their punishment. Those hung on a tree were considered accursed by God. Although crucifixion was accepted as part of the culture, both Jews and Romans abhorred it (Jos. 10:22; Dt. 21:22,23; Gal. 3:13).

How, then, did the Cross become so important to our faith?

The Bible teaches us that Jesus came to earth for several reasons. He came to show us what God is really like (Jn. 14:9). He modeled for us how we should walk with God and with others (Jn. 13:13-15). He came to destroy the works of the devil (1Jn. 3:8). And, foremost, the One without sin came to atone for sin—to die on the Cross that we might be forgiven and reconciled to God. Through His shed blood, we are made able to have a relationship with a holy God. The Cross of Christ disarmed Satan's power and authority in our lives (Col. 1:19-22, 2:13-15), and it empowered us to walk in peaceful relationship with others (Eph. 2:11-22). It serves as a reminder of the depths to which God was willing to go to rescue the worst of sinners, that we might enjoy His love, forgiveness, peace and joy.

That's why Christians celebrate the meaning of the Cross. It is the centerpiece of Christian faith because it represents God's expression of love for us. It is the means by which we know forgiveness from sin. And it is the prelude of all God's promises to us in Christ, rooted at the very center of the gospel message: Once we were separated from God, but now we have been reconciled to Him because of the death of Jesus on the Cross. How awesome is that!

In this chapter, we will further explore the dynamics of man's sin and separation from God, and the role of the cross in our reconciliation to God. We will also take a practical look at how repentance from sin and expressions of forgiveness can be applied in our lives in light of the work of the Cross.

SETTING SAIL

Throughout Scripture, contrasts are used to differentiate between the things of God and the plight of man. Darkness and light, mortal and immortal, flesh and spirit. Our salvation represents a crossing over from one realm to another—from the kingdoms of this world to the Kingdom of our Lord and Christ. As we look at the cross, sin and repentance, we see just how integral these things are to our faith's foundation. It allows us to not only see who God is and what He has done on our behalf, but who we are and our desperate need of a Savior.

Created in God's Image*

Have you ever wondered what makes you *you*? Sadly, people tend to define who they are by measuring themselves against who everyone else appears to be. This usually leaves people feeling confused, frustrated and insecure. The Bible provides us with the only standard by which man can judge. The wonderful news is that it tells us you and I are God's workmanship (Eph. 2:10). Imagine. God chose us and knew us before He laid the foundations of the Earth. With anticipation, He waited for the precise time in history to introduce us into His created world. For such a time as this, He ordained that we should live.

Man—Made in the Image of God – Gen. 1:26-27
- Man was made out of the dust of the ground (Gen. 2:7; 3:19).
- If our physical bodies were, in fact, reduced to dust, the minerals would value less than $100. Our true worth exceeds physical attributes. We are infinitely valuable because God breathed life and spirit into us (Gen. 1:26-27).
- Man is unique from the rest of creation in that he is made in the image of God, capable of having relationship with the Creator.

Man—Made to Reflect the Image of God
- Together, men and women reflect God's being (Gen. 1:26-27).
- Men and women were made to reflect God's character to the world around them, revealing His love, grace, truth, mercy, holiness, etc.
- Men and women demonstrate the dominion of God by stewarding creation (Gen. 1:26).

THOUGHTS & NOTES

* I would like to acknowledge Dr. J. Rodman Williams, a professor at Regent University's School of Divinity in Virginia Beach, VA, whose lectures and materials on God, the World and Redemption have helped shape my understanding of the nature of man, sin, and the atonement. I have gleaned from his material on these subjects and it is used here with his expressed permission.

Man—Made to be Free

God's original intention was that man should be aware of good only, that he would walk in obedience and blessing. By choosing to disobey God in the garden, man was introduced to sin and evil. Because of this choice man began to reap the consequences of sin. In Christ, we are free to fellowship with God (Gen. 1:31; 2:9, 16; 3:8-9; Rom. 8:2, 21).

- In Christ, we are free from sin and bondage.
- In Christ, we are free to enjoy creation.
- In Christ, we are free to live according to God's personal design.
- In Christ, we are free to do God's will.
- In Christ, we are free to make choices, free to obey God. (True freedom involves choice. If there is no option but to do God's will, freedom is only a word.)

An Overview of Sin

Human nature is inherently sinful. Scripture tells us, "There is no one righteous, not even one... all have sinned and fall short of the glory of God" (Rom 3:10, 24). But what is sin?

Sin Defined

- Sin is willful rebellion against God, His will, and commands (Is. 53:6; Eph. 4:18).
- Sin is a personal act against God, turning away from Him and His purposes (Ps. 51:4).
- Sin is failing to live up to God's intentions.
- Sin is failing to do what you know is right to do (Jam. 4:17).

Sin's Nature—Unbelief

- In the garden, the serpent laid the seeds of unbelief by asking, "Did God really say...?" (Gen. 3:1).
- Sin is often a mix of truth and error with just enough truth to make it an attractive lie (Gen. 3:1-5).

Our salvation represents a crossing over from one realm to another — from the kingdoms of this world to the Kingdom of our Lord and Christ.

One great power of sin is that it blinds men so that they do not recognize its true character.

Andrew Murray, 1828-1917, South African Pastor, Missionary and Writer

- Disbelieving who God is and what He has said lies at the root of every sin; it is a failure to have faith in God (Rom. 14:23).
- Sin entered the world when mankind turned its back on who God is and what He had said and was carried away by what was forbidden (Gen. 2:15-17).
- A note on temptation: when anyone allows something forbidden to become an object of focused attention, it may soon become so alluring that everything else, including God, is abandoned to obtain it.

Sin's Nature—Pride
- In the garden the serpent said, "You will be like God" (Gen. 3:5).
- The sin of Lucifer was one of pride, ambition and self-exaltation—to be like God (Is. 14:12-15).
- Temptation focuses on self (my interests), seeking to fulfill our own potential (my goals, gifts and dreams) and desires (lust of the flesh, lust of the eyes and the pride of life) (1 Jn. 2:15-17).

Sin's Nature—Disobedience
- In the garden they ate of the fruit in direct disobedience to God (Gen. 2:15-17; 3:6-7).
- Sin is not in opposition to a rule, but in opposition to a person—God. At the core of every sin is a turning away from the love of God.
- Disobedience is the fruition of sin, rising from the fertile soil of unbelief and pride.
- Sin's progression: unbelief in the mind moves to pride in the heart and bears the fruit of disobedience in the will.

The Consequences of Sin

Romans 1:18-32
Sin takes man through a maze of detours, separating him from open fellowship with God. When we lend ourselves to sin, we're held within its grasp longer than we would have expected. All sin has consequences.

Sin Leads to Futility
- Futility breeds darkness and confusion in man's thoughts and actions.
- Man pursues a course of absolute selfishness, forgetting God in the pursuit of everything else.

THOUGHTS & NOTES

Sin Leads to Idolatry

- When God is removed from our lives, something else takes His place in our hearts. When we choose sin, we dethrone God and crown a counterfeit as king of our lives.
- This always results in immoral thoughts and actions (Rom. 1:24-27).

Sin Leads to Guilt

- Adam and Eve hid in the garden, which signifies a deep sense of wrong and a break in their relationship with God (Gen. 3:7-8).
- Deep within man he knows he is guilty—the conscience is the inner court of judgment that produces the guilty or not guilty verdict.
- The only way to freedom from guilt is through repentance and forgiveness (1Jn. 1:9)

Sin Leads to Punishment

- In the garden there was the blaming of others to avoid punishment (Gen. 3:9-13).
- Whenever sin occurs there are consequences that follow (Num. 32:23; Gal. 6:7).

Sin Leads to Separation

- Sin results in spiritual death which separates man from God (Gen. 3:23-24).
- There resides within the heart of man a haunting sense that things should not be this way.

Sin Leads to Estrangement

- Man's relationship with God has been broken.
- Man is estranged from relationships with others, finding his condition as one of aggressiveness toward others in his life.

Sin Leads to Bondage

- Men and women no longer enjoy the freedom God gave them.
- Sin has become the master enslaving its object (Eph. 2:1-3).
- Man is stuck, absolutely incapable of reconciling himself to God.

Sin takes man through a maze of detours, separating him from open fellowship with God.

Turn to God from idols. For the sword of His wrath that had been aimed at you has been sheathed into the heart of His Son. And the arrows of His anger that had been put against your breast were loosed into the Lord Jesus Christ. Because He has died for you, you were forgiven.

Paris Reidhead, 1919-1992, Missionary Leader and Bible Teacher

The Biblical Realities of Sin

Our sinful choices alter our life circumstances, sometimes even complicating the life circumstances of those whom our sin impacts. Regardless of the diverse ways sin may deter us, the Bible assures us that all sin simultaneously produces one same effect—a separation from God.

- Man has a sinful nature and therefore a bent towards sin (Rom. 7:14-25).
- Everyone has sinned and has fallen short of God's glory (Rom. 3:23-24).
- Each person is responsible for his or her own sin (Ez. 18:4, 20).
- The results of sin are spiritual and physical death and eternal separation from God (Rom. 6:23; Rev. 20:11-15).
- Man is absolutely incapable of being made right with God and desperately needs a Savior (Tit. 3:3-8).

 # Deeper Waters

Sin is a reality of our earthly life. Each of us will fall to sin's temptation, and each of us will be sinned against. Through Jesus, however, we are invited to repentance and forgiveness. As we look to the Cross of Christ, we may receive atonement for our sins, and experience wholeness of heart and oneness with our heavenly Father.

Atonement

Atonement is the crux of the gospel message. It is through atonement that we are made pure and blameless and able to come before the Father.

Atonement Defined

- Atonement means *to be*, or *cause to be*, "at one." It is the overcoming of a serious breach between two parties.
- Atonement signifies some action taken that can bring satisfactory repair for an offense or injury, and to cancel the evil effects so two parties can be one again. Atonement is the process of reconciliation.
- Atonement between God and man refers to God's action that repairs the separation caused by man's sin. Man cannot make atonement or overcome his separation from God through his own strength and resources.

THOUGHTS & NOTES

_____

_____

_____

_____

- God took it upon Himself, at a supreme cost, to provide a way through His Son, Jesus Christ, to restore the relationship between God and man—to bring about an "at-one-ment".

Setting the Stage for God's Atonement

Who God Is

- He is a God of love and mercy reaching across the wide divide to sinners (Gen. 3:21; Hos. 11:8-9; Jn. 3:16; Rom. 5:8).
- He is a God of holiness and righteousness whose wrath is due upon the disobedient (Gen. 3:24; Hab. 1:13; Rom. 1:18, 3:10; Eph. 2:3, 5:6).
- He is a God of truth and faithfulness acting with integrity to maintain every promise from His Word (Ps. 51:6; Is. 45:19; Ps. 57:10, 119:75).

What Man Has Become

- Man is a sinner before God, walking in unbelief, pride and disobedience (Rom. 3:23).
- Man has become an idolater, becoming deeply committed to the things of this world (Rom. 1:21-25; Col. 3:5-6).
- Man is a guilty sinner deserving punishment and knowing that he will stand under the judgment of God (Rom. 6:23).
- Man is enslaved to sin, unable to free himself (Eph. 2:1-3).

The Emerging Conflict

Two opposed conditions set the stage for God's act of atonement.

- God, who is loving and merciful, does not desire the punishment and death of any of His creation. Yet, in His holiness and righteousness He cannot tolerate sin.
- Man, on the other hand, has no power to change his sinful condition. He cannot free himself from guilt and bondage. Man cannot keep the commands of God. He cannot enter God's presence. Because he is unable to help himself, his lot is death.
- God's divine plan, the reconciliation of the world to Himself, displays His infinite wisdom, where love, mercy, holiness and righteousness, truth and faithfulness come together in the supreme sacrifice of the atonement.

God took it upon Himself, at a supreme cost, to provide a way to restore the relationship between God and man.

Evidence of our hardness is that we are more concerned about our sufferings than our sins.

Matthew Henry, 1662-1714, English Preacher and Scholar

The Method of Atonement – Jesus' Death on the Cross
Who Jesus Is
- Jesus, the Son of God, became flesh and lived as a man among men (Jn. 1:14; Gal. 4:4-5; Phil. 2:7-8).
- He was without sin (2 Cor .5:21; Heb. 4:15).
- He lived a life of complete obedience to His Father's will so that His death was of One who was blameless, holy and righteous (Mt. 26:36-42; Jn. 17:4).
- The death of Jesus was on behalf of our sins (1 Cor. 15:3; 2 Cor. 5:17-21).

What Jesus Became
- His death on the cross, a sacrifice for man's sin, was foreshadowed in the Old Testament's Day of Atonement (Lev. 16).
- It also reflects the Passover lamb (Ex. 12:21-30; 1 Cor .5:7).
- Jesus is called the Lamb of God (Jn. 1:29; Rev. 5:12).
- His sacrificial death conquered death once and for all (Rom. 6:10; Heb. 9:12,26).
- It was the sacrifice of Himself (as priest and victim/sacrificer and sacrifice) (Heb. 7:27).
- He offered a sacrifice without blemish (Ex. 12:5; 1 Pet. 1:18-19).
- Our salvation is by the blood of the Lamb (Col. 1:19-20; Rev. 7:14).
- Redemption was brought about by God through the blood of Jesus, the Lamb of God.

The Results of the Atonement
Jesus Identified with Mankind
- On the cross, Jesus identified with the people that He had identified with in his ministry, the sick, the helpless, the sinner (Is. 53:4).
- All the sin of the human race was put upon Him, taking our place as the "One Great Sinner."
- God, in His infinite love and mercy, and in human flesh, was made sin and a curse that we might know His salvation and blessing forever (Is. 53:4-12).

Jesus Received Our Punishment – Is. 53:5, 10
- As the "One Great Sinner," He received the full measure of divine wrath in direct proportion to the sin of the world, past, present and future. This is a vicarious punishment on our behalf that is beyond comprehension.
- Becoming sin, the Father could no longer look upon Him and Jesus experienced the horrible God-forsakenness that belongs to hell itself. In the midst of this He cried out, "My God, my God, why have you forsaken me?" (Ps. 22; Mt. 27:46).
- Jesus experienced our lostness, our condemnation and damnation while on the Cross.

THOUGHTS & NOTES

- In the Old Testament, an animal was slain as the substitute, thus receiving the penalty of death due the Israelites. Such a sacrifice was inadequate to deal with the depth of human sin. Only the death of Jesus, representing both God and man, could accomplish the payment for the penalty of sin, the full extinguishing of guilt and the cleansing necessary to restore relationship between God and man. (Lev. 16)
- This was God, in Christ Jesus, reconciling the world to Himself (2 Cor. 5:17-21).

Jesus Took Away Our Sin
- Not only has Jesus received the just punishment for our sins, but He also has freed us from the bondage of sin through His death (Is. 53:6-12; Rom. 8:1-4).
- We are completely forgiven through the death of Jesus on the cross (Eph. 1:7).
- We have been ransomed, bought with a price, so that we might be free from sin (Mt .20:28; Mk .10:45; 1 Cor. 6:19-20; 1 Tim. 2:5-6; Rev .5:9).
- We have been redeemed, or released from sin, to pursue righteousness (Lk. 4:18; Col. 1:13).
- We are free from the dominion of Satan and the fear of death (Col. 2:15; Heb. 2:14-15; 1Jn. 3:8).

Jesus Reconciled Man to God
- Jesus' death on the cross is the solution to man's broken relationship with God (2 Cor .5:17-21; Eph .2:1-10; Col. 1:21-22).
- Jesus is worthy to receive the rewards of His sufferings (Rev. 5:9-14).

Jesus' Walk to the Cross

Jesus' journey to the cross allows us to better understand the price paid for our sin. Follow along with the accompanying Scriptures taken from the gospels and take the time to meditate on the reality of what Jesus experienced physically, mentally, emotionally, spiritually and relationally. Ask God for a fresh revelation of His passion for you on the Cross.

Jesus at the Passover Meal (Last Supper)
- Jesus was eagerly desiring to enjoy this meal with His disciples (Lk. 22:14-16).
- Satan enters Judas, one of the Twelve, who then betrays Jesus (Mt. 26:20-25; Lk. 22:3-6).
- Jesus gives thanks and serves His disciples the bread and wine (Lk. 22:19-20).

There is no mystery in heaven or earth so great as this—
a suffering Deity, an almighty Saviour nailed to a Cross.

Samuel Zwemer, 1867-1952, Missionary and Princeton Theological Seminary Professor

- When Jesus tells them that they will all fall away on account of Him, Peter vehemently denies that he would ever do such a thing. Jesus tells him that before the rooster crows he will deny Him three times (Lk. 22:31-34; Mt. 26:31-35).

Jesus at the Garden of Gethsemane
- Following the Passover meal, Jesus and His disciples went to the Garden of Gethsemane (Lk. 22:39; Mt. 26:36).
- As Jesus went off to pray, he asked His friends to stay awake and pray with Him. Nonetheless, they fell asleep (Mt. 26:37-44).
- While in prayer, He asked the Father to take this cup of suffering from Him. His prayer was so intense that an angel came to minister to Him (Lk. 22:43).
- Jesus was in such anguish that He began to sweat blood. Although this is a very rare phenomenon, blood sweat, or hematidrosis, results from great emotional stress as tiny capillaries in the sweat glands burst. This experience surely produced weakness and a physical state of shock (Lk. 22:44).
- Judas and the mob arrived and he betrayed Jesus with a kiss (Lk. 22:47-48; Mt. 26:47-50).
- Peter drew his sword and cut off the ear of the servant of the high priest. Jesus touched the servant and healed him (Lk. 22:49-5; Jn. 18:10).
- The disciples deserted Jesus and fled (Mt. 26:56).

Jesus brought before Annas, Caiaphas, and the Sanhedrin
- After responding to Annas, one of the officials standing nearby struck Jesus in the face (Jn. 18:20-22).
- The men guarding Jesus began mocking Him, beating Him and insulting Him (Lk. 22:63-65).
- By daybreak Jesus was found guilty by the Sanhedrin of blasphemy, a crime punishable by death (Lk. 22:66-71).
- It was during this time that Peter denied Jesus three times (Lk. 22:56-62).

Jesus' journey to the cross allows us to better understand the price paid for our sin.

THOUGHTS & NOTES

Jesus before Pontius Pilate

- Since permission for an execution had to come from the governing Romans, Jesus was taken early in the morning by the temple officials to the Praetorium of the Fortress Antonia, the seat of Pontius Pilate, the Procurator of Judea (Lk. 23:1).
- By this time Jesus probably was exhausted, having been battered and bruised and denied sleep.
- Jesus was presented to Pilate by the Jewish leaders, not as a blasphemer but as a self-appointed king who would undermine the Roman authorities (Lk. 23:2).
- After examining Jesus, Pilate found nothing wrong with Him and sent Him to Herod, the Tetrarch of Judea (Lk. 23:4-7).

Jesus before Herod

- Herod asked Jesus many questions, but Jesus remained silent (Lk. 23:8-9).
- Herod and his soldiers ridiculed and mocked Jesus, dressing Him in an elegant robe and then sending Him back to Pilate (Lk. 23:10-11).

Jesus before Pontius Pilate a Second Time

- Once again, Pilate found no basis for legal charge against Jesus (Lk. 23:13-16).
- In the midst of this Pilate's wife had a dream about Jesus (Mt. 27:19).
- It was the governor's custom to release a prisoner chosen by the crowd, and the chief priests and elders persuaded the crowd to ask for Barabbas and have Jesus executed (Lk. 23:18-25; Mt. 27:15-23).
- Pilate appeals to the crowd, trying to release Jesus, but the crowd insists that Barabbas be released and Jesus crucified. Pilate granted them their demand, had Jesus flogged and handed Him over to be crucified (Lk. 23:13-25; Mt. 27:15-26).
- Jesus was flogged by the Roman soldiers (Mt. 27:27-31) with a flagrum, or short whip, comprised of several strips of leather embedded with sharp pieces of sheep bone or small iron balls.
- The soldiers removed Jesus' clothing and tied His hands to a post above His head. His back, buttocks, and legs were flogged repetitively. Though Jewish Law allowed a forty lash maximum, the scourging of the Romans persisted until the victim collapsed or died.
- At first, the blows cut through Jesus' skin only. Then as the flogging continued the lacerations would tear into the underlying skeletal muscles and produce quivering ribbons of bleeding flesh.
- Near fainting, Jesus was untied and allowed to slump to the pavement wet with His blood.

There are some things that can be learned by the head, but...
Christ crucified can only be learned by the heart.

Charles Spurgeon, 1834-1892, English Preacher and Author

- The Roman soldiers, amused that this heap of flesh had claimed to be king, began to mock Jesus. They placed a robe on Him and put a crown of thorns on His head and wooden staff in His hand.
- The soldiers spat on Jesus and struck Him on the head with the wooden staff driving the thorny crown deeper into His scalp.
- Finally, as their mockery came to an end, the robe was torn off His back, opening the wounds once again, causing Jesus excruciating pain.
- Jesus was then led away to be crucified.

The Crucifixion of Jesus – Mt. 27:32–56; Lk. 23:26–49; Jn. 19:16–37
- A heavy crossbar weighing around 75-125 pounds was placed across the exposed muscles of Jesus' neck and tied to his shoulders and arms as He began the 650 yard journey to the place of His execution.
- In spite of Jesus' efforts to carry the cross bar, His body crumbled under the strain. He stumbled and fell, causing the rough wood to rip into the muscles of His shoulders.
- A centurion, wanting to get on with the crucifixion, selected a North African named Simon, from Cyrene, to carry the cross for Jesus.
- After arriving at the place of execution, a hill called Golgotha (meaning The Place of the Skull), the cross bar was placed on the ground and Jesus was thrown backward with His shoulders against the wood.
- A Roman soldier then drove a heavy, square, wrought-iron nail through the wrists and deep into the wood of the cross bar. One foot was then pressed backward against the other while a nail was driven through the arches of each, with His knees left moderately flexed.
- Fiery pain shot through Jesus' body while it cramped in relentless spasms.
- Jesus fought to raise Himself in order to catch one short breath. To do so was difficult. Though He was able to draw air into His lungs, He could not exhale. Slowly, He was suffocating, as is the objective of crucifixion.
- Attempts to move up and down to breathe further shredded Jesus' back.
- Insects fed upon His open wounds and the blood that poured into His eyes and ears.
- Jesus spoke seven times while hanging on the Cross.
    - To the Father regarding those who were crucifying Him—
    "*Father, forgive them, for they do not know what they are doing*" (Lk. 23:34).
    - To the repentant thief—
    "*I tell you the truth, today you will be with me in paradise*" (Lk. 23:39-43).

THOUGHTS & NOTES

- To His disciple John, and His mother, Mary—
  "Dear woman, here is your son. Here is your mother" (Jn. 19:25-27).
- To the Father—
  "My God, my God, why have you forsaken me?" (Mt. 27:46).
  "I am thirsty" (Jn. 19:28).
  "It is finished" (Jn. 19:30).
  "Father, into your hands I commit my spirit" (Lk. 23:46).

- At the sixth hour of the day, darkness came over the land. This darkness clung to the Earth until the ninth hour (Noon to 3:00 PM) (Lk. 23:44-45).
- When Jesus died there was a great earthquake and the curtain of the temple was torn from top to bottom. Tombs broke open and the bodies of holy people who had died were raised to life, appearing to many people (Mt. 27:50-53).
- When the Roman centurion who was overseeing the execution saw all that had happened, he exclaimed, "Surely He was the Son of God!" (Mt. 27:54; Lk. 23:47).
- Finally, a sword was driven through Jesus' side, and blood and water flowed out. This may reveal that Jesus didn't die from suffocation, which was the normal result of crucifixion, but rather of a ruptured heart. Our Savior, the Lord Jesus, died of a broken heart for the sin of the world.

The Resurrection of Jesus
- Jesus rose from the dead in the early morning on the first day of the week and appeared to His disciples (Mt .28:1-15; Mk. 16; Lk. 24:1-49; Jn. 20, 21; 1 Cor .15).
- He then ascended into Heaven (Mk. 16:19; Lk. 24:50-53; Acts 1:1-11).
- The disciples went out and preached everywhere, and the Lord worked with them confirming His word through signs and wonders (Mt. 28:18-20; Mk. 16:15-20; Acts).

Jesus didn't die from suffocation, which was the normal result of crucifixion, but rather of a ruptured heart. Our Savior, the Lord Jesus, died of a broken heart for the sin of the world.

Lord Jesus, you are my righteousness, I am your sin.
You have taken upon yourself what is mine and given me what is yours.
You have become what you were not so that I might become what I was not.

Martin Luther, 1483-1546, German Theologian and Reformer

Our Response to the Cross: Repentance

The work of our salvation is complete in Christ. We need only to repent from sin and receive what had been done on the Cross as atonement for our sins.

A Brief Introduction – Mt. 4:17, 12:41; Mk. 6:12; Acts 2:38, 17:30; 2 Cor. 7:10
- Because of what the atonement accomplished through Jesus' death on the cross we can experience forgiveness as we repent and confess our sins to God (1Jn. 1:9).
- Our sin hinders our walk with God. It also cost God the life of His Son, the Lord Jesus. It is appropriate that we come to a place in our lives of hating sin just as God hates it (Ps. 66:18; Prov. 8:13).
- Repentance is different from being sorry. Repentance brings about a heart and life change, while being sorry is simply feeling bad for getting caught (2 Cor. 7:9-11).
- Repentance is not only something one does as a part of becoming a Christian, but something that becomes a way of life in response to our sin and selfishness.
- We cannot repent for something we are not aware of doing. Nor can we repent of something we don't believe is wrong. We need God's light in our lives to see things as He sees them.
- Repentance is taking responsibility for our actions in relation to God and people.
- Repentance is a gift God grants us to bring about the changing of our hearts (Acts 11:18).
- As believers, it is important for us to cultivate an attitude of correctability, desiring to walk in God's light and truth.

The Meaning of Repentance
- A Turning Around:
    - It means *to turn around*, or to *head back home*.
    - It is not as much a command, as it is an invitation, to set our hearts toward home.
- Exchanging
    - It carries the meaning to convert or exchange.
    - Exchanging the currency of the world's ways with the currency of God's ways.
- Restoring
    - Because our sin has disfigured our lives, God will not only help us to turn away from our sin, but also restore us to our intended design and condition through repentance.
- A Turning Toward
    - Repentance is about turning from sin toward God.

THOUGHTS & NOTES

A Few Working Definitions of Repentance
- A radical heart change in one's attitude toward God, sin and others.
- A complete turning around of one's life toward God and His ways.
- Seeing sin as God sees it, hating it and turning away from it toward Jesus in love, trust and obedience.

Five Steps to Heart Change Through Repentance
- As the Holy Spirit convicts you of your sin, ask Him to show you the commands of God that you have broken by committing that sin.
- Ask the Holy Spirit to reveal to you all the people you have hurt through your sinful choices.
- Invite the Holy Spirit to uncover the motives of your heart that led you to sin.
- Ask the Holy Spirit to show you how you have hindered God's work and have helped Satan's cause through your sin.
- Invite the Holy Spirit to reveal to you the influences in your life that pointed you toward sin.

Restitution
- True repentance is also expressed by making things right with those you've sinned against (Lk. 3:8; Acts 26:20).
- Restitution is going to those you've sinned against with the intention of restoring the relationship by confessing your sin and doing all that is within your ability to right the wrong that has been done.
- It is a practical way to take revenge on sin.
- When you confess your sin to God you are forgiven. Restitution is necessary to walk rightly and integrally with those around us.
- Biblical pictures of restitution:
    - The Prodigal Son (Lk. 15:11-32)
    - Zacchaeus (Lk. 19:1-10)
    - Paul's conscience clean before God and man (Acts 24:16)

Practical steps in making restitution with others:
- Confess to the extent of your sin.
- Avoid the details and name the basic sin(s) committed.
- Be brief and intentional, and do it as soon as possible.
- Don't involve others in your confession. Take responsibility for your own actions.
- Think through what you need to say ahead of time.

He became what we are that He might make us what He is.

St. Athanasius, 296-373, Bishop of Alexandria

Repentance is to leave
The sin we loved before,
And show that we in earnest grieve
By doing so no more.

Charles Spurgeon, 1834-1892, English Preacher and Author

- Look for a time that is appropriate.
- Don't attempt to witness about Jesus while making restitution. Making things right is the testimony of what Jesus is doing in your life.
- Approach others in humility and with a right heart attitude.
- If others have wronged you and confess sin to you, respond from the heart by saying, "I forgive you."

Once you make restitution with someone, receive the Lord's cleansing. The offended person(s) may or may not forgive you. Regardless of how others respond, you have done what God requires of you. Pray for those who choose not to forgive, as their unforgiveness will destroy them.

A Second Response: Forgiveness

Unforgiveness clings to the pain and effects of sin. God gives us the ability to forgive others not only to restore their freedom to them, but particularly to restore our freedom and wholeness to us. Unless we forgive those who have sinned against us, we will never regain peace in our lives.

A Brief Introduction
- All of us have been sinned against and have experienced pain in our lives.
- Pain tempts us to execute revenge on those who have wronged us.
- Unforgiveness is like a disease that consumes us from the inside out until it kills us.
- Unforgiveness also hinders our walk with God and others (Mt. 6:14-15).
- Unforgiveness opens the door to bitterness, rage and anger in our lives (Eph. 4:31-32).
- Jesus died not only so we could be forgiven, but also so we might forgive others.
- Forgiveness is the ripping up of the "I owe you" of the heart.

Unforgiveness clings to the pain and effects of sin. God gives us the ability to forgive others not only to restore their freedom to them, but particularly to restore our freedom and wholeness to us.

THOUGHTS & NOTES

Lessons of Forgiveness — Mt. 18:21-35
- Jesus gives us grace to forgive others—to forgive beyond what we think we are able (Mt. 18:21-22).
- Forgiveness should flow freely from our hearts toward others (Mt. 18:21-22).
- This does not always mean that once you forgive, trust is immediately restored. Sometimes it takes a period of time, even years, to restore and rebuild trust, depending on how deep the wounding is.
- We must give God room to work in our hearts, and extend grace to those with whom we are trying to restore relationship. God cares about each of us and is able to bring about healing in His way and time.
- God's heart is to "settle accounts" — He desires us to walk in right relationship with Him and with the people in our lives. He has provided a way for us to do so through forgiveness (Mt. 18:23).
- When it comes to holding unforgiveness within our own hearts, we must remember how much we have been forgiven by God. In this parable there is a contrast between the millions of dollars owed by the slave who had been forgiven, and the fellow servant who owed literally just a few dollars (vv. 28-33).
- Unforgiveness keeps people in prison in their hearts where they will feel bound and tortured (v. 34).
- We must forgive people from our hearts (v. 35).

Applying Forgiveness — Eph. 4:30-32
- We are not to grieve the Holy Spirit by walking in unforgiveness (Eph. 4:30).
- We are not to allow bitterness, rage and anger to be cultivated within our hearts (Eph. 4:31).
- We are to forgive each other as Jesus has forgiven us (Eph. 4:32). We are to forgive those who sin against us before they even ask, as Jesus did on the Cross (Lk. 23:34).
- We are to cultivate attitudes of kindness and compassion towards one another (Eph. 4:32).

It is impossible for a man to be freed from the habit of sin before he hates it, just as it is impossible to receive forgiveness before confessing his trespasses...

Ignatius, 50-117, Bishop of Antioch

 # CASTING THE NET

What are the greatest sin issues that you currently face in your life?

_____

_____

_____

_____

_____

_____

_____

_____

Can you identify the sources of unbelief, pride and disobedience in your life?

_____

_____

_____

_____

_____

_____

_____

_____

_____

_____

THOUGHTS & NOTES

_____

_____

_____

_____

What did you take away from the truths you've learned about the atonement and Jesus' walk to the cross?

_____

_____

_____

_____

_____

_____

_____

Where do you need to repent? Is there anyone you need to make restitution with? Make a list here now.

_____

_____

_____

_____

_____

_____

_____

_____

Are you walking in unforgiveness? Is there someone that you have not "let off the hook?" Go before God now and ask Him to help you see that person through the lens of His love and a personal understanding of the parable in Matthew 18:21-35.

_____

_____

_____

_____

A baptism of holiness, a demonstration of godly living is the crying need of our day.

Duncan Campbell, 1898-1972, Scottish Pastor and Evangelist

CATCH OF THE DAY

Chapter Summary

- Because of man's sin we are separated from God and unable to be restored to Him apart from His initiative.
- Jesus died on the cross so man might be reconciled in his relationship to God and others.
- Repentance is a gift God gives us to bring about a change of heart.
- Restitution is making things right with those whom we have sinned against.
- God asks us to forgive others as He has forgiven us.

What are the two or three things the Holy Spirit spoke most clearly to you through this chapter, and how will you respond to Him?

_____

_____

_____

_____

_____

_____

_____

_____

_____

_____

THOUGHTS & NOTES

_____

_____

_____

_____

A VIEW FROM THE SHORE

"The sheep hear his voice, and he calls his own sheep by name and leads them out. When he has brought out all his own, he goes before them, and the sheep follow him, for they know his voice."

John 10: 3-4

In the book of Acts we observe various ways in which God spoke to and guided the Apostle Paul. While traveling on the road to Damascus, Paul audibly heard the voice of Jesus (Acts 9:1-9). He then heard God speak His will to him through a man named Ananias (Acts 9:10-19). Later, Paul was launched on the first of his three missionary journeys by hearing from God during a time of worship and fasting with other leaders (Acts 13:1-3). While on one of his journeys, he sensed guidance from the Holy Spirit, preventing him from going to preach in Asia (Acts 16:6,7). He once had a vision that led him to Macedonia (Acts 16:9-10). Acts also tells us that the Holy Spirit led Paul to travel to Jerusalem, and then records some prophetic words he received from others along the way (Acts 20:22-24, 21:1-16). Towards the end of Acts, in the midst of a storm, an angel appears to Paul on board a ship telling him that the crew will remain safe (Acts 27:21-26).

As a father desires to share his heart with his children, so God longs to speak into our lives and share His heart with us. We see in the scriptures that He chooses a variety of ways to communicate (or speak) to His people.

When was the last time you heard God speak to you? Was it today, yesterday, several weeks ago? Maybe it's been a while, even

years. Do you question whether you've ever heard God speak? If you've felt as though God only speaks to other people and never to you, I want to encourage you that God has spoken to you, but perhaps you haven't yet learned to recognize His voice.

Have you ever tried to tune in a radio station, but all you got was static with a faint sound in the distance? What do you do in that situation? Do you try to nudge the dial ever so slightly, hoping to bring clarity so you'll be able to understand what's being broadcasted? If that doesn't work, do you wiggle the antenna and try to find an angle that will enable you to hear. If all else fails, maybe you're like me—maybe you move the radio in an attempt to locate a position that will receive a better signal? I know the signal is out there. There are times, however, when we need to better align our antenna or radio to receive it.

God desires for us to hear to His voice. Sometimes we don't know how to remove the 'static' or align our hearts and lives to hear from Him. In this chapter, we'll look at a few people in the Bible who heard from God. We'll observe various scriptural principles for hearing His voice and we'll learn some of the ways in which He speaks. You will also receive discernable tools to help you recognize when it is God that is speaking to you.

SETTING SAIL

In the very beginning, starting with Adam and Eve in the Garden of Eden, we find a God who consistently desires to communicate with His people (Gen. 1-3). He made us to enjoy relationship with Him, and He pursues us until we know Him and allow Him to permeate the most intimate places of our lives. As with any intimate relationship, communication is absolutely essential. This is why God speaks to man. This is why He desires to speak to you and me.

The Purposes of Hearing God's Voice

A relationship is only as good as the willingness of two people to talk and to listen. Without healthy, thriving communication, it can hardly be said that one person can know another. How can anyone understand the heart and nature of a friend unless these two share their thoughts, feelings and ideas, their inspirations and goals, their triumphs and their struggles?

God, too, is a Person. While He is not a carnal man like you and I, He is a Being able to know and be known. God speaks. He spoke in Biblical times and He speaks today. Forever, God will keep in close confidence those who call on His name. He communicates with us in order that:

- We would grow in our relationship with Him (Ex. 33:7-11).
- We would know His desires and direction for our lives (Is. 30:21).
- We would be used by Him to minister to others (Acts 8:26-40).

God's Promises of Guidance

God has never left His people to wonder which way they should go. He speaks and gives direction to those who seek His counsel.

- He guides the humble in heart (Ps. 25:9).
- He will guide us in His way (Is. 30:21).
- He will lead us as a shepherd leads their sheep (Jn. 10:1-5,27).

THOUGHTS & NOTES

God Speaks to People in Scripture

Look up the following passages of Scripture and notice how God spoke to His people.

- Adam & Eve (Gen. 1-3)
- Abraham (Gen. 12:1-3)
- Moses (Ex. 3:1-6)
- Joshua (Jos. 1:1-9)
- Gideon (Jud. 6:11-24; 6:36-40)
- Samuel (1 Sam. 3:1-23; 16:1-13)
- David (1 Sam. 23:1-5)
- Elijah (1 Ki. 19:9-18)
- Jeremiah (Jer. 1:4-12)
- Mary (Lk. 1:26-38)
- Jesus (Jn. 8:26-28)
- Paul (Acts 9:1-9; 13:1-3)

Cultivating a Hearing Heart

The Parable of the Sower: Mark 4:1-20

It is essential as a disciple of Jesus that we learn to listen to the voice of God. Many other "voices" compete for our attention, including our own thoughts, the opinions of others, the world around us, and even the enemy of our souls—the devil. With these competing sounds pulling on our hearts and minds, how does one go about positioning themselves to hear from God? The tending of our hearts can put us in a place where we can become more sensitive to the voice of God.

A Hard Heart: the word sown "along the path" – 4:14-15

- A hard heart produces unbelief that hinders you from hearing from God (Heb. 3:12-19).
- When our hearts are not tender to the voice of God, the devil will attempt to rob us from hearing what He wants to say.
- Cultivate an open, tender, and clean heart through confession of sin and by forgiving those who have sinned against you (Ps. 66:18; 1Jn. 1:9).

There is not in the world a kind of life more sweet and delightful than that of a continual conversation with God.

Brother Lawrence, 1605-1691, French, Carmelite Lay Brother

A Shallow Heart: the word sown on "rocky ground" – 4:16-17

- A shallow heart does not allow what God is saying to take root within one's life.
- When we do not know who God is and His ways as revealed in Scripture, we can miss what He is saying to us. When trouble comes, our tendency is to rely on our own wisdom and experiences instead of on God and His ways revealed in His Word.
- Cultivate a hearing heart by allowing your roots to go deep in the Scriptures, where you will come to know God's character and ways.

A Crowded Heart: the word sown "among thorns" – 4:18-19

- A crowded heart is one that is consumed with many other things, including worries and desires for other things, therefore choking out what God may be saying to us.
- When we allow other voices (influences) to consume our lives we may miss what God is saying to us through His Word, by His Spirit and through other believers.
- Cultivate a hearing heart by learning to wait quietly upon God and by not allowing busyness to sacrifice your times alone with Him (Lk. 10:38-42).

A Fruitful Heart: the word sown on "good soil" – 4:20

- A fruitful heart is one that simply listens to God and obeys Him, born out of relationship with Him and walking in His ways.
- Cultivate a hearing heart by keeping it clean before God, by being rooted in God's truth of Scripture, and by listening to the Holy Spirit throughout your day. This will bring forth much fruit for the Kingdom of God.
- Cultivate a hearing heart by being obedient to what God speaks to you.

> God consistently desires to communicate with His people. He made us to enjoy relationship with Him, and He pursues us until we know Him and allow Him to permeate the most intimate places of our lives.

THOUGHTS & NOTES

DEEPER WATERS

As we search the Scriptures we see that God spoke to people in various ways, according to His choosing. Moses heard from God via a burning bush (Ex. 3), Ezekiel saw a vision of dry bones (Ez. 37), Esther heard from God while fasting (Est. 4:12-17), Mary received God's message through a visit from an angel (Lk. 1:26-38). Still others heard from God through his prophets, leaders and teachers. The book of Acts, in the New Testament, gives an account of many ways in which God spoke to and led His people.

Some of the Ways God Speaks

God, the Creator of all things, can use whatever means He chooses to communicate to you and me. Sometimes He uses the words of a friend or the messages preached by a preacher. Other times, we gain a certain knowing inside of us that comes in the place of prayer. He may provide a peace that passes all understanding. He may even speak to us while we sleep. He desires to talk with us. We can open our ears to His voice by:

Reading Scripture
- God's Word is a lamp to our feet and a light to our path (Ps. 119:105).
- We are directed as we walk in daily obedience to the truth revealed in the Bible (2 Tim. 3:16-17).
- Meditating on and studying God's Word invites the Holy Spirit to speak to us (Ps. 1:1-3; Jos. 1:8).

Listening for the Holy Spirit
- Quieting ourselves to hear the Spirit's leading within us (Is. 30:21).
- Sensing the Holy Spirit's confirmation, or "bearing witness" to the things in our heart (Acts 16:6-10).

Pursuing Peace (Col. 3:15).
- The word "rule" in Colossians 3:15 has the meaning "arbitrator" or "umpire," giving us a picture of a sporting event where the umpire makes the call on whether something is right or wrong. We can let the peace of Christ be an "umpire" in our hearts—as we seek God and gain His peace, we can discern His will. A lack of peace may also reveal God's heart to us.

God is our true Friend, who always gives us the counsel and comfort we need. Our danger lies in resisting Him; so it is essential that we acquire the habit of hearkening to His voice, or keeping silence within, and listening so as to lose nothing of what He says to us. We know well enough how to keep outward silence, and to hush our spoken words, but we know little of interior silence. It consists in hushing our idle, restless, wandering imagination, in quieting the promptings of our worldly minds, and in suppressing the crowd of unprofitable thoughts which excite and disturb the soul.

François Fénelon, 1651-1715, French Archbishop, Theologian

By Waiting on God
- Waiting on God in the place of worship (Acts 13:1-3).
- Waiting on God in the place of prayer (Lk. 6:12-16).
- Waiting on God in the place of prayer with fasting (Dan. 9-10).
- Waiting on God for His counsel (Ps. 106:13).
- Waiting on God to act on our behalf (Is. 64:4).

Through Circumstances
- By observing "doors" God may be opening or closing (Acts 16:6-10).
- By being aware of what God is actively doing and aligning yourself to it.
- By paying attention to repeated circumstances, situations and opportunities.

Through People
- Through family members (Ex. 18).
- Through spiritual leaders (Josh. 1:10-18).
- Through other believers functioning in their spiritual gifts (Acts 11:27-30).

Through Supernatural Means
- Through visions and dreams (Acts 10:9-48; Mt. 1:18-25).
- Through angelic visitations (Acts 12:6-19).
- Through the audible voice of God (Acts 9:1-9).
- Through whatever means God chooses (Num. 22:21-35; Dan. 5).

Some Ways to Test Your Guidance

We can and should expect to hear God speak to us, as we are reminded in Scripture that the sheep hear the Shepherd's voice (John 10:4). But how can we know when it is really God and not our own thoughts and imaginations? We should test the spirits, as we are cautioned in Scripture (Rom 12:2; 1 Thes. 5:21; 1Jn. 4:1-3). Here's how. Ask yourself:

Is it Biblical?
The Holy Spirit will never ask us to do something that is contrary to the Scriptures. He will never violate the value of people, nor will He lead someone to do something outside the biblical attitude of walking under authority.

THOUGHTS & NOTES

Is it in line with God's character and ways?

God will not contradict who He is. He will not tell us to do something that opposes His nature.

Does it glorify Jesus and draw people closer to Him?

God will not command us to walk outside of love, or to do something that will communicate a distorted image of God to others.

Does it bear witness to you? Does it bear witness to other believers that you walk closely with? Is there a sense of hope and courage within you that accompanies God's direction?

Do you sense God's peace concerning the matter which you believe He has spoken to you? Do others confirm your hearing from God? What do your leaders sense God is saying?

Apply the Triple Confirmation to make sure it holds up:
- Does it align with God's Word, the Bible?
- Is the Holy Spirit bearing witness within you?
- What is God saying to you through other believers and your spiritual leaders?

Practical Helps

To help you discern God's voice, always remember that the ultimate end of hearing from Him is to strengthen your relationship with Him and direct you to walk in agreement with His ways and in obedience to His will. Consider the following practical advice:
- Don't make it complicated. Remember, God desires to speak to you.
- Always allow God to speak to you in the way He chooses.
- If you become a bit lost in your direction, do the last thing that God spoke clearly to you.
- Don't talk about your guidance too quickly:
  - You may not have full understanding yet.
  - You might miss God's timing, which is just as important as His direction.
  - You could bring confusion to others who are still seeking God.
- Be careful not to move in pride when sharing with others what "you heard from God."

Receiving Prophetic Words
- Listen carefully to what is being said. Consider writing it down or recording it.
- Thank the one who gave you the word of prophecy.
- Test it to see whether all or part of it is from God. Examine what might apply to you now. Leave the rest for God to bring back at a later time, or dismiss altogether (1 Th. 5:19-21).
- Remember, most prophetic words will usually confirm things God has already spoken to you.

If honesty of heart and uprightness before God were lacking or if I did not patiently wait on God for instruction, or if I preferred the counsel of my fellow-men to the declarations of the Word of God, I made great mistakes.

George Mueller, 1805-1898, English Evangelist and Philanthropist

CASTING THE NET

How has the Lord spoken to you in the past? How do you tend to hear from Him the most?

_____

_____

_____

_____

Based on the portion covered in this chapter on Cultivating a Hearing Heart, did the Holy Spirit show you anything that might be preventing you from hearing God?

_____

_____

_____

_____

_____

When was the last time you sensed the Lord speaking to you? What did He say? How did you respond to what He said?

_____

_____

_____

_____

_____

THOUGHTS & NOTES ━━━━━━

_____

_____

_____

Think of a time, either in the past or recently, when you thought the Lord might have spoken something to you, only to find out later that it really wasn't God on that occasion. Take a moment now and analyze it a bit, asking the Holy Spirit to show you insights on how you could have handled it differently.

_____

_____

_____

_____

_____

_____

_____

_____

Carve out a few minutes, either right now or sometime today, to let the Lord speak to you. It may help to find a quiet place or to go on a walk. If it has been a while since you have taken the time to listen to His voice, ask Him to forgive you, receive His love for you, and invite Him to share His heart with you. Record what He says to you.

_____

_____

_____

_____

_____

_____

_____

[A truly humble man] is sensible of his natural distance from God;
of his dependence on Him; of the insufficiency of his own power and wisdom;
and that it is by God's power that he is upheld and provided for,
and that he needs God's wisdom to lead and guide him, and His might
to enable him to do what he ought to do for Him.

Jonathan Edwards, 1703-1758, American Preacher and Theologian

CATCH OF THE DAY

Chapter Summary

- God desires to speak to His people.
- We can cultivate a hearing heart that enables us to hear from God more effectively.
- God can speak to us in many ways, including:
  - Through Scripture
  - Listening for the Holy Spirit
  - Pursuing Peace
  - By waiting on God
  - Through circumstances
  - Through people
  - Through supernatural means
- It is wise to test our guidance from God, using among other things, the Triple Confirmation.
- The end result of hearing from God is building our relationship with Him, and walking in obedience to what He says.

What are the two or three things the Holy Spirit spoke most clearly to you through this chapter, and how will you respond to Him?

_____

_____

_____

_____

_____

_____

THOUGHTS & NOTES

_____

_____

_____

_____

 # A VIEW FROM THE SHORE

"Endure hardship with us like a good soldier of Christ Jesus.
No one serving as a soldier gets involved in civilian affairs—
he wants to please his commanding officer. Similarly, if anyone competes
as an athlete, he does not receive the victor's crown unless he competes
according to the rules. The hardworking farmer should be the first
to receive a share of the crops. Reflect on what I am saying,
for the Lord will give you insight into all of this."

2 Timothy 2:3-7

Olympic athletes compete against the world's best to prove they're champions. Whether runners, weightlifters, swimmers or ice skaters, individual competitors or team players, they aim for nothing short of winning the gold medal.

But Olympic athletes aren't born—they are developed over many years. They hone their raw skills and talents through hours of hard work and coaching by those equipped to guide them. Becoming masters of discipline, they forsake comforts to lift a few more pounds or better their times by milliseconds. Their sights are set on the ultimate prize.

I have a friend who was an Olympian. Becoming a world-class athlete required commitment, sacrifice, endurance, and focus. It meant doing the things that others weren't willing to do. In the end, my friend was honored to wear his country's colors while representing his nation on the world's stage.

To walk as a disciple of Jesus is no less daunting an undertaking. It, too, requires commitment and sacrifice, endurance and focus. We represent God and His Kingdom as ambassadors in this world, all the while battling our fleshly desires and the devil's lures. To resist the onslaught of these threats and to develop strength in our inner person, we must exercise discipline.

Discipline is not legalism (religious acts designed to gain God's approval). We received God's favor and approval when we accepted His work for us on the Cross. The spiritual disciplines position us before God where He can change us to become more like Him. We choose to make ourselves accessible and to invest in our relationship with Him through our steady and sincere commitment, with our sights set on the ultimate prize.

In this chapter, we will look at five spiritual disciplines. As we develop our relationship with God through Scripture, worship, prayer (including fasting), waiting on Him, and giving, we will reap the wonderful fruit of knowing God in our lives. As God's Word promises, discipline will produce a harvest of righteousness and peace for those who have been trained by it (Heb. 12:1-11). We have much to look forward to.

setting sail

The disciple's disciplines are practices that position us before God so He can transform us. Through activities like Scripture study and meditation, prayer, worship, waiting on God, and giving, we invest in our relationship with Jesus. These disciplines are not a means to make Him love us more—there is no earning His love. Such exercises merely open within us a deeper awareness of how completely our heavenly Father loves us. The disciplines of discipleship allow us to partner with the Holy Spirit on the task of molding us into what God wants us to be. As we draw close to Him, we become more like Him, taking on His heart and His mind.

Searching the Scriptures

The first spiritual discipline we want to examine is searching the scriptures. Because the Bible is a divinely inspired book used by the Holy Spirit to help us hear from God—to know His character, discover His ways, and rest in His promises—the study of scripture is essential to becoming spiritually mature and equipped for His calling on our lives (2 Tim. 3:16-17). Let's begin by taking a look at the uniqueness of scripture and the place it is to have in the Christian walk.

The Bible is a Unique Book
- The Bible was written over a period of some 1500 years by 40-plus authors from varied backgrounds.
  - Moses, the author of the first five books of the Bible, was a ruler trained in Egypt.
  - Joshua was a military leader.
  - Nehemiah was a cupbearer.
  - Peter and John were fishermen.
  - Luke, who wrote the gospel named after him and the book of Acts, was a physician.
  - Paul was a Jewish teacher and leader.

The study of scripture is essential to becoming spiritually mature and equipped for His calling on our lives.

THOUGHTS & NOTES

- The various books of the Bible were written in different times and places—some in times of peace, others in times of turmoil and upheaval.
    - Genesis through Deuteronomy were most likely penned in the wilderness.
    - Jeremiah wrote from a dungeon.
    - Paul wrote several of his letters (books) while he was imprisoned.
    - Luke wrote Acts while on the road.
    - John recorded Revelation while exiled on an island.
    - Portions of the scripture were written in Africa, Asia, and Europe.
    - The Old Testament was written in Hebrew, and the New Testament in Greek.
- Although Biblical writers dealt with hundreds of topics over many centuries, there is harmony and continuity in all 66 books.
- Those who put the 27 books of the New Testament together used a certain standard to include or exclude first century writings. The selection of the *canon* ("measuring rod") came from the following six criteria:
    - **Apostolic Authority**: It was written by one of the disciples of Jesus or someone who was under their influence.
    - **Orthodoxy**: It held to the rule of faith in both the oral and written tradition.
    - **Catholicity**: The church accepted it universally.
    - **Antiquity**: It was written between the time of the birth of Jesus and the death of the last of the twelve disciples.
    - **Inspiration**: There was an internal witness of the Spirit by those judging it.
    - **Traditional Usage**: It was something already being used by the church in faith and practice.
- The Bible has endured more attacks by its enemies than any other book in all of history. From the days of the Roman Empire until today, skeptics have tried to destroy its influence. Voltaire, one of France's greatest thinkers, once said that in 100 years, the Bible would be forgotten and copies only found in museums. History tells us that 100 years after his death, the Geneva Bible Society used his house as their headquarters and his press to mass-produce Bibles for the first time!
- No historical book has such a large number of surviving copies as the Bible. Written on perishable material and being hand-copied over and over again hundreds of years before the creation of the printing press did not lessen its existence or its accuracy. The Jews had special groups of men whose sole responsibility was to preserve the scriptures, making sure every paragraph, word and letter was transmitted absolutely perfectly.

The Bible is one of the greatest blessings bestowed by God on the children of men. It has God for its Author, salvation for its end, and truth without any mixture for its matter. It is all pure, all sincere; nothing too much; nothing wanting!

John Locke, 1632-1704, English Philosopher

- Science and scripture always support each other, because both are authored by the One who created the universe. Galileo (who invented the telescope and discovered that the sun, not the earth, was the center of the universe), Newton (who developed the laws of physics), and Pascal (a mathematician and philosopher) are among the many great minds that searched the scripture and had a relationship with its Author.
- Science can define for us the *what*, analyze the *how*, and probe the *why*, but it cannot tell us the *where from* or the reasons *for which* the universe exists. It cannot tell us *who* we are or *why* we live. While science can tell us *what* we are able to do, it cannot teach us *what* we ought to do. God's revelation in science is superseded by His revelation in scripture. Science reveals God's awesome might, while scripture reveals His purposes and our destiny.
    - Before Christopher Columbus sailed around the world in 1492, the scriptures recorded that the world was round (Is. 40:21-22).
    - When science, in its infancy, thought the world was held up by *three elephants on the back of a tortoise*, the Bible spoke of its free float in space (Job 26:7).
    - Hundreds of years ago, it was documented that physical life resided within our blood systems. The Bible recorded it thousands of years ago (Lev. 17:11).
- A book's true nature is revealed in the effect it has on society. History tells us that wherever scripture has been circulated in the language of a people, it has elevated society by overthrowing superstition, stimulating a reverence for human life, and a respect for all segments of society. In the United States, the Ten Commandments hang on the wall of the Supreme Court. A trial witness is required to take an oath for truth by placing his hand on the Bible. At the inauguration of elected officials, their left hands are placed on the Bible when they take the oath of office
- The Bible is also the best-selling book of all time.
- The greatest proof of the supernatural power of the scriptures is the testimony of the millions of lives that have been radically changed as they have encountered Jesus through it. Only the truths revealed in the Bible are able to make bad people good on the inside, transforming rebels into servants of humility.

The disciplines of discipleship allow us to partner with the Holy Spirit on the task of molding us into what God wants us to be.

THOUGHTS & NOTES

The Bible's Place in a Disciple's Life

The study of a subject is the pursuit of that subject's truth—we seek to understand something as it truly is. When we gain understanding, we become equipped to respond and relate to it rightly. To understand the human body, for instance, we would study physiology. This would teach us how to become physically fit and remain healthy and, therefore, to enjoy an active lifestyle. For us to understand who God is and what it means to be His disciple, we must study His Word. Only through a firsthand knowledge of God's truth can we be certain that we know Him—that we see and hear God, and that it is indeed His ways we determine to keep. The Bible proves integral to the disciple's life as it becomes the foundation on which we are rooted and our new lives grow. Unlike any other source we study, the Bible is uniquely effective because God's words are pure, promising blessing to those who pursue their truth.

In Psalm 119, we catch a glimpse of one man's passion for Scripture. He writes, "Oh, how I love your law! I meditate on it all day long. Your commands make me wiser than my enemies, for they are ever with me. I have more insight than all my teachers, for I meditate on your statutes. I have more understanding than the elders, for I obey your precepts. I have kept my feet from every evil path so that I might obey your word. I have not departed from your laws, for You Yourself have taught me. How sweet are Your words to my taste, sweeter than honey to my mouth! I gain understanding from your precepts; therefore I hate every wrong path" (Ps. 119:97-104). May you, too, find God's Word indispensable to your life.

What the Bible Says About Itself
- Scripture is divinely inspired (2 Tim. 3:16-17).
- It will never pass away (Is. 40:8).
- It is food for the soul (Ps. 119:103).
- It illuminates our path (Ps. 119:105).
- It is loved by God's people (Ps. 119:72, 97).
- It is living and active (Heb. 4:12).
- Its influence is powerful (Jer. 23:29).
- It is a spiritual weapon (Eph. 6:17).
- It purifies a life (Ps. 119:9).
- It was written with a purpose (Jn. 20:31).
- It is absolutely trustworthy (Ps. 111:7).
- It always accomplishes what God desires for it to (Is. 55:11).

Do not have your concert first, and then tune your instrument afterwards.
Begin the day with the Word of God and prayer, and get first of all
into harmony with Him.

Hudson Taylor, 1832-1905, English Missionary to China

Some Commands to Obey
- From Joshua (Josh. 1:8):
    - Disciples of Jesus are to not let truth depart from their mouths.
    - Disciples of Jesus are to meditate on God's truths day and night.
    - Disciples of Jesus are to be careful to obey God's truth.
- From Deuteronomy (Dt. 6:4-9):
    - Disciples of Jesus are to keep God's truths in their hearts.
    - Disciples of Jesus are to impress God's truth upon their children by example and teaching.

Some Promises to Trust
- You will be prosperous and successful (Josh. 1:8).
- You will not wither spiritually and you will bear good fruit (Ps. 1:1-3).
- You will have a firm foundation (Mt. 7:24-27).
- You will know great rewards (Ps. 19:7-11).
- You will know true freedom as you hold to Jesus' teaching (Jn. 8:31-32).

It's Role in the Disciple's Life – 2 Tim. 3:16-17
- *Teaching* – so we may know God's character and ways, His truth and His will.
- *Rebuking* – so we may know God's truth regarding our sin.
- *Correcting* – so we may change our motives, attitudes and behaviors and align with God's truth.
- *Training in Righteousness* – so we may live a life that reflects Jesus to the world around us.
- *Equipping for Good Works* – so we may have the tools we need to fulfill God's call on our lives.

Considerations for Bible Reading
- Make time in your schedule to read the scriptures on a regular basis.
- Try to read through the whole Bible in a systematic way so you continually receive the whole counsel of God's Word.
- When reading a portion of Scripture, pay close attention to what it says about God's character and ways. Also look for obedience points you can immediately apply to your life.
- Always remember to read Scripture in the context in which you find it.

THOUGHTS & NOTES

Studying the Scriptures

Inductive Bible Study Basics

Studying the Bible is not primarily for information, but for the transformation of heart. As the scriptures reveal God's heart to us, we become more like Him. But where do we begin?

Often, people search the scriptures to find passages that support conclusions they've already made. This approach, the Deductive Method, can lead to error in application because interpretation is based on preconceptions, rather than on what God says. By contrast, the Inductive Method uses Scripture for an understanding of Scripture, allowing God's Word to speak for itself. The Inductive Method relies on three sequential steps—observation, interpretation, and application. Included below are some Inductive Bible Study basics that will help you begin a lifetime journey of studying the scriptures.

Observation – What does it say?
- Always begin by inviting the Holy Spirit to illuminate your understanding and to teach you.
- Study the Bible as it is, leaving aside commentaries until after you have had an opportunity to look at it yourself.
- Observation has to do with what the text of Scripture actually says (and doesn't say). The key here is to look, look, look! Pay close attention to what is written in the passage you are studying.
- A good place to start is by reading and re-reading the book or passage you are studying several times through. Continue to read it until you begin to see the structure, themes and the main message emerging.
- Begin by looking at the book as a whole, then narrow your focus to chapters, paragraphs, verses and words.
- Ask the following questions of the book you are studying. Answer the ones you can, and leave the rest until later.
  - Who is the author?
  - What is the purpose or occasion of the writing?
  - Where was it written?
  - When was it written?
  - To whom was it written?
  - What is the book's big idea?
  - What is the key verse that summarizes the big idea?
  - What words, phrases, ideas, and themes are repeated?

No man is uneducated who knows the Bible,
and no one is wise who is ignorant of its teachings.

Samuel Chadwick, 1860-1932, English Revival Pioneer

- Observe people (biography), time (chronology), places (geography), events (history) and ideas (ideology) by asking who, what, when, where, why and how questions.
- Create an outline of the book based on what you are seeing from your observations.
- Provide each paragraph with a brief paragraph title using your own words.
- For deeper study, you may observe the literary style and devises used in the text. What do the following ten laws of composition reveal to you about the text you are studying?
    - Comparison – things that are alike.
    - Contrast – things that are unlike.
    - Continuity – similar (but not identical) terms, phrase, statements or events.
    - Completion – the progression of events or ideas to a conclusion or resolution.
    - Pivot – the movement to a crucial point on which the subject matter turns in another direction.
    - Cause/Effect – from source or reason to result.
    - Effect/Cause – from result to source or reason.
    - Instrumentality – the means by which an end or result is achieved.
    - Explanation – an event or idea followed by an interpretation or illustration.
    - Identification – the meaning of something is established by being equated with something else.
- Remember, it is of utmost importance to observe the text in context of what is said both before and after each verse or portion to interpret accurately what is being communicated.

Interpretation – What does it mean?
- Good interpretation is built on the foundation of solid observation.
- Proper interpretation is determining what the book or passage meant to the original writer and readers/hearers (audience).
- The interpretation process will take a little work and may require some Bible study aids.
- Here are three areas to consider in the interpretive process:
    - *Literary Structure* – This helps one understand how a book is structured and interpreted. Is the book structured geographically (Acts), chronologically (Luke), biographically (Ruth), logically (Romans), as a letter (Ephesians), as a drama (Revelation), etc.?
    - *Historical Setting* – When did this happen in history? What else was going on in the world at that time? When was this written in God's revelatory process in regard to Israel/Jesus?

THOUGHTS & NOTES

- *Cultural Context* – Where did these people live and work? What was the original language used? How would they have understood these words in light of their times and cultural mindsets?
- When interpreting Scripture, ask the following questions to help determine its meaning:
    - What does a particular word or phrase mean?
    - Why did that action/event or statement occur?
    - Why did the author include this? What did they want the readers to know/understand?
    - What are the ramifications of this passage?
    - What principles can be gleaned from this?

Principles for Interpreting the Scriptures
- We need the illuminating work of the Holy Spirit to enable us to understand the Scriptures.
- Scripture interprets Scripture—view truth through the whole counsel of Scripture.
- Stick to the natural use of language—use common sense instead of approaching it like a secret code.
- The text cannot mean what it never originally meant.
- Misinterpretation is missing the meaning altogether.
- Sub-Interpretation is not getting the entire meaning.
- Super-Interpretation is giving more meaning than was intended by the author.
- Always interpret in the framework of a book's literary, historical and cultural structure.
- The New Testament guides the interpretation of the Old Testament.
- Look for Jesus in all of Scripture— Jesus and the Kingdom of God are the fulfillment of the message of the whole of Scripture.
- Distinguish between the cultural (local applications) and the trans-cultural (universal applications). In other words, what applied only to the culture at the time and what applies to all races and generations, including today.

Studying the Bible is not primarily for information, but for the transformation of heart. As the Scriptures reveal God's heart to us, we become more like Him.

Be assiduous in reading the Holy Scriptures.
This is the fountain whence all knowledge in divinity must be derived.
Therefore let not this treasure lie by you neglected.

Jonathan Edwards, 1703-1758, American Preacher and Theologian

Application – How does it apply to my life?

- Application is the final goal of searching the Scriptures because it demands that our lives align to Jesus and His Kingdom.
- Effective application takes place on the foundations of solid observation and interpretation.
- Some questions to consider:
    - What have I learned about God's character and ways?
    - What are the basic truths from this book/passage?
    - What is God saying to me through this book/passage?
    - Is there sin I need to confess? Are there promises for me to cling to? Do I see an example to follow? What about commands to obey? Is there knowledge to embrace?
    - How does this apply to my thinking and attitudes, as well as my actions?
    - How does this apply to my relationships?
    - What changes do I need to make in my life and how do I plan to carry them out?
    - When trying to apply a passage of Scripture to your life, listen to the voice of God as He leads you in the process. Remember that He has promised to complete the work He began in you (Phil. 1:6).

Meditating on the Scriptures

Meditation, or reflection—the practice of regularly looking at the Scriptures and applying them to various circumstances and prayerfully asking God to illuminate our perspectives with the light of His truth—opens us to receiving a deeper deposit of God and His truth in our lives. As walking the streets of a city are to driving through it, meditation lingers where Scripture study keeps moving. Meditation notices nuances, ponders detail and digests insights, allowing passages of the Bible to become personal and familiar. Both activities greatly serve the disciple and their growing relationship with God.

What Scripture Says About Meditation

- The Lord instructed Joshua to meditate on God's Law day and night that he might be prosperous and successful (Josh. 1:8).
- The Psalmist declared that blessed and fruitful is the person who meditates on the Law of the Lord (Ps. 1:1-3).
- The Psalmist meditated on God throughout the watches of the night (Ps. 63:6).
- The Psalmist also meditated on God's promise (Ps. 119:148).

THOUGHTS & NOTES

- Jesus made a habit of getting alone with His Father (Mt. 14:13,23; Mk. 1:35; Lk. 5:16, 6:12).
- The source of a disciple's meditation is the Scriptures, which reveals God's character and ways, and the works of His hands. Reflecting on God's creation can also provide insights into what God is like.
- Meditation allows us to internalize and personalize the truths revealed in the Scriptures — it enables us to get truth from our heads to our hearts and into our lives. It provides an opportunity for us to create an inner sanctuary of reverence, reflection and intimacy that allows us to commune deeply with Jesus and His Word.

Considerations for Bible Meditation
- Find time when you will not be interrupted.
- Select a place that will allow you to get alone before God. Sometimes a beautiful setting in nature can enhance your time of meditation.
- Choose a passage of Scripture that you have been reading, or have come across recently, one you want to reflect on and make a part of your life.
- Invite the Holy Spirit to lead you to deeper places of revelation and understanding.
- Trust Him for new insights. Wait silently before the Lord as you ruminate on each paragraph, verse, phrase and word.
- Listen carefully for the voice of the Lord in your spirit as you reflect on the passage.
- When you receive insights, ask the Lord to imprint these truths on your soul.
- Don't rush—linger as long as you can in God's presence.
- Record what the Lord shows you for future reflection, life application, and to share with others.

Reading, studying, and meditating on God's Word tends to elicit an inner response of thanksgiving, praise and worship as we receive fresh insights from the wealth of His wisdom. The more we meet with God in His Word, the deeper our walk with Him becomes. We not only find grace and freedom for ourselves, but we gain revelation that the Holy Spirit will revisit as we minister to those He's placed in our lives.

Meditation notices nuances, ponders detail and digests insights, allowing passages of the Bible to become personal and familiar.

It is impossible to rightly govern the world without God and the Bible.

George Washington, 1732-1799, American President

DEEPER WATERS

Let's consider four other important spiritual disciplines that also allow us to encounter God so we might know Him better, learn His ways and be transformed to be more like Him. They are worship, prayer (including fasting), waiting on God, and giving.

Worship

The second spiritual discipline that positions the disciple before God is worship. Worship is our love response to Him – it is ministering to the heart of God. As we study His Word and meditate on His nature, the Holy Spirit reveals to us more of who God is. Worship then becomes an intimate and joyous expression, the engagement of our entire beings with the greatness of our Lord. In the book of Revelation (ch pts. 4-5) we see a picture of what is taking place in heaven at this very moment. We glimpse what one day we will partake in—a worship celebration of Jesus before His throne with men and women from every race and generation.

So important is worship that God set aside a tribe of the Jewish nation, the Levites, to spend their lives exclusively in worship. In the book of Numbers, we read the process that set them apart for this holy calling (Num. 8:5-26). When Jesus spoke to the woman at the well, He told her that God sought worshipers who would worship Him in spirit and truth (Jn. 4:23-24). As we express our worship to God, the Holy Spirit imparts life to all He has taught us from His Word. Peace and gratitude rise up within us as we fix our eyes on Truth Himself, and the deceptions of a dark world lose their hold.

What the Bible Says About Worship
- We worship because God is worthy (Rev. 4:9-11; 5:9-14).
- We worship because it gives us the opportunity to minister back to Him (1 Sam. 3:1-10). Worship allows us to touch the heart of God. Following a time of worship, whether personally or with other believers, our primary response should be God-focused, envisioning His pleasure from our worship—not whether we liked the songs chosen, or if we received something from the experience.

THOUGHTS & NOTES

- Worshiping God comes before service to God. Service to God flows out of worship for God (Is. 6:1-8). When our service for God becomes a substitute for worship then our service has become idolatrous.
- As we worship God dwells in the midst of His people's praise (Ps. 22:3).
- As we worship it releases God's power into our lives and circumstances (2 Chr. 20:1-30; Ps. 149:1-4).
- As we worship it allows God to share His heart with us (Acts 13:1-2).

Defining Worship

- Worship is our love response to God for who He is and what He has done for us. It is our response to His initiations and expressions of love to us.
- The Hebrew word used in the Old Testament to describe worship speaks of bowing or falling down, or prostrating oneself in reverence before God. A Greek word used in the New Testament provides the imagery of a dog expressing its affection for its master by licking the master's hand. It also conveys the meaning "to kiss towards" God.
- Worship, as observed in Scripture, may be regarded as the direct acknowledgement to God of His nature, names, attributes and ways, whether by expressions of the heart in thanksgiving and praise, or by an action or attitude.
- One aspect of worship is the giving of thanks to God. Thanksgiving is expressing gratitude to God for what He has done for you. Here are some Old and New Testament words describing thanksgiving:
  - Hebrew: *towdah* – an extension of the hand, adoration, a choir of worshipers, thanksgiving (Ps. 50:14, 95:2, 100:4: 147:7).
  - Hebrew: *yadah* – to use hands, throw, to revere or worship (Ps. 18:49, 107:1).
  - Greek: *charis* – gratitude, the divine influence upon the heart and it's reflection in the life (Rom. 6:17; 1 Cor. 15:57).
  - Greek: *eucharisteo/eucharista* – to be grateful, to express gratitude, grateful language to God as an act of worship (Jn. 11:41; Eph. 5:20, 5:4; Rev. 4:9).
  - Greek: *anthomologeomai* – to acknowledge fully, to celebrate fully in praise with thanksgiving (Lk. 2:38).

Worship is our love response to Him – it is ministering to the heart of God.

Missions is not the ultimate goal of the church. Worship is. Missions exists because worship doesn't.

John Piper, American Pastor

- Praise is also an expression of worship, declaring to God who He is through the use of His names, titles and attributes found in Scripture. Here are some other Old and New Testament words describing praise:
    - Hebrew: *tehillah* – laudation, hymn (Ps. 34:1, 35:28).
    - Hebrew: *halal* – to shine, make a show, boast, clamour foolishly, to rave, to celebrate (2 Chr. 20:19; Ps. 63:5, 150:1-6).
    - Hebrew: *shabach* – to address, loud, commend, glory, praise, triumph (Ps. 63:3, 147:12).
    - Greek: *epaninos* – commendation, praise (Eph. 1:6; Phil. 4:8).
    - Greek: *aineo* – to speak in praise of (Lk. 2:13; Acts 3:8-9).
    - Greek: *humneo* – to sing to the praise of (Heb. 2:12).

The Physicality of Worship
God has designed us in such a way that we can worship Him with our heart, soul, mind and strength, and express our love to Him through the use of our voices and bodies. Here are some of the ways Scripture says we can worship God.
- Singing – Ps. 33:1
- Shouting – Ps. 95:1
- Clapping – Ps. 47:1
- Laughing – Ps. 126:1-3
- Leaping – Lk. 6:23; Acts 3:8
- Lifting hands – Ps. 134:2
- Bowing – Ps. 95:6
- Kneeling – Ps. 95:6
- Dancing – Ps. 149:3
- Musical Instruments – Ps. 150
- Singing a new song – Ps. 149:1
- Falling prostrate – Neh. 8:6
- Loudly – 1 Chr. 15:28
- Making a joyful noise – Ps. 66:1-2
- Stillness – Ps. 46:10
- In tongues – Acts 2:1-10, 10:46
- With all that is within us – Ps. 103:1
- With our whole heart – Ps. 111:1

THOUGHTS & NOTES

When can we worship?

- From the beginning of the day until the end (Ps. 35:28, 113:3).
- As long as we live (Ps. 146:2).
- At all times (Ps. 34:1).
- Forever into eternity (Ps. 52:9).
- When we don't feel like worshiping is the time to remember why we worship—because Jesus is worthy and our greatest ministry is to worship Him. This is referred to as a sacrifice of praise (Heb. 13:15). We see this expression of praise when Jonah is in the belly of the fish (Jon. 2:9), and when Paul and Silas are in jail in Philippi (Acts 16:25-34).

Practical Expressions of Worship in the New Testament – Eph. 5:19; Col. 3:16

- Early Christians used the Psalms of the Old Testament to worship God.
- Hymns are composed songs addressed to God that contain truths about Him and His Kingdom.
- Spiritual Songs are spontaneous songs that express one's love in worship to God.

Steps to Cultivating the Heart of a Worshiper

- Ask God to give you a heart of worship for Him.
- Commit to live a life set apart (holy) as a worshiper (Ps.15, 24).
- Cultivate a heart of worship by seeing God's character in the Scriptures in His names, titles and attributes. Worship Him for *who* He is.
- Learn to quickly give God thanks (for what He does) and praise (for who He is) when you see Him move on your behalf in the midst of your day.
- Practice offering God sacrifices of praise when you don't feel like worshiping.
- Keep your sights set on the picture of worship in Revelation (ch. 4-5) recognizing that your destiny is before the throne of God worshiping with people from every tribe, language, people and nation (Rev. 5:9,10).
- The more you see God the more you will desire to worship Him. And the more you worship God the more you will desire to see Him.

Worship is an intimate and joyous expression, the engagement of our entire beings with the greatness of our Lord.

To worship God in spirit and truth means to worship God as we ought to worship Him. God is Spirit, so we must worship in spirit and truth, that is, by a humble and true adoration of spirit in the depth and center of our souls. God alone can see this worship; we can repeat it so often that in the end it becomes as if it were natural to us, and as if God were one with our souls, and our souls one with Him.

Brother Lawrence, 1605-1691, French, Carmelite Lay Brother

Prayer

History belongs to those who pray. God has chosen to allow us to work with Him in the place of prayer to influence the present and the future. Certain things will come to pass if we pray. If we do not pray, some things God had desired to happen will not (Gen. 18:16-33; Ezk. 22:30-31). Prayer is the power of God released through people to bring revival in the church and unreached peoples to Jesus. Prayer solves insurmountable problems and touches lives for God's glory.

Often we approach this third discipline as if prayer were a monologue. Prayer is more than talking to God. Prayer is a conversation. It involves speaking and listening. Because God is ever-present, we can "pray continually" (1 Thes. 5:17; Phil. 4:6). Asking God questions like, *"How would You like me to act in this situation?"* or *"How should I respond to that comment?"* transforms our lives to display His heart in everyday matters.

Some Examples of Biblical Pray-ers
To learn more about prayer, read the chapters surrounding each of the following passages.

- Abraham (Gen. 18:16-19:29)
- Moses (Ex. 32:1-14)
- Nehemiah (Neh. 1:4-11)
- Esther (Est. 4:12-17)
- Daniel (9,10)
- Jesus (John 17)
- Disciples in Acts (Acts 1:12-14, 2:42-47, 4:23-31, 6:1-7, 7:54-8:1, 10:9-48, 12:1-19, 13:1-3)

Principles for Effective Prayer
Prayer does not need to be complicated to be effective. It's not about saying the "right words," but rather being rightly aligned to God.
- Faith in Jesus (Mk. 11:22-24; Jam. 1:5-7)—A key to praying with faith is knowing God's will. This requires seeking and listening to God (1 Jn. 5:14-15).
- A Clean Heart (Ps. 66:18; Is. 59:1-2)—We must approach God in prayer with a clean heart, meaning that we first confess our sins before Him and release forgiveness to those who have sinned against us. Our prayers may be hindered because we have wrong desires (lust, fight, covet vs. friendship with God), or wrong motives (satisfying own pleasures vs. glorifying God) (Jam. 4:1-3).

THOUGHTS & NOTES

106

- The Holy Spirit's Power (Rom. 8:26-27)—Effective prayer is initiated, energized and empowered by the Holy Spirit.
- Endurance (Dan. 10; Lk. 18:1-8)—It is necessary to endure in prayer until we see our prayer answered, until the Holy Spirit gives us a sense that the battle is won, or until God says no.

The Lord's Prayer: A Pattern for Prayer – Mt. 6:9-13

Prayers are not said to impress others or to manipulate God. When Jesus taught his disciples to pray, He told them to use simple, straightforward speech (Matthew 6:7-13, 7:7-11). Here are the various parts of the Lord's Prayer along with areas to consider praying about on a daily basis.

- *Our Father Which Art in Heaven, Hallowed Be Thy Name*
     - Begin each day with thanks, praise and worship, acknowledging who He is (Father, Holy, etc.).
     - Cultivate an awareness of His presence in your life and His desire to fellowship with you.
- *Thy Kingdom Come, Thy Will Be Done on Earth as it is In Heaven*
     - Prayer recognizes that God is God and we are not. In prayer, we yield our desires to God's. Jesus prayed, "Not my will but yours."
     - Establish God's purposes each day in prayer led by the Holy Spirit—as in heaven, so on earth.
     - We ask God to change the way we see ourselves, to reveal things hidden from us or things we may be hiding from Him. In prayer, we invite God to come in and occupy all the rooms of our heart. We establish His purposes in our lives, placing ourselves under His Lordship, being filled with the Spirit, committing and aligning the plans of our day to His purposes.
     - In prayer, we ask God to change the way we see others. When He enables us to look into people's eyes and see His reflection, our hearts are transformed. We are able to love and serve those we pray for as though we are loving and serving Jesus.
     - God's purposes are established in our sphere of relationships as we pray for family, friends, leaders, those we work with, etc.
     - We establish His purposes in our world, interceding for our community, city, nation and peoples of the earth.
     - We also pray for the various spheres of society—family, church, government, education, arts and entertainment, media and business—so God's purposes will be established.

The men who have done the most for God in this world have been early on their knees. He who fritters away the early morning, its opportunity and freshness, in other pursuits than seeking God will make poor headway seeking Him the rest of the day. If God is not first in our thoughts and efforts in the morning, He will be in the last place the remainder of the day.

E.M. Bounds, 1835-1913, American Pastor and Man of Prayer

- *Give Us This Day Our Daily Bread*
    - God invites us to come to Him each day for the provision of our needs.
    - God cares about all of our needs—spiritual, emotional, physical, mental, financial, material, directional, etc.
- *Forgive Us Our Debts as We Forgive Our Debtors*
    - Walking in truth and freedom each day in our relationships.
    - Check your heart to make sure you are walking in forgiveness towards those who have sinned against you, offended or hurt you. Don't let unforgiveness grow within you. Pray blessing over those you have forgiven.
- *Lead Us Not Into Temptation But Deliver Us From Evil*
    - Stand humbly each day in God's power and protection.
    - Put on the Armor of God (Eph. 6:10-18).
    - Ask God for His power in your life to overcome temptation and to defeat the devil's schemes (1 Cor. 10:13; Jam. 4:7).
- *For Thine is the Kingdom, the Power and the Glory Forever*
    - Finish your time in prayer with declarations of God's character, ways, words and works.
    - Commit yourself to live daily for His glory alone.

Principles for Team Intercession

When praying together with other believers in a small group, you will find these principles for intercession helpful:

- Prepare Together
    - Acknowledge that you cannot pray without the direction and power of the Holy Spirit (Rom. 8:26-27).
    - Confess your sins and forgive those who have sinned against you (Ps. 66:18; Mt. 5:23-24).
    - Replace your thoughts and imaginations with God's truths, and set aside your desires and personal burdens (Is. 55:8; 2 Cor. 10:5).
    - Together, resist the enemy who would like to disrupt your prayer time (Mt. 4:1-11; Jam. 4:7).
    - Ask for the fear of the Lord to speak what God puts on your heart to pray for.
- Wait Together
    - Take a few minutes and quietly listen to God.
    - Have your Bible with you so He may speak to you from His Word.

THOUGHTS & NOTES

- Share Together
    - Allow each person in the group to share what the Lord spoke to them. Some may have received something and others nothing.
    - Compare what the Lord has said to each other, asking the Holy Spirit to help you discern His leading.
- Pray Together
    - Pray for the various things the Holy Spirit put on your hearts.
    - Pray through one area until the Holy Spirit releases you to move to the next.
    - Upon completion of the time of prayer, give thanks and praise to God for allowing you to partner in prayer with Him for the purpose of advancing His Kingdom.
- Obey Together
    - Make sure to be obedient to anything that God has asked you to do during your time of prayer.

Prayer with Fasting

- The Bible speaks about the blessing of God regarding prayer with fasting. Fasting is setting aside food (or another life necessity or pleasure) to focus on prayer and seeking God's face. There are many examples in the scriptures of those who fasted, some for a day and others for several.
- Scripture implies the practice of fasting in the disciple's life, saying when you fast, not if you fast (Mt. 6:16-18).
- A fast can be initiated by God, or by an individual or group as they set their hearts to seek God.

Why Fast?

- The disciple fasts to seek the Lord related to personal needs. Hannah fasted out of her desire to have a child (1 Sam. 1:1-20).
- The disciple fasts to seek guidance and direction. Esther fasted when her people were faced with extinction (Est. 4:12-17); Daniel fasted as he sought God for his nation (Dan. 9).
- The disciple fasts to seek the Lord in the midst of distress and spiritual warfare. Daniel fasted when faced with hindrances (Dan. 10); Jesus fasted in the wilderness when tempted by the devil (Mat. 4:1-11).

*I know of no better thermometer to your spiritual temperature
than the intensity of your prayer.*

Charles Spurgeon, 1834-1892, English Preacher and Author

Prayer is reaching out after the unseen; fasting is letting go of all that is seen and temporal. Fasting helps express, deepen, confirm the resolution that we are ready to sacrifice anything, even ourselves to attain what we seek for the kingdom of God.

Andrew Murray, 1828-1917, South African Pastor, Missionary and Writer

- The disciple fasts to seek the Lord when facing a national crisis. Jehoshaphat called a national fast when threatened by another nation (2 Chr. 20:3), and Ezra proclaimed a fast as God's people were returning to the land (Ezra 8:21); the Ninevites responded to Jonah's message with fasting (Jon. 3).
- The disciple fasts for the advancing of God's Kingdom purpose. The Church's missionary activity was birthed as the disciples fasted (Acts 13:1-3).

Kinds of Fasts
- Common Fast – The most common fast in the Scriptures has to do with refraining from solid food, but drinking liquids (Dan. 10:2-3; Mt. 4:1-11).
- Complete Fast – This fast involves no food or drink and should only be done for a short period when directed by the Lord (Acts 9:9).
- Partial Fast – This type of fast has to do with abstaining from certain kinds of food for a period of giving oneself to prayer and God's purposes (Dan. 1:8-21).
- Sacrificial Fast – Due to physical ailments or limitations some people fast something of value other than food to give themselves to focused prayer.

Lengths of Fasts
- Sunset to Sunset – This 24 hour fast was common in Scripture (Jud. 20:26; 2 Sam. 1:12, 3:35).
- Three Day Fast – As seen in the book of Esther (Est. 4:12-17).
- Extended Fast – Lasting several days or weeks (Ex. 34:28; Dan. 10:2,3; Mt. 4:1-11).
- A fast can last for a short or long period as directed by the Lord.

Practical Considerations for Fasting
- If you have never fasted, begin with one meal and then attempt one day.
- Drink lots of water; some juices are fine as well.
- You may experience a headache and other kinds of physical effects from a fast, most of which fade after the first three days.
- When attempting an extended time of fasting, make sure you join with one other person who will be standing with you in prayer and keep an eye out for your well-being. Do not attempt an extended fast until you have built up to it.
- If you are on medication, always consult your physician before commencing a fast.
- When breaking a fast, do it slowly. Begin with small amounts of food for the first meal or two. Avoid highly acidic foods. Eat softer foods such as small amounts of bread and vegetables. Continue to drink water.

THOUGHTS & NOTES

- Consider fasting one meal, or one day a week, along with an occasional three day fast to seek God's face. Add a more extended fast at a time where you can be away from your normal activities and routines for the purpose of hearing from God for your life.
- Fasting with prayer is a powerful tool that God will use. It is not, however, a means to prove our spirituality, gain favor with God (we already have it in Christ), or just to lose weight. It is an act of humility and obedience that God will honor when approached with the right attitude of heart.

Waiting on God

The Bible speaks about waiting on God. This refers to setting aside time to sit before God to enjoy friendship with Him and to listen to what He wants to say to us. As disciples of Jesus, it is our privilege to be able to wait before the King of Kings! Creation is completely dependent upon God. A plant or flower needs to know the soil, sun and rain from its Creator, otherwise it will not survive. Animals are dependent on their Maker for provision of food and shelter. All of creation waits upon Him with eager expectancy and He provides in due season. He is their source and their strength. Surrounded by a creation robed in splendor lovingly reminds us that we, too, have been made to wait on God. He alone is our source and strength (Ps. 104:27-28).

Waiting on God refers to a state of active stillness. God says, "Be still, and know that I am God" (Ps. 46:10). As we quiet our hearts, we ready them to receive. Solitude and silence with a mind attuned to our heavenly Father enables us to hear His counsel and wisdom, and to view life as He reveals it. Waiting presents us with an opportunity to weigh our ideas and actions and consider our motives. We become prepared to consider the actions of others and allow God to season our responses with compassion and forgiveness because our stillness has kept us aware of His compassion and forgiveness for us. While our natural inclinations are to make decisions based on our knowledge and experience, waiting on God rests in knowing His will and settling for nothing less.

There are times we wait on God in silence for a matter of moments. And there are seasons when we wait weeks, months, even years to receive God's direction for our lives. It is as we wait that the infinite hole in our souls is filled, not with the finite things of this world, but with the Infinite One who is everlasting.

*It is a glorious thing to get to know God in a new way in the inner chamber.
It is something still greater and more glorious to know God as the all-sufficient One
and to wait on His Spirit to open our hearts and minds wide to receive the great
things, the new things which He really longs to bestow on those who wait for Him.*

Andrew Murray, 1828-1917, South African Pastor, Missionary and Writer

The Fruit of Waiting On God
- We will not be ashamed or disappointed (Ps. 25:2-3; Is. 49:23).
- We will receive courage (Ps. 27:14).
- We will receive hope and help (Ps. 33:18-22).
- We will receive rest in the midst of difficulty (Ps. 37:5-9).
- We will inherit the land God wants to give us (Ps. 37:34).
- We will know His deliverance (Ps. 40:1-3).
- We will receive His counsel (Ps. 106:13).
- We will know His salvation (Gen. 49:18; Is. 25:9).
- We will know His blessing (Is. 30:18).
- We will receive His strength (Is. 40:28-31).
- We will see Him act on our behalf (Is. 64:4).
- We will experience His goodness (Lam. 3:25).
- We will know that He hears us (Mic. 7:7).
- We will experience the proper birthing of ministry, as the church was birthed in the place of waiting on God (Acts 1:4).

How and when are we to wait on God?
- In stillness (Ps. 37:7)
- Patiently (Ps. 37:7, 40:1).
- Silently (Ps. 62:1)
- All day long (Ps. 25:5)
- Continually (Hos. 12:6)
- With the expectancy of the watchman waiting for the morning (Ps. 130:5-6).

Giving

God is generous, and a giver, therefore He desires for His people to be as well. It is the power of the Holy Spirit working in us that produces generous, giving hearts. We recognize that we have received all things as gifts from God and we share a portion of what we have been given with others. We can give God our time, our treasures and our talents for Him to use for His glory and the advancement of His Kingdom.

THOUGHTS & NOTES

God is a Giver

In His very nature God is a giver. It is who He is. Here is a small sampling of God as a giver from the Scriptures:

- Giver of creation – "I *give* you every seed bearing plant...I *give* every green plant for food" (Gen. 1:29, 30).
- Giver of food – "The eyes of all look to you, and you *give* them their food at the proper time" (Ps. 145:15).
- Giver of sleep – "For He *grants* sleep to those He loves" (Ps. 127:2).
- Giver of life and breath – "...because He Himself *gives* all men life and breath and everything else" (Acts 17:25).
- Giver of the days of life – "...all the days of the life God has *given* him under the sun" (Eccl. 8:15).
- Giver of wisdom – "For the Lord *gives* wisdom" (Prov. 2:6).
- Giver of beauty for ashes (Is. 61:1-3).
- Giver of His Son – "God so loved the world that He *gave* His one and only Son..." (Jn. 3:16).
- Given for our sins – "Grace and peace to you from God our Father and the Lord Jesus Christ, who *gave* Himself for our sins to rescue us from the present evil age..." (Gal. 1:3-5).
- Giver of the Kingdom – "Do not be afraid little flock, for your Father has been pleased to *give* you the Kingdom" (Lk. 12:32).
- Giver of His Life (Jesus) – "The good shepherd *gives* his life for the sheep" (Jn. 10:11).
- Given as a Ransom – "...the man Christ Jesus, who *gave* Himself as a ransom for all men" (1 Tim. 2:5-6).
- Giver of grace – "...to the praise of His glorious grace, which He has freely *given* us in the One He loves" (Eph. 1:4-6).
- Giver of gifts – "We have different gifts, according to the grace *given* us" (Rom. 12:6).
- Giver of rest – "Come to me, all you who are weary and burdened and I will *give* you rest" (Mt. 11:28).
- Giver of peace – "My peace I *give* you" (Jn. 14:27).
- Giver who meets our needs – "Seek first the Kingdom...and all these things will be *given* to you as well" (Mt. 6:25-34).
- Giver of love – "How great is the love the Father has *lavished* on us..." (1 Jn. 3:1).
- Giver of the Holy Spirit – "We know it by the Spirit He *gave* us" (1 Jn. 3:24, 4:13).
- Giver of Eternal Life – "God has *given* us eternal life, and this life is in His Son" (1 Jn. 5:11).

There are three conversions necessary:
the conversion of the heart, mind and the purse.

Martin Luther, 1483-1546, German Theologian and Reformer

For it is in giving that we receive.

St. Francis of Assisi, 1182-1226, Founder of the Franciscan Order

Foundations on Giving

- Everything belongs to God (Job 41:11).
- The true essence of Christianity is giving because that is what God is like.
- The Scriptures teach, "Freely you have received – freely give" (Mt. 10:8).
- We are to freely pass on to others what we have received from God (Acts 3:1-10).
- Giving is not an issue about money—it is a Kingdom attitude that reflects God.
- There is a releasing of the graces of God to others as we give to them.
- From God's perspective it is more blessed to give than to receive (Acts 20:35).
- As we give to others there is a promise of blessing into our lives (Lk. 6:38).
- How we give inevitably impacts how we live and how we relate to other people.
- To the degree we give of ourselves is the degree we also grow.

Becoming Givers

- Giving of our Time – Eph. 5:15-17
    - Time is a gift. We all have the same amount each day. What do you do with your time?
    - Submit your time to God so that He can order your day for Kingdom purposes. Pay attention to where the enemy is trying to steal, kill and destroy your time. Pay attention to God's *divine interruptions*.
    - We spend our time based on our values. Our values determine our priorities. If our values are properly aligned we will spend our time wisely for the Lord.
    - God has determined that one day in seven is to be a Sabbath. Honor it in faith and obedience and watch God honor you (Ex. 20:8-11).
    - Ask the questions: *"How much of my time is going towards the establishing and advancing of God's Kingdom?"* and *"Are any of my activities hindering the devil in any way?"*
    - Understand what season of life God has you in so you can maximize it for His purposes.

God is generous, and a giver, therefore He desires for His people to be as well.

THOUGHTS & NOTES

- Giving of our Treasures – Mt. 6:25-34
  - Ultimately, God is the one who provides us with all that we have.
  - As Christians, we give back to God in the form of tithes, offerings and our possessions.
  - The tithe, or 10 percent of our income, is to be given to the Lord. This tithe is part of the Old Testament Covenant and is an acknowledgement by believers that everything belongs to God. We see this evidenced in the New Testament as well, and validated by Jesus (Mt. 23:23). God asks us to bring the tithe to Him, and He promises blessing as we give it (Lev. 27:30; Mal. 3:8-12).
  - Offerings, which are given above the tithe, may be given to the poor, to the needs of those in God's family, and to the advancement of God's Kingdom and purposes (Acts 4:32-35, 11:27-30; Rom. 15:26; 2 Cor. 8:1-4; Phil. 4:14-19).
  - Our possessions belong to God. He has provided them for us to use and be blessed by. Therefore, we make them available for His purposes as they are His tools in our hands to steward.
  - When deciding where and to whom to give, listen to the Holy Spirit and obey. Pay special attention to those relationships that God partners you with, and those who share a common vision for Kingdom advancement. Also be aware of those who have invested much of God's truth in your life (1 Tim. 5:17,18).
- Giving of our Talents
  - God has uniquely created each one of us. He has given us each various talents, abilities and giftings for His glory.
  - What natural abilities has God given you? What about acquired skills? What are your spiritual gifts? How are you using them for God's purposes to bless others and to advance His Kingdom?
  - We are stewards who one day will give an account of how we have used what God has given us (Mt. 25:15-30; 2 Cor. 5:9,10).
- The Heart of a Giver
  - Gives Cheerfully (2 Cor. 9:6-8).
  - Gives Sacrificially (Mk. 14:3-9; Lk. 21:1-4; Acts 4:32-35).
  - Gives with Faith (Lk. 6:38).
  - Gives in Obedience (Mal. 3:10-12).

God's work done in God's way will never lack God's supply.

Hudson Taylor, 1832-1905, English Missionary to China

CASTING THE NET

When will you spend time in Scripture—reading, studying and meditating on it? How will you make this a more central part of your life?

_____

_____

_____

_____

_____

Do you have the heart of a worshiper? In what ways can you grow in this area?

_____

_____

_____

_____

_____

Are you a history-maker in your prayer life? What did the Holy Spirit speak most clearly to you about prayer from this chapter?

_____

_____

_____

_____

_____

THOUGHTS & NOTES

_____

_____

_____

_____

How are you going to apply the truth of waiting on God in your life? Remember, your Heavenly Father longs to give you His counsel in all areas of your life.

_____

_____

_____

_____

_____

_____

_____

In what area do you give the most—your time, your treasures, your talents? Which of those is the weakest? Yield that area to God, asking Him to expand your capacity to give in that manner.

_____

_____

_____

_____

_____

_____

_____

_____

_____

The one concern of the devil is to keep Christians from praying.
He fears nothing from prayerless studies, prayerless work, and prayerless religion.
He laughs at our toil, mocks at our wisdom, but trembles when we pray.

Samuel Chadwick, 1860-1932, English Revivalist

CATCH OF THE DAY

Chapter Summary

- God invites us to interact with Him through these spiritual disciplines so we may know Him more and be transformed to His likeness.
- Among the many disciplines we may engage in as believers, there are five that stand out as essential to our spiritual growth—time in the scriptures, worship, prayer (including fasting), waiting on God and giving.
- Remember that it's not our involvement in these disciplines that earns God's favor. It's simply what God does in us when we spend time with Him.

What are the two or three things the Holy Spirit spoke most clearly to you through this chapter and how will you respond to Him?

_____

_____

_____

_____

_____

_____

_____

_____

_____

THOUGHTS & NOTES

_____

_____

_____

_____

CHAPTER 7
RELATIONSHIPS

 A VIEW FROM THE SHORE

> "A new command I give you: Love one another.
> As I have loved you, so you must love one another.
> By this all men will know that you are my disciples, if you love one another."
>
> *John 13:34,35*

God pursues relationship with man. He is a relater—the ultimate relater. Even before the creation of man, God was relating within the Trinity. The Father loved and served the Son and the Spirit, the Son loved and served the Father and the Spirit, and the Spirit loved and served the Father and the Son. Relationship is an expression of the Godhead—it exists at the core of who God is and what He most values.

To relate more intimately with man, God sent us His Son, Jesus. Through a revelation of God as man, Jesus showed us what the Father is like. As well, He demonstrated for us how to relate to those around us. Jesus loved others to the extent that He laid down His life on their behalf (jn. 15:13). He walked in grace and humility, mercy and forgiveness. He treated others with honor and sought to serve them. He encouraged and cared for people and ministered to their deepest needs. Jesus called His disciples friends, while He Himself was called a friend of sinners (Jn. 15:14,15; Mt. 11:19).

Did you know that when you became a Christian you also became a member of God's household (Eph. 2:19, 3:15)? You now have brothers and sisters dispersed throughout the nations and throughout time. You belong to a multi-generational, inter-racial,

mega-gifted, international and eternal family of men and women, boys and girls all devoted to Jesus. Those who have gone before you cheer you on as you run the course God has marked for you (Heb. 12:1,2)

The way we relate to others is important. Outside of our relationship with God, there can be nothing more important than becoming good relaters. Our love for each other has eternal consequences. Jesus said that the world would recognize that we belong to God because of the way we regard each other (Jn. 13:34,35). He said that if we walk in love and unity, the world would know that the Father has sent Jesus and loves them, even as He loves Jesus (Jn. 17:23). No wonder the devil works so hard to steal, kill and destroy relationships (Jn. 10:10).

Just about every problem in the world is a relationship problem. Pride, sin and selfishness, independence and rebellion, along with unmet expectations and hurt, all hinder our attempts to build meaningful and lasting relationships.

In this chapter we will examine the various spheres of friendship and see what the Scriptures say about the pillars of godly relationships, maintaining unity of the Spirit, walking under authority, as well as guy-girl relationships, marriage and family life.

SETTING SAIL

God uses our relationships in the discipling process of our lives. Through others, we catch a glimpse of His heart for us, as well as a greater understanding of Himself, His ways, and even ourselves. Because of our backgrounds and past experiences, we come to relationships with different perspectives. Problems sometimes emerge, particularly in the area of expectations. Having been loved imperfectly—some of us more so than others—we're prone to expect friends to mend our self-esteem and fill the emptiness within us. On occasion we confront our inability to quench the places of rejection in others. At other times, we square off against the reality that no person can satisfy the longing of our own hearts. Through the struggle for balance and grace, we learn compassion and the limits of human nature. We discover that no matter how loving and godly people are, they cannot meet our needs, hopes, fears and expectations— only God can do that. He alone is our Father in heaven, and Jesus, our one true Savior.

An Introduction to Relationships

We experience varying degrees of relationships. Some people we relate to as team members working toward a particular goal. Others we meet through the services we've rendered them, or they us. Some people become acquaintances seen around town, people who greet us regularly at the market or school. There are those who share common interests with us— those we enjoying getting together with when opportunities arise. And, then, there are those whom God has linked to our hearts, people who share a genuine affection. Within this bond of friendship, hearts and lives are shared. Encouragement, trust, honesty, understanding and commitment mark these relationships in good times and in bad.

As wonderful as it would be to share a heart-link with everyone in the Body of Christ, it's simply impossible. God places each member of the Body of Christ right where each person needs to be. He is in perfect control, enacting the plans He has for our lives. As He promises, He uses all things—and people—to work His purposes into us, to *disciple* us in His ways.

THOUGHTS & NOTES

Spheres of Relationship

We see, even in Jesus' life, that He had varied *spheres*, or circles of relationship. Crowds followed Him to hear His teaching and receive healing. From the multitudes, people approached Him, engaging Him one-on-one. Nicodemus *knew* Jesus, as did the woman at the well and the rich young ruler. In the gospels, we're told about a party at Matthew's house, the wedding in Cana, and a meal at the home of Zacchaeus. Following a night of prayer, Jesus chose 12 men to walk closely with Him. Of these 12, three disciples came to possess an even closer place in His heart. While Jesus loved all, He experienced people differently, just like you and I do. Concentric circles of relationship surrounded His life—the largest representing the more distant relationships, and the smallest depicting the intimate few.

As various spheres of relationships emerge in our lives, each takes on its own set of characteristics, responsibilities and tending points. These basic dynamics allow people to understand their relational boundaries and create healthy expectations. The four categories listed below are not indicators by which to ascertain the value of our relationships, but rather, they are markers to help gauge godly response to the people who share life with us.

The Crowd (Acquaintances)
- *Characteristics*
  - Occasional contact.
  - Talk centers on general information and friendly conversation.
- *Responsibilities*
  - Acknowledge them with love and grace.
  - Discern what questions are appropriate to ask at this point in the friendship.
- *Tending Points*
  - Greet and receive them in a friendly manner.
  - Learn and remember their name.
  - Be a good listener.
  - Get to know them better by asking appropriate questions.
  - Consider how God may use you to be a blessing in their lives.

Within the bond of friendship, hearts and lives are shared.

Has it ever occurred to you that one hundred pianos all tuned to the same fork are automatically tuned to each other? They are of one accord by being tuned, not to each other, but to another standard to which each one must individually bow. So one hundred worshipers [meeting] together, each one looking away to Christ, are in heart nearer to each other than they could possibly be, were they to become 'unity' conscious and turn their eyes away from God to strive for closer fellowship.

A.W. Tozer, 1897-1963, American Preacher and Writer

The Casual (Casual Friendships)
- *Characteristics*
    - Based on common interests, activities, concerns; neighbors.
    - Personal conversation that centers on information about each other, our opinions and desires.
- *Responsibilities*
    - Recognize what God has done, and is doing, in their lives.
    - Affirm strengths and encourage them.
    - Discern what questions are appropriate to ask at this point in the friendship.
- *Tending Points*
    - Watch for their strengths.
    - Learn about the hopes and desires they have by being a good listener.
    - Come alongside of them in prayer and encouragement should they disclose a problem to you.
    - Reflect interest in them and display trustworthiness and faithfulness in your friendship.
    - Consider how God may use you to be a blessing in their lives.

The Committed (Close Friendships)
- *Characteristics*
    - Based more on mutual enjoyment and life purpose.
    - More deliberateness in the friendship due to a deeper heart-link.
    - Purposeful conversation often revolving around issues of life purpose and speaking into each other's lives.
- *Responsibilities*
    - Be available to come alongside them in life's journey as invited.
    - Look for ways to affirm character traits, gifts and call.
    - Actively help each other in the fulfilling of life purpose.
- *Tending Points*
    - Talk about what God is doing in areas of character development in each other's lives.
    - Take the 'given level' of responsibility to help them grow personally and fulfill their life's purpose.
    - Pray regularly for them.
    - Listen to the Holy Spirit as He gives you something for them.
    - Actively encourage them and be available to help them in whatever ways you can.

THOUGHTS & NOTES

The Core (Intimate Friendships)

- Characteristics
  - Based on a mutual commitment to walk together in God at a deep level. Besides spouse (if married) only a few will be part of your core relationships.
  - Intimate conversation – totally honest, vulnerable, transparent sharing of the heart; total freedom to speak into each other's lives with wisdom .
- Responsibilities
  - Love, commitment to walk together, integrity, encouragement.
  - Used by God to help each become more like Jesus.
  - Walk alongside each other to finish well as it relates to living life and fulfilling God's call.
- Tending Points
  - Actively look for ways to help them grow and pursue God's purposes for their lives.
  - Learn how to comfort and strengthen them through trials.
  - Assume a personal level of responsibility for their reputation – always stand with them.
  - Pray for them, obey what God asks you to do for them and look for ways to bless them.
  - Continue to speak honestly as you both strive for integrity.

A relationship with someone cannot be forced. It must grow naturally, as well as intentionally. We can only establish a level of friendship that both parties desire. The person with the lesser commitment determines the extent of the friendship. The other party should accept the friendship offered and trust God to build on it if He desires to do so.

Always remember that we are permitted to speak into others' lives only to the degree they allow us. If we try to share beyond what they have opened to us, we can damage our friendships. If someone asks for our input about their job, we shouldn't offer counsel regarding their marriage. We should go only where we've been invited. Once someone gives us blanket freedom to speak into their life, we must walk in the Fear of the Lord and speak only as God directs us. While these kinds of friendships are invaluable, they cannot be rushed. By providing them time and trust, they become vehicles for the Lord's use in our lives.

Never has the world had a greater need for love than in our day.
People are hungry for love. We don't have time to stop and smile at each other.
We are all in such a hurry! Pray. Ask for the necessary grace. Pray to be able to
understand how much Jesus loved us, so that you can love others.

Mother Teresa of Calcutta, 1910-1997, Missionary to the Poor

Pillars of Godly Relationships

The Lord says much through Paul about relationships in his thirteen letters (Romans-Philemon). In his book to the Romans, in chapter 12, we find a number of foundational principles, or relational pillars, for walking in healthy relationships. Let's take a closer look at some of them.

A Renewed Mind – Rom. 12:1-2
- Relationships in the Kingdom are based on a different set of values than we may have learned through experiences in our family, friendships and in encounters with authority figures. God wants us to view our relationships through His set of lenses. This text of Scripture speaks of not being conformed to the patterns of this world (squeezed into its mold), but to be transformed (metamorphosis – the process of the caterpillar becoming the butterfly) by the renewing (the gradual conforming to God's perspective) of our minds (the organ of perception, the way we look at life).
- We first need to allow God to renew our thinking about other people, helping us to value them as He values them.
- Second to our relationship with God is the way we relate to others (Mt. 22:34-40).
- All of our relationships need to be based in truth (Eph. 4:15).

Grace – Rom. 12:3
- Because God's grace has been given to us we have the privilege of extending His grace to others through our lives.
- Grace is getting what we don't deserve. It is freely giving to others, regardless of whether or not we think they deserve it.
- Grace is how God responds to our failures. Likewise, we need to give room to those who fail us.
- Those with gracious hearts use words to build others up according to their needs (Eph. 4:29).
- People hurt others because they have been hurt. God's grace makes a way through our lives to be a source of healing and health to the hearts of those in the place of need (Heb. 4:14-16).

THOUGHTS & NOTES

Humility – Rom. 12:3, 16

- Pride destroys relationships, while humility breeds healthy ones.
- Pride conveys the subtle attitude that ultimately we want everyone to be like us. Humility accepts people the way they are. To "think of yourself with sober judgement" means to think of yourself in reality of who you are in the context of everyone else. This means accepting who you are and who you are not. It applies to how we view others as well.
- God did not create personality conflicts. Conflicts of personality have more to do with a lack of humility then anything else.
- Humility freely admits when they are wrong and others are right.
- If we walk in true humility it is impossible to evade peace and getting along with others.
- Humility is the building block upon which all other relational qualities depend. Without humility, for example, we won't be able to offer our forgiveness, trust and understanding.
- The fruit of humility includes openness, teachability, flexibility rather than stubbornness, an ability to receive correction without needing to defend or be right, and a willingness to follow those in a position to lead.

Celebrating Diversity – Rom. 12:4-8

- God made each of us different and unique—and He likes it that way! To be more like Jesus means we must adjust our hearts and minds to His way of thinking on this matter.
- God made people of different genders, races, generations, languages, bodies, personalities, with a variety of interests and passions, gifts and calls.
- We need to learn to appreciate and celebrate our diversity, rather than fear differences and be threatened by change.
- Pride requires everyone to be like them. It is at the root of all prejudice.
- Our differences, combined with humility, allow us to walk in a godly dependence on one another, keeping us from an attitude of independence.
- Even though we are different, we belong to one body and each member belongs to all others.

Relationships in the Kingdom are based on a different set of values than we may have learned through experiences in our family, friendships and in encounters with authority figures.

He is your friend who pushes you nearer to God.

Abraham Kuyper, 1837-1920, Dutch Theologian and Statesman

Love – Rom. 12:9-10

- Love is a choice; a choosing of someone else's highest good.
- We are to love God above everyone and everything, and our neighbors as ourselves (Mk. 12:28-34).
- Since God has commanded us to love (Jn. 15:12-17), it means He will give us the ability to do it.
- Our love is to be sincere, or without hypocrisy. In the New Testament, the word *hypocrite* referred to an actor who played a part. We are not called to act lovingly—we are called to love, to sincerely love each other.
- We are to be devoted to one another with a brotherly, or family kind of love.
- Biblical love is giving and self-sacrificing. It expresses kindness, care and servanthood.
- Take a further look at the attributes of love in 1 Corinthians 13.

Honor – Rom. 12:10

- We are to outdo one another in showing honor.
- What is pictured in the Scriptures is an entire society, the Kingdom, built on the principle of mutually honoring one another.
- Honor has to do with recognizing a person's worth or value, and the expression of it.
- Honor not only encourages the heart, but nourishes and refreshes the spirit.
- A biblical value system has three measures of honor:
    - Honor due to performance, which is earned, not given; recognizes what a person has done or achieved (Rom. 13:7; 1 Tim. 5:17).
    - Honor due to character, which is earned and not given; it recognizes who the person is in character or what they have become (1 Tim. 3:1-13).
    - Honor due to a person's intrinsic value and worth, which is given, not earned; it recognizes the person's eternal worth in the sight of God. Because men and women have been made in the image of God, and have had the priceless blood of Jesus shed for them, they are worthy of honor (Gen. 1:26; Heb. 2:6).
- Expressions of honor:
    - *Acceptance* enables another to feel like a valuable addition to our lives.
    - *Affirmation* draws attention to another's gifts, strengths and achievements.
    - *Appreciation* expresses heart-felt gratitude for contributions made to one's life.
    - *Approval* commends for how one behaves and what he or she does.
    - *Admiration* praises another for the standard they set and our desire to emulate their example.
    - *Acknowledgement* offers public recognition of another's character or achievements.

THOUGHTS & NOTES

Joyful and Patient – Rom. 12:12

- We are to be joyful in hope. People enjoy being around those who live life out of joy and hope.
- Those who bring joy and hope to relationships bring tremendous encouragement to others.
- We are also to be patient in affliction. Just as there are times of joy, there are times of difficulty in our lives and relationships. In the latter times, patience expresses our trust in God and our love for one another.

Prayer – Rom. 12:12

- The encouragement here by Paul is to be faithful, or constant, in prayer.
- Praying for those we are in relationship with creates a spiritual bond, or heart-link, with them.
- This also allows the carrying of each other's burdens with opportunities to hear from God on behalf of each other.

Sharing – Rom. 12:13

- This speaks of partnering with people to see their needs met (Acts 4:32-35).
- God has given us each various resources at our disposal so we can share to help others.
- Partnering with someone at this level means we must know them well enough to know their needs.
- We are to share what we have to meet the needs of the poor. We must have Jesus' heart for the poor. A reading of the gospels will reveal this.
- Practicing hospitality speaks of opening up our homes to those who may need our help or ministry.

Blessing – Rom. 12:14

- Paul echoes the words of Jesus, "Love your enemies and pray for those who persecute you...bless those who curse you" (Mt. 5:44; Lk. 6:27,28).
- We are to speak kindly and constantly be a blessing to those who persecute us that they might see who God really is and be won to Him.
- We are to minister in the opposite spirit when someone mistreats us; in this case we respond to a curse with a blessing.

Assuredly there is but one way in which to achieve what is not merely difficult but utterly against human nature: to love those who hate us, to repay their evil deeds with benefits, to return blessings for reproaches. It is that we remember not to consider men's evil intention but to look upon the image of God in them, which cancels and effaces their transgressions, and with its beauty and dignity allures us to love and embrace them.

John Calvin, 1509-64, French Protestant Theologian of the Reformation

Understanding and Trust – Rom. 12:15

- We are to sincerely identify with where people are at.
- This speaks of a selflessness that allows us to connect with and understand them.
- One of the most basic needs that people have is the need to be understood.
- When people feel understood it relieves them from the need to justify their actions and intentions.
- People won't feel understood unless they can reveal themselves to you, and they won't do that until they trust you. Trust is necessary for any relationship to be successful.
  - Trust is choosing to make oneself dependent upon another person.
  - Trust occurs when the one trusting has made no back-up plans to protect themselves, should the person in whom they are trusting fail them.
  - Trust is fragile and must be built one step at a time through honesty, truth, faithfulness, and responsibility.
- Understanding pertains to communication between people. To aid understanding, learn to communicate clearly and listen intently so the person sharing feels heard and understood.

Harmony – Rom. 12:16-21

- The greatest obstacle to harmony is pride.
- Regardless of another's position in life, we are to walk together in harmony.
- Pride, arrogance and conceit have no room in the Kingdom community of believers.
- Harmony may mean accepting 'humble duties' for the purpose of serving others.
- We are never to return evil for evil, nor is it our responsibility to take revenge. Instead, we are to overcome evil with good.
- As far as it depends on you, live in peace with everyone.

> We are one Body, one Spirit, called to one hope, one Lord, one faith, one baptism, and one God and Father of all. It is our responsibility as believers to maintain the unity and peace—the oneness— that God has provided.

THOUGHTS & NOTES

Maintaining Peace & Oneness in Relationships

Through His death on the cross Jesus has made believers one (Eph. 2:11-22). We are one Body, one Spirit, called to one hope, one Lord, one faith, one baptism, and one God and Father of all (Eph. 4:4-6). God has made us one already—it is our responsibility as believers to maintain the unity and peace—the oneness—that God has provided. The Scriptures exhort us to "make every effort to keep the unity of the Spirit through the bond of peace" (Eph. 4:3). So how do we maintain the unity of the Spirit and the bond of peace?

Walk Worthy
- Jesus died for us. He has called us to Himself and recreated us for His glory. We, then, should live in a manner worthy of who He is and what He has called us to.
- Regardless of who we are or what we do, if we live to bring God glory, we will enjoy peace and unity among ourselves. A focus on the glory of God keeps all of our eyes on Jesus.

Walk in Humility
- Jesus walked in humility (Mt. 11:29).
- Pride brings contention, humility breeds peace. Disunity originates in pride (Prov. 13:10; Phil. 2:8-11; 1 Pet. 5:5).
- Humility can be defined as being *"willing to be known for who we really are".*
- Humility allows us to be real and honest with our selfishness, weaknesses and failures.
- Humility enables us to be honest about what we do well and where God has gifted us.
- Humility recognizes our creatureliness and our desperate need for God.
- Humility yields to God's right to do what He wishes with whom He wants. Humility does not need to play God by exercising control over other people's lives.
- Humility allows us to cheer for people who are like-gifted and further along in development.
- Humility also recognizes its need for others in their lives.
- Humility knows how to say, "I was wrong and you were right."
- Unity, in its simplest form, is nothing more than corporate humility.
- God is attracted to humility and establishes His presence among humble people.
- We are to humble ourselves under God's mighty hand. Because He values humility so much, He will humble us if we refrain from humbling ourselves (1 Pet. 5:6).

_____

_____

_____

_____

_____

Walk in Gentleness (Meekness)

- Jesus was gentle (Mt. 11:29).
- Gentleness is the picture of an animal being trained until it is completely under control. Its spirit is not broken, but it is now yielded to its trainer's will.
- Gentleness is part of the Fruit of the Spirit (Gal. 5:22-23).
- Gentleness speaks of a "softness of heart" as opposed to being harsh or violent.
- Gentleness may be defined as "a sensitivity of the heart towards others, a desire not to harm due to a valuing of the other person."
- Gentleness takes tremendous strength of character to walk in.
- Gentleness is unwilling to provoke others, and is not easily provoked.
- Gentleness does not lash out at others around them.
- Gentleness produces a heart that is not easily offended, or that causes offense.
- Gentleness does not assert its own importance.
- Gentleness accepts the dealings of God without dispute or resistance.
- People who are gentle nurture others and provide a safe place for them to share their hearts.

Walk in Patience

- God is patient (2 Pet. 3:9).
- Consider God's patience in bearing with the ungratefulness and utter foolishness of man; He is slow to anger (Neh. 9:17; Ps. 103:8).
- Patience has to do with longsuffering and steadfast endurance.
- Patience is slow to anger and bears insult and injury without complaint.
- Patience might simply be defined as "to endure with unruffled temper".
- Patience defers what may be due; it has the power to take revenge but doesn't.
- A lack of patience is often rooted in being driven by our agendas.
- Patience values other people enough to give them room and time to fail, learn and develop.

Bear With One Another in Love

- Bearing with one another in love literally means "putting up with each other"— bearing each other's attitudes, activities and choices.
- Things will go awry with people, even in the Kingdom of God. It is important that we bear with one another through mistakes, miseries and the trials of life.

THOUGHTS & NOTES

- Bearing with one another in love might be defined as "putting up with another's weaknesses and differences, not ceasing to love them because of those things in them which perhaps might irritate or displease us."
- Bearing with one another in love means not writing people off or giving place to bitterness or revenge.
- All of us at times are a burden to someone, but if we bear with one another in love we can maintain unity and peace in our relationships.
- We are to bear with one another in love by choosing another's highest good as we relate to them.

deeper waters

Four foundational kinds of relationships require us to lay down our lives for one another so that we may value others as God values them. They include walking under those in authority, relationships among guys and girls, husbands and wives, and parents and children. Let's take a closer look at these important relational spheres.

Walking Under Authority

Authority comes from God – Rom. 13:1-2
- Ultimately, we are all under God's authority.
- Authority is delegated by God, and He has set up various spheres of authority over our lives:
    - Family (Eph. 6:1)
    - Government (Rom. 13)
    - Church (Heb. 13:17)
    - Employers (Eph. 6:5-8)
    - Teachers, coaches, etc.
- Choosing to rebel against authority is choosing to rebel against God (Rom. 13:2).
- If authority is God-given then why do we rebel against authority?
    - Because our sin nature wants our own way.
    - Because we've been hurt, wounded and disappointed in the past by authority figures.
    - Because we don't see God for who He really is, so we don't trust Him.

O divine Master, grant that I may not so much seek
to be consoled as to console; to be understood as to understand;
to be loved as to love; for it is in giving that we receive,
it is in pardoning that we are pardoned...

St. Francis of Assisi, 1182-1226, Founder of the Franciscan Order

- Walking under authority is meant to be a blessing in our lives (Rom. 13:3,4).
  - Given for protection, to keep us safe.
  - Given for provision, as resources for life.
  - Given for direction, as guidance, wisdom and counsel.
  - Given to develop character qualities in our lives—truthfulness, obedience, dependability, orderliness, diligence, faithfulness, reverence, loyalty, patience, forgiveness, responsibility, etc.
  - Given to help us become fruitful people in the Kingdom, to help find our place and purpose in God.
- The blessings of walking under authority:
  - It will go well with you (Eph. 6:1-3).
  - It brings delight to the Lord (Col. 3:20).
  - We avoid fear, condemnation and punishment (Rom. 13:5).
  - We maintain a good conscience (Rom. 13:5).
  - We obtain a good report (Heb. 13:17).
  - We won't blaspheme God and His Word (1 Tim. 6:1).
  - We walk in protection and guidance (Pr. 6:20-22).
  - We gain discernment (Pr. 15:5).
  - We will be commended (1 Pet. 2:13-14).
  - We will bring honor to those over us (1 Th. 5:12-13).

Understanding Submission – 1 Pet. 2:13-25

- Submission is *an attitude of voluntarily placing oneself under God-given authority as an act of faith in the sovereignty of God.* Ultimately, when we submit to someone in authority we are submitting to God.
- It is important to note that submission to authority is a command of God, yet it is voluntary by the person doing the submitting, and should not be something "lorded over" and forced upon by those in authority. *Submission demanded by authority is an abuse of authority.*
- God Himself sets the tone by commanding all men to walk under His authority while simultaneously giving them volition. Leaders, especially, must be aware of the dynamic tension of this Kingdom truth.
- Once someone agrees to become part of something like a church or a company, they must walk under the guidelines established by those positioned as leaders. Should they choose to subvert authority, leadership has the responsibility to address the situation with their authority.

THOUGHTS & NOTES

_____

_____

_____

_____

- We are to submit "for the Lord's sake" (1 Pet. 2:13).
- We are to submit "to every authority instituted among men" (1 Pet. 2:13).
- We are to submit "with all respect" (1 Pet. 2:18-20).
- We are to submit as Jesus did (1 Pet. 2:21-25).
    - He walked in radical submission to God all the way to the cross (Phil. 2:6-8).
    - He yielded, not demanding His way (Mt. 26:36-46).
    - He submitted and learned obedience (Heb. 5:7-10).
    - He let go and entrusted Himself to God because He knew the Father's character (1 Pet. 2:23).
- The disciples of Jesus followed their Savior's model, as seen throughout the book of Acts.
- The obsession to demand that things always go our way is one of the greatest bondages in society and the church today. Submission is the ability to lay down this compulsion.
    - Submission gives us the freedom to lay our lives down for others.
    - Submission exposes our hearts regarding what we really believe about God – whether or not we'll trust Him.
    - Submission reveals what is in our hearts when we don't get our way, providing us a platform for character growth.
- Often, when we have an issue with authority, it is over a difference of opinion between us and the leader and not matters that are illegal, immoral, unethical or unbiblical. This reveals, once again, our desperate need to try to get our own way.
- When does submission come to an end?
    - When we are asked to disobey God and the Scriptures (Acts 5:29).
    - When we are asked to do something that is illegal, immoral, unethical or unbiblical.
    - When it becomes destructive through the denial of love and the loss of value of an individual—for example, a parent abusing a child in the name of discipline.
    - When manipulation and control are exercised by a leader, not allowing those under them to have the freedom to make choices in regards to their own personal lives, those under authority may need to consider whether God may be releasing them from the situation.

Submission is an attitude of voluntarily placing oneself under God-given authority as act of faith in the sovereignty of God.

Properly Appealing to Authority

What do we do when the leader is wrong or mistaken?

- We have two tendencies when we don't like what authority is doing—react in anger and leave, or passively succumb to erroneous direction. Neither is a godly response.
- Consider first if you are being asked to do something that is illegal, immoral, unethical or unbiblical. Or, is it simply a difference of opinion that you merely need to accept?
    - Be wise in appealing to authority as appealing too many times can undermine your place of influence.
- Next, before appealing, spend time in prayer asking God for wisdom.
- If you are to appeal to the one in authority, use these principles from the life of Daniel (Dan. 1:8-20).
    - *Keep your heart clean before God towards them.* Daniel did not defile himself. He did not allow the issue at hand to corrupt his life, causing a bad attitude that could be reflected in his words and actions (Dan. 1:8).
    - *Meet with the authority figure with a right heart attitude of humility.* Daniel sought an audience with the chief official. He went to him and placed himself under his authority, demonstrating an attitude of humility and openness (Dan. 1:8).
    - *Listen for the reasons behind the authority figure's decision(s).* Daniel discovered the intentions of the one in authority. He discovered why authority was doing the things in question (Dan. 1:10).
    - *Be ready with a creative alternative, and the reasons you think that will serve them better.* Daniel was ready with a creative alternative (Dan. 1:11-13).
    - *Pray to receive favor from the one in authority.* Daniel received favor and permission from the chief official (Dan. 1:9, 14).
    - *Ask God to make you and your creative alternative a blessing to everyone.* Daniel, and all associated with Him, were blessed by God (Dan. 1:15-20).
- What do you do if you walk through these steps of appealing to authority and the answer is no?
    - Identify the cause: Is it you? Was it the way you appealed? Is it the authority figure? Or might it be God's way of moving you on?
    - Trust God and give Him some time to change their minds.
    - Consider carefully if you need to appeal to your authority's supervisors. If you do, use the same process again with them.
    - Recognize when God is leading you to stay the course or telling you that it is time to leave.

THOUGHTS & NOTES

Guy-Girl Relationships

Principles for Guy-Girl Relationships
- God made men and women and intends for them to enjoy godly relationship with each other.
- All relationships, these included, are to walk together out of the relational pillars of Romans 12 described earlier in this chapter.

Attraction and Love
- Just because you are attracted to someone of the opposite sex does not mean it is supposed to turn into a romantic relationship.
    - Guy-girl relationships cannot be based on attraction and feelings alone. Feelings come and go, while love and commitment endures a lifetime.
    - It is fine to be attracted to someone's looks, personality or gifts. But attraction does not serve as an indicator, validating that the relationship will meet a romantic end.
    - As a Christian, one turns the corner from good friendship to romantic relationship only after both people are willing to choose to love and be committed to each other, by hearing from God, and receiving wise counsel from others in their lives.
    - Love is a choice, based on a commitment to the other person that grows from a healthy friendship. Lust, in contrast, is an abnormally strong desire to selfishly use someone for one's own gratification and purposes. Love gives, while lust takes what it can get.

Tending a Growing Friendship
- When it comes to developing a more serious relationship with someone of the opposite sex, one that could possibly lead to a marriage relationship, it is essential that both people be Christians (2 Cor. 6:14-18).
    - It is important that both people be committed to Jesus, not only in obedience to Scripture, but also for the purpose of living from a common set of values based in scriptural truths.
    - For someone to engage in a romantic relationship with a non-Christian is disobeying the Lord, and it is also setting up themselves, and the other person, for tremendous disappointment.

- As a relationship between a man and woman grows into a deeper friendship, wisdom dictates that they surround themselves with godly counsel (Pr. 11:14, 15:22, 24:6).
    - This can begin with their parents (Eph. 6:2,3).
    - It can also include other spiritual leaders and mentors in their lives (Heb. 13:7).
- As it grows, enjoy the friendship and give it plenty of time. There is rarely ever a need to hurry the relationship along (Eccl. 3:11; Pr. 20:25).
    - The pacing of this kind of relationship is important. Allow lots of time to lay a solid foundation of genuine love and friendship. The deeper the friendship before marriage, the more solid the foundation in marriage.
    - Time provides the opportunity to truly see each other's strengths and weaknesses.
    - Time provides the couple with the kinds of experiences they need to explore compatibility, which is essential for the long-term.
    - Time lets both people in the relationship get to know each other's families. It is a true saying, that when one marries he or she marries the whole family.
    - Time allows a couple to count the cost of marriage—where the question can be asked within each heart, *"Is this the one I believe I am to forsake all others for and to commit the rest of my life to?"*
- As the friendship deepens, serious consideration must be given to each person's gifts and callings.
    - What has God said to each about their calling before the other person came into their lives?
    - How similar and different is each one's calling? Gifts?
    - Where and how might there be teaming for Kingdom purposes?

Love is a choice, based on a commitment to the other person that naturally grows out of a healthy friendship.

THOUGHTS & NOTES

- A deep love for the other person, a choice to commit to the other for a lifetime—along with hearing from God—is necessary to move the relationship from friendship to engagement to marriage.
    - Who you marry is the single most important relational decision of your life. In light of this, a season of seeking God in prayer and fasting is appropriate before making a commitment to marriage.
    - If you are wise, you will seek the counsel of godly people who really know and love you to get their impressions. Ask them to be totally honest with you and listen carefully to what they say.
- Ultimately, marriage is intended to offer mutual love, joy and giving to one another, secured by a deep and lasting commitment, and walking in oneness of heart to fulfill God's purposes together.

What the Bible Says About Sex in Relationships
- Sex is God's idea, therefore it is holy and a blessing (Gen. 2:24-25).
- Sex was given by God to be a source of deep spiritual, physical and emotional pleasure between a husband and wife, and for the purpose of creation of the human race by reproduction (Gen. 1:27,28; Pr. 5 :18,19).
- Scripture does not hesitate to extol the joys of sexual love in marriage (Song of Solomon).
- Sex is to be reserved for a husband and wife in marriage (Heb. 13:4).
- A married couple is to fulfill their partner's sexual needs (1 Cor. 7:1-5).
- The Bible gives stern warnings about the misuse of sex:
    - *Lust* – an abnormally strong desire to selfishly use somebody for one's own gratification (Mt. 5:27-28).
    - *Sensuality* – a planned appeal to the physical senses to excite sinful desires for selfish purposes (this includes pornography) (Mt. 5:28; Gal. 5:19; 1 Thes. 4:3-8; 1 Pet. 2:11).
    - *Sexual Immorality or Fornication* – sexual relations among unmarried people (1 Cor. 6:13-20).
    - *Adultery* – sexual relations with another's married partner (Ex. 20:14; Rom. 13:9-10).
    - *Homosexuality or Lesbianism* – sexual relations between those of the same sex (Lev. 18:22; Rom. 1:18-32; 1 Cor. 6:9-11).
    - *Incest* – sexual relations with family members other than a spouse (Lev. 18:8-18).
    - *Rape* – sexual relations forced on someone against their will (Dt. 22:25-29).
    - *Prostitution* – sexual relations with a prostitute (Prov. 7:1-27; 1 Cor. 6:13-20).
    - *Bestiality* – sexual relations with an animal (Lev. 18:23).

The first service one owes to others in the fellowship consists in listening to them.
Just as love of God begins in listening to His Word, so the beginning of love
for the brethren is learning to listen to them. It is God's love for us that He not
only gives us His Word but lends us His ear. So it is His work that we do
for our brother when we learn to listen to him.

Dietrich Bonhoeffer, 1906-1945, German Theologian and Writer

- Ungodly sexual relationships produce severe consequences (Jdg. 16:1-31; 1 Ki. 11:1-13).
- Sex outside of marriage will/can result in:
    - Sin and guilt for disobeying God and His Word.
    - Spiritual bondages created by unhealthy bonds to another (1 Cor. 6:16-20).
    - Emotional hurt caused by a deep sense of loss or being used, destroying trust in future relationships.
    - Hurt family members due to your choices.
    - Ruining your reputation.
    - Marrying or becoming a parent too soon, forcing important life choices to be made.

Walking in Sexual Purity

- Spiritual Purity
    - Walk in the light and truth of the Scriptures (Ps. 119:9-11).
    - Renew your mind in the ways of God (Rom. 12:1-2).
    - Be honest and recognize the leaning towards sin and selfishness within (Rom. 7:14-8:4).
    - Live by the Spirit, keep in step with the Spirit (Gal. 5:16-26).
    - Choose to walk in honest, accountable relationships with others (Eccl. 4:12).
    - Remember, God will not allow you to be tempted beyond what you can bear and will provide a way out (1 Cor. 10:12-13).
    - Jesus will help you in your time of need (Heb. 4:12-16).
- Emotional and Physical Purity
    - It is important to guard your heart by allowing God to show you how much of it you should open and give to another.
    - Make a gift of your whole being, including your body, to the Lord (Rom. 12:1,2; 1 Cor. 6:18-20).
    - Men can become sexually aroused by what they look at, so they must be careful to guard their eyes (Job. 31:1; Mt. 5:27-28).
    - Women may become sexually aroused through a man's tenderness and touch, so they must be careful how far they go emotionally with a man, and must avoid inappropriate touching by a man.

THOUGHTS & NOTES

- When tempted sexually, flee from the source of temptation. Follow the example of Joseph (Gen. 39:1-21).
    - Joseph didn't listen to the temptation (39: 6-9).
    - Joseph realized that ultimately he would be sinning against God if he gave in to the temptation (39:9).
    - Joseph didn't place himself in the path of temptation (39:10).
    - Joseph fled when temptation appeared (39:11-12).
- How far is going too far physically before marriage? Whatever begins to arouse you sexually, creating a desire for more, needs to become the line that you will not cross. Being honest with each other, and walking in a mutual commitment of purity before God and others, is the only way to succeed in this area.

Some Steps to Sexual Freedom
- If you have already sinned in this area, confess your sin(s) to God and ask Him to forgive you (1 Jn. 1:9).
- Seek Him for a fresh filling of His Spirit (Ps. 51:10-12).
- Commit yourself to walk purely before God in this area of your life by dedicating your whole being, including your body, afresh to Him (Ps. 119:9-11; Rom. 12:1-2).
- Ask God to lead you in making things right with those whom you have sinned against, and forgive those who have sinned against you.
- Seek out someone who is further along spiritually you can talk to and pray with. Ask them to pray a prayer of cleansing over you.
- Set your heart to sin no more and to glorify God in this area of your life (Jn. 8:1-11; 1 Cor. 10:31).

Sex was given by God to be a source of deep spiritual, physical and emotional pleasure between a husband and wife.

Family Life Basics

God's Intentions for the Family

- Family is to be a great place of love, laughter and the sharing of life with one another.
- Family is a place where the love of God can be demonstrated:
    - To the parents as they catch a glimpse of God's heart for them as His children.
    - To the children as they catch a glimpse of what God is really like through their parents.
- Family is a place of comfort and safety when times are difficult.
- Family is a place of nurturing, discipline and training both spiritually and practically.
- Family is a place of modeling and mentoring.
- Family is for encouraging and helping each other fulfill God's purposes in life.
- Family can be a little picture of what the Kingdom of God is like for the watching world.

Things Satan Uses to Destroy Family Life – Jn. 10:10

- *Our Own Hearts* – Satan will attempt to use our own pride, sin and selfishness to wreak havoc upon family life.
- *Lack of Lordship* – When Jesus is not Lord of family life it opens the doors for the devil to influence it in even greater measure.
- *Low Commitment* – To be successful in family life, each family member must be unconditionally committed and available to the others.
- *Not Choosing Love* – Love is primarily a choice for someone else's highest good.
- *Wrong Priorities* – A person's primary sphere of relationship is their family, thus the devil attempts to destroy it by placing greater importance on other relationships, activities, pursuits or possessions.
- *No Training* – Because everyone is new to marriage and family life when they begin, it is necessary to receive training and mentoring from others who have gone before them.
- *Neglect of Roles* – God has laid out a structure for family life in His Word. When it is not followed, problems erupt, opening doors for the devil to bring confusion and frustration.
- *Independence* – Isolation of family members from each other will not repair itself. They must learn to consider one another in all things.
- *Communication Problems* – Learning to listen and understand, and to communicate deeply and clearly, is essential to good family life.
- *Trials* – Difficult times will either bring a family closer together or drive them further apart.

THOUGHTS & NOTES

Marriage: The Husband and Wife Relationship

God is the one that brought the first man and woman together in the Garden of Eden. Marriage is His idea (Gen. 2:22-25). It is to be honored by all (Heb. 13:4) and is not to be separated by anyone (Mt. 19:6).

- Two Shall Be One – Gen .2:24-25; Eph. 5:31; Mk. 10:6-9
    - *Leaving* – A couple has a responsibility to establish an independence from their parents for the purpose of creating an entity of their own. Parents are to be honored, enjoyed as friends, and remain sources of wise counsel when called upon, but they are no longer the primary source for the couple's physical, emotional or financial needs.
    - *Cleaving* – A couple has a responsibility to establish that their primary relational commitment in life is to each other. The idea of cleaving is actively pursuing one another, being joined, glued or welded together. It is receiving each other as God's gift, embracing natural differences and seeing God's purposes in building oneness through each other's weaknesses.
    - *One Flesh* – A couple has a responsibility to cultivate intimacy with one another. Along with the sexual relationship, this speaks of growing deeper in love, trust, dependence and purpose. It is learning to function as one by completing and complimenting one another, thus reflecting God to the world through the marriage relationship.
- Companionship – Gen. 2:18
    - *Companionship is enjoyed through the mutual sharing of love and life together.* God has provided a married couple with a best friend they can love deeply and share life's joys and challenges with. Companionship is enhanced through life experiences, spending time together, the honest sharing of hearts, engaging in each other's areas of interest and accomplishing God's purposes together.
    - *Companionship grows from good communication and mutual understanding.* Communication is achieved when the person listening understands what the person talking really meant. To facilitate better communication, use the expressions "I feel" when expressing emotions; "I think" when pondering or processing something and inviting another's input; and "I believe" when expressing a belief, conclusion or a decision made. Understanding takes time, which builds trust, which opens the door to transparency and the deep sharing of thoughts, feelings and opinions.
    - *Companionship is hindered through wounding one another.* A person's spirit

There is no more lovely, friendly and charming relationship,
communion or company than a good marriage.

Martin Luther, 1483-1546, German Theologian and Reformer

Two great forgivers makes a great marriage.

Anonymous

becomes closed to another when they are offended or hurt by them. A wounded person's reactions are evidence of their pain. To attempt to re-open someone's spirit requires tenderness and a willingness to listen with humility to the point of understanding, and sincerely seeking their forgiveness for whatever role was played in causing the hurt. The longer one waits to heal this wound, the more difficult it becomes as hurt is piled upon hurt. Pray for openness and do it as soon as possible. Don't let the sun go down on anger and hurt (Eph. 4:26-27).

- *Companionship grows in the correct handling of conflict.* The tendency in conflict can be for men to dominate and women to manipulate – both are ungodly. The choices made by a couple in the midst of conflict will either drive them apart or draw them closer. When hurt occurs, most people will either stuff it and withdraw from their spouse or erupt in anger. Either way, it reveals that the marriage partner has been hurt, not understood, or that their expectations were not met. If left untended it will lead to bitterness and resentment that can undermine the relationship.

  - A few keys to appropriately handling conflict:

    - Begin in prayer by asking for God's leadership in the conflict.
    - Ask God to forgive you if you have sinned and contributed to the problem.
    - Humbly approach the situation making sure your own heart attitude is one of love and reconciliation.
    - Gently reaffirm your love and commitment to your spouse.
    - Ask your spouse to forgive you where you have hurt or offended them.
    - If there needs to be confrontation on a matter, speak the truth lovingly and work together to solve the problem. Remember that God has made you one, so in dealing with conflicts and problems your greatest strength as a couple is in tackling it together.
    - Listen well to each other to discover the root issue behind the conflict.
    - Allow humility and forgiveness to flow freely in the conversation. This allows trust to be rebuilt.
    - Talk through the issue at hand. Take the time to talk to God about it together and ask Him for divine insight. Come to a conclusion together regarding any changes that can prevent this situation from recurring.
    - Determine the process you will use in the future to bring reconciliation and resolve to future conflicts.

THOUGHTS & NOTES

- Compliment – Gen. 2:20-23
    - God made Eve out of one of Adam's ribs and brought her to Adam as a compliment to him.
    - God has made men and women different physically and emotionally, yet in marriage, those differences are meant to compliment each other.
    - Although respectful of each other's dreams and desires, a couple learns to function as a team for God's purposes.
    - A healthy marriage cultivates an interdependence on each other that prompts an abandoning of self-centeredness and an attitude of giving to one another.
    - God will also actively use a person's marriage partner as His primary source of disciple ship for them.
    - Outside of hearing from God themselves, a person's marriage partner is the primary person through whom God will speak to them. Thus, it is important to listen to the voice of God through a spouse.

To compliment his wife, a man must understand her greatest needs:

- To Feel Secure—safe and free from fear, protected in areas of vulnerability.

- To Feel Cared For—listened to, understood, invested in by his time and attention; validating and attempting to meet her needs.

- To Feel Adored—expressions of praise, being highly prized and valued above all else.

To compliment her husband, a woman must understand his greatest needs:

- To Feel Trusted—believing in who he is, receiving her confidence and loyalty.

- To Feel Supported—helped, comforted, and encouraged in the pursuit of God-given dreams.

- To Feel Admired—championed before others through expressions of honor and affirmation.

God made men and women different... yet in marriage those differences are meant to serve as compliments to one another.

- Commitment – Gen. 2:24
  - Marriage is a covenant before God. Therefore, the most important relational commitment in a married person's life is to their spouse. No other relationship should ever come between this covenant commitment (Mk. 10:6-9).
  - There is to be a commitment to advance God's purposes in and through each other's lives.
  - There is to be a commitment to love each other by choosing each other's highest good.
  - There is to be a commitment to walking in oneness by not allowing anything or anyone to ever come between them as a couple.
  - There is to be a commitment to guard the "affairs of the heart" — the meeting of needs through other sources that should rightfully be met through a spouse.
  - There is to be a commitment to relational health by actively tending the marriage:
    - Spiritually – by knowing the condition of each other's walk with Jesus, to encourage intimacy with God and obedience to His Word and Spirit.
    - Emotionally – by knowing the condition of each other's hearts and feelings, to strengthen and comfort one another.
    - Mentally – by knowing what is on each other's minds, to carry each other's burdens and to be used by God to impart peace.
    - Physically – by knowing the condition of each other's physical well being, to nurture rest, refreshment and health.
    - Relationally – by knowing the condition of each other's friendships, to provide opportunities for recreation and meaningful sharing, and to console in times of difficulty and disappointment.
    - Calling – by knowing the condition of each other's calling from God, to pursue the growth and development of gifts and to discover God-given outlets for their unique expression.

The Role of the Wife

Support – Gen. 2:18, 20-23

Support offered through unconditionally loving her husband (Tit. 2:4).
- Support offered by coming alongside her husband to help him (Gen. 2:18, 20-23).
- Support offered by being the kind of woman he can rejoice in (Pr. 5:18).
- Support offered by developing godly character and an inner beauty (Pr. 12:4, 31:10,11; Tit. 2:5; 1 Pet. 3:3-6).
- Support offered by tending to the home (Pr. 31:15,21,27; Tit. 2:4,5)
- Support offered by using her skills and gifts at home and beyond (Pr. 31:12-29).

THOUGHTS & NOTES

- Support offered through her words, providing wise counsel (Pr. 31:26).
- Support offered by walking in the fear of the Lord (Pr. 31:30; 1 Pet. 3:1-2).
- Support offered by respecting and expressing honor to her husband (Eph. 5:33; Pr. 12:4).
- Support offered by praying for her husband (1 Tim. 2:1,2).
- Support offered by walking in peace with her husband (Pr. 19:13, 21:9).
- She will be openly honored by her husband and family for the support she has given (Pr. 31:23,28,29,31).

Submit – Eph. 5:21-24; Col. 3:18; Tit. 2:4-5; 1 Pet. 3:1

- The verses in Ephesians are in the context of examples of life in the Spirit, and come after Paul's exhortation to "submit to one another out of reverence for Christ" (Eph. 5:21). This means all Christians are to submit to one another—not some Christians to other Christians, but all Christians to each other.
- These passages were not placed here for husbands to use to force their wives into submission. Throughout the centuries many husbands have quoted these verses selfishly to use and abuse their wives, treating them as servants compelled to meet their desires.
- The backdrop of Paul's letter to the Ephesians:
    - At the time of the writing of Ephesians, women were treated poorly by their husbands. In the Jewish world, the process of divorce was disastrously easy. A man could divorce his wife for something as minor as spoiling his dinner with too much salt.
    - Among the Greeks, prostitution was an integral part of their culture and wives were only for having legitimate children and overseeing the household. Companionship within marriage was next to impossible.
    - For the Romans, family life was in ruins. It was stated that women "were married to be divorced and divorced to be married", and that the best days of a woman's life were the day she wed and the day she was buried.
    - At the time of the writing of Ephesians women were already submitting to their husbands. When Paul wrote this passage he was calling men and women to a mutual commitment to purity and companionship in marriage that had not yet been seen in the culture of the times.
    - The real challenge by Paul in this passage was for men to love their wives to such an extent that they lay their lives down for them, just as Jesus did for the church.

The most extraordinary thing in the world is an ordinary man and an ordinary woman and their ordinary children.

G.K. Chesterton, 1874-1936, British Writer

What Does Submission Mean?
- Submission was important to the writers of the New Testament as it described the selfless love, humility and a willingness to lay down one's lives for Christ.
- Jesus submitted to the point of death in obedience to His Father (Phil. 2:6-8).
- Submission here in Ephesians means to "arrange oneself under." As a part of her submission to the Lord, a wife should voluntarily arrange herself under her husband's authority.
- It is not about a husband bossing his wife around, nor is it about a wife walking independently from her husband. It is about both loving and serving the other.
- Paul is asking that wives place themselves under their husband's authority, "as unto the Lord" as a disciple of Jesus, and to take seriously their companionship with their husbands, doing all they can to benefit the life of their spouse. They are to stand in a giving relationship towards their husbands, just as their husbands are to stand in a giving relationship towards them.
- A couple is to function as a team, hearing from God and following His lead together. If it becomes necessary for someone to make a final decision, it is to be the husband, but only after seeking the wise counsel of his wife and praying together with her about it. Extremely rare should be the moments in a marriage where a wife feels like she just has to go along with her husband's decision. When this situation arises, a wife should be so lovingly led by her husband that she trusts him completely, knowing he will always choose her highest good.

The Role of the Husband

Lead – Eph. 5:21-33
- The head of the wife, the husband, is also part of the church that submits to Jesus and other Christians (which includes his own wife).
- Paul's emphasis in this Ephesians passage is focused on the husband, but contrary to the culture around them, it is for the benefit of the wife.
- The word "head" here in Ephesians does not mean boss or the person in charge, but rather that *the husband has God-given authority to take responsibility for his wife.*
- The husband does have a leadership role in his home, not to order his wife or to use his position for privilege, but to take responsibility to love, to give of himself, and to serve and tend his wife. Just as Jesus redefined greatness as being a servant, Paul redefines being the head of the home as loving and serving one's wife.
- The actions of both husband and wife loving and serving each other is based on both of them being disciples of Jesus who desire to walk in obedience to Him.

THOUGHTS & NOTES

- The function of a Christian marriage is revealed in this portion of Scripture. Both the husband and wife live foremost for the Lord. Jesus is the real head of family life and both partners live in submission to His Lordship, and in mutual submission to each other.

Love – Eph. 5:25, 28, 33
- While wives are asked to submit, husbands are not told to rule. Husbands are commanded to love by replicating the self-sacrificial love demonstrated by Jesus for His Bride, the church.
    - Jesus demonstrated love through self-sacrifice, giving, serving and laying His life down for others. He provides the model for husbands to follow in relation to their wives.
    - Jesus loved the church, not for what she would do for Him, but so that He might give Himself to her.
- The quality of love here seeks not its own satisfaction, or even affection responding to affection, but is a complete giving of oneself for the highest good of the one being served.
- The husband is to forego his own rights and desires so that he can place the well being of his wife first. The choice to lay his life down for his wife is a husband's way of expressing his discipleship to Jesus.
- In his loving and serving, a husband is to nurture and care for his wife so that she will be holy (set apart) and radiant, fulfilling God's purposes through her life and through their lives together as a couple (Eph. 5:25-33).
- As a husband loves his wife by laying his life down for her, she is able to freely submit herself to him. The greater the husband loves his wife, the more delighted she is to follow his lead. The more a wife supports her husband, the more the husband wants to give himself for his wife. This demonstrates the relationship of Jesus and the church, and models for the world who God is and what a joy-filled marriage can look like.

Both the husband and wife live foremost for the Lord. Jesus is the real head of family life and both partners live in submission to His Lordship, and in mutual submission to each other.

A Parent's Relationship to Children

Loving Children – Ps. 127:3-5

- Children are gifts from God and must be held within the hearts of parents as such.
- Children need to know the unconditional love and acceptance of their parents. The child's greatest inner needs are for love, security and self-worth.
- Tell them often how much you love them and what a valuable addition they are to your life.
- Openly express that love by demonstrating physical affection.
- Children receive love from their parents through eye contact, physical affection and focused attention. Spend quality time with them in these expressions of love.
- Let them know that God loves them even more than you do, pointing them to the Heavenly Father whom they will one day know, love and serve.
- Love them by praying often for and with them and speaking words of affirmation and affection to them. Seek God on their behalf, catching glimpses of who He has created them to be and speaking loving words of destiny over their lives.
- Learn to be sensitive to a child's needs and lovingly look for ways to meet those needs.

Training Children – Dt. 6:4-9; Pr. 22:6; Eph. 6:4

- Teaching a child is necessary to gain knowledge and understanding; training is essential so godly principles and habits can be established in their lives.
- Children should be trained in the ways of God:
    - The character of God.
    - The beginning of a working knowledge of the Scriptures.
    - Hearing God's voice.
    - Obedience to God by obeying their parents as children.
    - To honor and respect others, and to walk under authority.
    - Being responsible.
    - How to walk in godly relationships.
    - Loving and serving others.
    - Discovering and developing of God-given skills and gifts.
    - To pursue God's call on their life, etc.
- Children should be trained in the practical and necessary things of life by their parents – basic life skills, manners, how to behave in various settings, etc.

THOUGHTS & NOTES

Models & Mentors
- Training requires modeling and intentional mentoring by parents.
- Instruct children in the "whys" and demonstrate for them the "hows."
- Be a consistent example for them by the way you live your life in front of them.
- Hold children accountable to do things as you have instructed, demonstrated and modeled for them.

Discipline – Pr. 13:24, 19:18, 22:15, 23:13–14, 29:15,17
- Discipline is a necessary expression of a parent's love and training (Heb. 12:7-11).
- Discipline is to grow out of a healthy loving relationship between the parent and the child.
- Discipline builds inner control and security in a child as they learn right from wrong and grow to understand their boundaries.
- Family guidelines and rules should be based upon love and the truth of Scripture. They should be expressed to a child in a way in which they can be clearly understood. When children are little they need to be told in a concrete manner when they are not to be doing something. As they become older, they also need to understand why they should not do it.
- Some guidelines for discipline:
    - Parents must set the standard. A child must clearly know what is expected of them. When they do something they should not have done it must be discerned whether it was not clearly communicated and understood, truly forgotten by the child, unintentionally done, or done willfully.
    - When a child does something wrong, it is a parent's responsibility to bring correction. If the child did not know it was wrong or it was done unintentionally, parents only need to tell the child it was wrong, thus giving them a warning while setting the standard. If a child does something that they know is wrong to do, the parents must correct them, the child must acknowledge the wrong and seek forgiveness, and willingly reap the consequences of their actions. If a child refuses to admit wrong or accept correction for breaking a known standard, then parents must exercise godly discipline.

The child's greatest inner needs are for love, security and self-worth.

Religion was established first in families and there the devil seeks to crush it.
The family is the training ground for both the Church and the State and
if children are not well-principled there, all will fail. The fathers of families have
as truly the charge of the souls in those families, as pastors have of the churches.

Thomas Manton, 1620-1677, English Puritan Preacher

- The purpose of disciplining a child is to restore the proper relationship between the parent and the child. God desires for children to walk under the loving leadership of their parents. When a child deliberately refuses to accept the God-given authority of the parents, they are in rebellion. Discipline is God's way of ending the rebellion and restoring the child to their rightful place under the parent's loving authority. Without discipline being administered in a child's life, they will live self-centeredly as a teen and adult, with little to no self-control, wrestling with rebellion towards those in authority, including God.
- When a child directly and purposeful disobeys a parent, acting in rebellion, it is a parent's responsibility to exercise appropriate discipline in their child's life.
  - A parent is not to discipline out of anger. Discipline is never an excuse to hurt or abuse a child or to take out one's frustrations. Discipline is to be expressed out of true love for the child with a desire to guide them on to the right path.
  - The consequences of wrong choices must fit the offense, be appropriate and consistent. Consequences change with the age of the child.
  - The last resort of discipline should be spanking a child, which can become necessary due to willful defiance. When using this form of discipline, it is important to make sure the child understands exactly what it is that they have done wrong, and it is to be administered carefully so as to not inadvertently hurt another part of a child's body. Spanking is not to be done by a parent's hand (a hand is for loving), but with an instrument such as stick or wooden spoon to swat a child's bottom just enough to bring about the brokenness that is needed to affect the child's attitude and behavior. When the defiant will is broken, the child, who may be in tears, can ask for and receive forgiveness and be rightly restored in relationship with their parents. This is also a time for parents to reaffirm their love for their child.
- The disciplining of teenagers takes on other forms such as allowing them to reap the natural consequences of poor choices, limiting their freedom, and removing privileges. The success of raising and disciplining teenagers is directly related to the degree of time invested in building relationships of love and understanding.

The purpose of discipline is to restore the proper relationship between the parent and the child.

THOUGHTS & NOTES

A Child's Relationship to Parents

Love
- Love them by choosing their highest good.
- Express love to them in words and actions.
- Accept them for who they are in their strengths and weaknesses.

Obey – Eph. 6:1; Col. 3:20
- God's command to children is for them to obey their parents; this pleases Him.
- Obedience should be exercised in both actions and in attitude.
- A child should set their heart to obey their parents – the only exceptions are if they are asked to do something illegal, immoral, unethical or unbiblical.
- When needed, a child can appeal to authority (see notes on appealing to authority in the section of this chapter on *Walking Under Authority*).

Honor – Ex. 20:12; Eph. 6:2
- God commands children to honor their parents; with this command comes a promise from God, "that it may go well with you and that you may enjoy long life on the earth."
- Honoring is recognizing the parent's place of love and God-given authority in your life.
- Parents can receive honor in the way a child lives their life; dishonor can also come in the same way.
- Honor can be expressed by a grateful heart for all they do, or have done, for you.
- As parents get older, they need to feel like they still have a place of honor, or value, in the lives of their children. Make room for them to contribute into the life of the family.

Carefully Consider their Counsel – Pr. 6:20-22,
- Although children will come to a place in life as adults where they are no longer expected to obey their parents, they are always to express honor towards them and to carefully consider their counsel.
- Take advantage of the many years of experience that has cultivated wisdom in the lives of parents and glean as much as possible from their wisdom and insights.
- The first seven chapters of the Book of Proverbs speak much about listening closely to the words, commands, teachings and instructions of fathers and mothers for the gaining of wisdom.

In essentials, unity. In non-essentials, liberty. In all things, charity.

Rupertus Meldenius, 17th Century German Lutheran Scholar

CASTING THE NET

What needs, hopes, fears and expectations do you bring to a relationship? Who are the people in your life that God has forged a heart-link with? What do you do to cultivate these friendships?

_____

_____

_____

_____

_____

Which two or three of the Pillars of Godly Relationships from Romans 12 do you need to most apply to your current relationships?

_____

_____

_____

_____

Are you making every effort to maintain unity and the bond of peace in your relationships? Where is there room for growth and what are you going to do about it?

_____

_____

_____

_____

_____

THOUGHTS & NOTES ━━━━━━

_____

_____

_____

_____

What spoke the most to you about walking under authority?

_____

_____

_____

_____

_____

_____

_____

_____

_____

_____

Which portion of the Guy-Girl Relationships or Family Life Basics section applies the most to your life today? Are there any action steps that you need to take?

_____

_____

_____

_____

_____

_____

_____

_____

_____

catch of the day

Chapter Summary

- God is the ultimate relater, and to accurately reflect Him to the world around us we must become good relaters.
- We all have various spheres of relationships in our lives. Although we are to be loving, gracious and have an attitude of serving towards all people, there are some that God has linked our hearts with and we should be intentional about growing those friendships.
- Among other places in the Scriptures, Romans 12 reveals some key pillars on which to build our relationships.
- God has placed authority over our lives and it is important that we learn how to walk under authority, and to know how and when to properly appeal when necessary.
- Whether you are currently single or growing in a relationship with someone of the opposite sex, whether you're married, have children, or are children living at home, the Word of God has much to offer by way of wisdom for walking in godly relationships.

What are the two or three things the Holy Spirit spoke most clearly to you through this chapter and how will you respond to Him?

_____

_____

_____

_____

_____

_____

_____

_____

THOUGHTS & NOTES

_____

_____

_____

_____

A VIEW FROM THE SHORE

> "Behold, I have given you authority to tread on serpents and scorpions,
> and over all the power of the enemy, and nothing shall hurt you."
>
> *Luke 10:19*

Have you ever imagined what it will be like in heaven? Think about it for a moment—being with Jesus in His royal splendor, enjoying friendship with the saints from all generations. No worries. No bills to pay. No illness or aging. No tears. Sometimes I wonder why we didn't go directly to heaven and into God's presence when we gave our lives to Jesus! That would have been wonderful.

One day we will find ourselves standing before Him, immersed in the beauty of God's glory and heaven itself, but not quite yet. When we gave our lives to Jesus we were enlisted in a spiritual army, commissioned to an ongoing battle of spiritual warfare. You and I have an enemy—the very same enemy that opposes God. He is known as Satan, or the devil. He is real—he exists as surely as you and I, and he has set himself to prowl vigilantly for those from whom he can "steal, kill and destroy"(Jn. 10:10). Peter depicted Satan as "a roaring lion seeking someone to devour" (1 Pet 5:8). Paul referred to him as "the god of this world," (2 Cor. 4:4) and Jesus called him a "liar" (Jn. 8:44).

Satan aims to distort, disfigure and defame the character and ways of God. He intends to derail God's purposes in the nations of the Earth and to destroy the lives of the precious people Jesus died for. He actively opposes any attempts by believers to advance God's kingdom and to glorify Jesus.

The Bible gives us the clear impression that Satan, or Lucifer, was created as an angel in heaven who was to minister to God. He was created absolutely perfect, full of wisdom and amazing in beauty (Ez. 28:11-19). However, Scripture also tells us that he became so enamored with himself that pride compelled him to rebel with the presumption that he deserved to be God. For this, God expelled him from heaven, and he exists today as the adversary of God and man (Is. 14:12-15).

The good news is that Jesus came "to destroy the works of the devil" (1 Jn. 3:8) And He accomplished this end—guaranteeing our victory—through His life, death and resurrection. Now, Jesus desires to exercise His authority through His church, which is you and me.

God has provided us with weapons to enforce the rights He has won for us. Unfortunately, many Christians don't realize their authority in the Name of Jesus. This, too, is a ploy of Satan to keep us from becoming fully free and effective. It is a strategy used to divide relationships and obstruct the advancement of God's kingdom. While Satan works to hinder God's purposes, we can thwart his efforts through godliness, intercession, fasting, praise and worship, and the preaching of the gospel.

In this chapter we will take a look at the authority we have in Jesus to defeat our enemy, learn to recognize and anticipate his tactics, and become acquainted with the arsenal of weaponry at our disposal as believers.

setting sail

Every disciple of Jesus eventually discovers that spiritual warfare is a reality. A battle persists in the supernatural dimension where God is all-powerful and Satan prowls like a roaring lion (1 Pet. 5:8-9). To understand the topic of spiritual warfare, we must examine what the scriptures say about Satan and his strategies against God and His people. It's important to have God's knowledge about our enemy, who he is, what he is like, and why God permits him to exist. Throughout church history, some have tried to ignore the devil's existence, while others have attempted to exaggerate his influence. Only through a biblical balance can we humbly and effectively work with God to advance His kingdom in our lives, families, neighborhoods, cities and the nations of the earth.

Satan's Origin and Power

For the most part, the world views Satan as a caricature with horns and a tail, diminishing the reality of his existence and the threats he poses. God's Word tells us that his appearance can vary dramatically—"And no wonder; for Satan himself masquerades as an angel of light" (2 Cor. 11:14). Gaining an understanding of this spiritual being equips us with an awareness of who he is and how he may try to hinder us and the advancement of God's Kingdom.

A few of the biblical basics on Satan:
- He was originally created as a beautiful angel in heaven to minister to God, but he became enamored with himself and in pride tried to become like God – Ez. 28:11-19; Is. 14:12-15.
- Due to his pride and rebellion he was expelled from heaven, along with other angels – Lk. 10:18; Rev. 12:9.
- He is a finite spirit-being created by God, and he is not all-knowing, not all-powerful, and not personally present everywhere, as is God – Ez. 28:13-15.
- Because God is sovereign and in control, Satan can only act with limited influence. God always has something higher in mind when the enemy attacks so we must focus on the activity of God in the midst of spiritual battles – Job 1:6-2:10.
- Satan has already been defeated by the death of Jesus on the cross and it is the role of the church to enforce and implement this victory on the earth – Col. 2:15; Rev. 20:10.

THOUGHTS & NOTES

Satan's Names and Titles Reveal His Character

Satan plays many roles. Learning his names and titles from scripture can give us an understanding of some of the methods he employs.

Some of His Names

- Satan (means "adversary") (1 Pet .5:8).
- Devil (means "accuser") (Rev. 12:9-10).
- Lucifer (means the "morning star") (Is. 14:12).
- Beelzebub (means "prince of demons") (Mt. 10:25).
- Abaddon / Apollyn (means "destruction" and "destroyer")(Rev. 9:11).

Some of His Titles

- Accuser (Rev. 12:10).
- Dragon (Rev. 20:2).
- Enemy (Lk. 10:18-19).
- The Evil One (Eph. 6:16).
- The god of this world (2 Cor. 4:4).
- Prince of the power of the air (Eph. 2:2).
- Roaring lion (1 Pet. 5:8).
- Serpent (Rev. 12:9-10).

What Jesus Called Satan

- A liar (Jn. 8:44).
- A murderer (Jn. 8:44).
- A thief who steals, kills and destroys (Jn. 10:10).
- A tempter (Mt. 4:3).

Some have tried to ignore the devil's existence, while others have attempted to exaggerate his influence. Only through a biblical balance can we humbly and effectively work with God to advance His kingdom.

If you yield to Satan in the least, he will carry you further and further, till he has left you under a stupefied or terrified conscience: stupefied, till thou hast lost all thy tenderness. A stone at the top of a hill, when it begins to roll down, ceases not till it comes to the bottom. Thou thinkest it is but yielding a little, and so by degrees are carried on, till thou hast sinned away all thy profession, and all principles of conscience, by the secret witchery of his temptations.

Thomas Manton, 1620-1677, English Puritan Preacher

Why Does God Permit Satan to Exist?

Many have wondered, *If Satan lives to destroy us, then why does God allow him to exist?* The question is a good one and goes back to the beginning of time.

When Adam and Eve disobeyed God, they chose something that God did not create—sin. As a result, evil entered the world. Since that moment, known as the Fall, everything in creation—nature, animals, people—no longer existed in their original corrupt-free condition. Every person since Adam and Eve who have been born possesses a sin-nature— a bent toward sin and selfishness—that makes him or her susceptible to Satan and in need of God's redemption.

The Old Testament reveals this conflict, telling stories of people killing the prophets who were sent by God to preach His love and commandments. The apostle Paul warns the Christians in Rome not to be conformed to the ways of this world (Rom. 12:2), and Jesus Himself referred to Satan as "the ruler of this world" (Jn. 14:30). Conflict between people, has plagued mankind for generations since.

From the foundations of time, the Father knew He would send His Son to win back what we had given over. On the cross, Jesus won the ultimate victory over Satan. And one day He will return to inflict Satan's final defeat, conquering every shred of evil the Earth has ever known (Rev. 20:10). Until that appointed hour, God uses Satan's destructive efforts for His purposes and our welfare (Gen. 46; Rom 8:28). Among the reasons why God allows Satan to exist:

To Conform Us into the Image of Jesus

A focus of God for our lives is to make us more like Jesus in character. God will use the process of spiritual warfare to cause us to seek His face, to trust Him and to follow His leadership. He allows battles we face for our good, because He is a good God. In the midst of these experiences, it is important to lean into Him for His perspective and for the gains He is trying to develop in us. God will use spiritual warfare to move us into greater places of humility and dependence, as well as teach us how to flex our "spiritual muscles" in His Name (Rom. 8:18-30; 2 Cor. 12:1-10).

THOUGHTS & NOTES

To Reveal God's Character and Glory

To bring glory to God means to enhance His reputation in the eyes of others. We do not add to God's glory; our obedience simply draws others to Him. God uses the process of spiritual warfare to display His awesome power through the transformation of our own sinfulness and susceptibility to Satan. God's wonderful character contrasts with the evil ends of the devil. Though Satan tried to diminish God's reputation by nailing His Son to a tree, God used the cross to redeem mankind. He raised His Son from the dead that "every knee may bow and every tongue confess that Jesus Christ is Lord, to the glory of God the Father" (Phil. 2:5-11).

To Accomplish God's Purposes

Nothing catches God by surprise. He is never oblivious to Satan's doings. Instead, He uses the enemy of our souls to accomplish His purposes in the Earth. When the devil attempts to inflict harm, God is able to turn it to good. While the devil desired to keep Israel in Egyptian bondage, God delivered them, setting them free to worship Him. To that end, He used the ten plagues to show His almighty power and expose the frailty of the Egyptian gods (see Exodus). When Satan attacked Job, a man blessed with every kind of abundance, he ends up more blessed by God after Satan's worst onslaught. Summarizing results of his fiery trials, Job said, "I had heard by the hearing of the ear, but now my eye sees You" (Job 42:5). God remains actively involved in the business of redeeming Satan's attempts to "steal, kill and destroy." We must remind ourselves that God limits Satan's freedom to act - which invariably means that God has something greater in mind than the finite struggle at hand (Job 1:1, 2:10).

To Advance the Kingdom of God in the Earth

Advancing the kingdom often comes through conflict and testing responded to by the prayer and obedience of God's people. Among the many accounts of kingdom advancement recorded in Acts is the persecution and death of Stephen. Jesus had commanded the twelve to make disciples of every nation, but their focus hadn't yet spread beyond Jerusalem. When God allowed the attack on the church, which resulted in Stephen's death at the hands of Saul, the remaining disciples were forced to move outside the city and focus on other people. Stephen's death ultimately contributed to Saul's conversion, who, as Paul, became the writer of thirteen of the books of the New Testament and the lead missionary of his time, advancing the Kingdom to the very borders of his known world (Acts 13-28)!

The riches of His free grace cause me daily to triumph over all the temptations of the wicked one, who is very vigilant, and seeks all occasions to disturb me.

George Whitefield, 1714-1770, English Evangelist and Preacher

We should know Satan's purposes

"The Lord said to Satan, 'Where have you come from?' Satan answered the Lord, 'From roaming through the Earth and going back and forth in it'" (Job 1:7). Though people typically cannot see into the spiritual realms, Scripture tells us that they are none less real (Col. 1:16). Jesus, the commander of the Lord's army, has commissioned us to remain vigilant and aware of the ways Satan incites conflict, and to set free those he has ensnared in his deceptions (Mk. 16:15-20; 2 Co. 2:10-11). With real casualties and real victories at stake, how we fight—and live—has real consequences. Therefore, it is essential for us to know Satan's primary purposes.

Satan's Purposes

- To disfigure the character and ways of God in the hearts and minds of people (Gen. 3:1-7).
- To keep people from coming to the light of the gospel of Jesus (2 Cor. 4:4).
- To use sin and selfishness, and sin committed against us, to hinder people from knowing God and fulfilling their God-given destiny (Jn. 10:10).
- To tempt people to act independently from God (Lk. 4:3). The devil tempted Jesus to depart from His Father's agenda and turn stone into bread to meet His own needs.
- To tempt people to abandon love and loyalty to God (Lk. 4:6-7). The devil invited Jesus to abandon God and worship him (Satan) instead.
- To tempt people to test God (Lk. 4:9). The devil challenged Jesus to do something not in alignment with God's will.

Jesus has commissioned us to remain vigilant and aware of the ways Satan incites conflict, and to set free those he has ensnared in his deceptions. With real casualties and real victories at stake, how we fight—and live—has real consequences.

THOUGHTS & NOTES

Deeper waters

Identifying the Enemy's Schemes

In Ephesians 6:11 we see that Satan has schemes, actual core strategies and plans. He lies in wait for the right time to employ them against God's people. Scripture sites examples of those who were led to do things contrary to God's will. In 1 Chronicles 21:1, Satan rose up against Israel, inciting David to take a census. And most of us are familiar with Judas Iscariot, but did you realize it was the devil who had prompted him to betray Jesus? (Jn. 13:2).

The apostle Paul made it his business to know Satan's tactics (2 Cor. 2:11). This wasn't his sole or even predominate focal point. Paul preached balance, teaching the Romans, "I want you to be wise about what is good, and innocent about what is evil. The God of peace will soon crush Satan under your feet shortly" (Rom. 16:19-20). We need to be aware of Satan's basic strategies in order to recognize when we are under attack and to know how to restore our freedom from his assaults. More often than not, Satan's schemes will include some or all of the following:

Pride

This sin originated in the devil himself. In Isaiah 14:12-15, we see five *"I wills"*—each relating to Lucifer's desire to ascend and make himself like God. This is the basis of Satan's kingdom. Many of our sin issues are rooted in pride. Pride opens our life to the attack of the enemy. We give Satan a grip on our soul to the degree that we choose to walk in pride and independence from God. Pride breeds such things as selfishness, independence, following the desires of our sinful nature and rebellion. Because God is humble, He will see to it that our pride is opposed (Jam. 4:6-7). Beware of the enemy's attempts to isolate you from God and others through an attitude of pride.

Unbelief

We find this sin in the very beginning, in the garden with Adam and Eve. Satan, in the form of a snake, asks the question in Genesis 3:1, "Did God really say...?" From that moment, Satan has tried to sow distrust of God in the deepest places of the human heart. The enemy loves to use

The reason why many fail in battle is because they wait until the hour of battle. The reason why others succeed is because they have gained their victory on their knees long before the battle came...Anticipate your battles; fight them on your knees before temptation comes, and you will always have victory.

R.A. Torrey, 1856-1928, American Pastor, Evangelist and Educator

this tool to lead us to believe things about God, others, and even ourselves, to rob us from all that God has promised us as His children. God desires for us to have faith in who He is, believing His Word fully (Heb. 11:6), yet our unbelief opens the door for the enemy to bring spiritual blindness and deception into our lives (2 Cor. 4:4).

Deception
Can you believe the devil quoted Scripture? We see in Matthew 4:1-11 that he used the very words of the Old Testament to try to deceive Jesus. Sometimes deception is obvious, but most often it comes to us woven in a cloak of truth. The devil knows the formula well—the unique blend of falsehoods mixed with a portion of truth to suit our individual vulnerabilities. He's adept at concocting tailor-made deceptions to put each of us in a strategic stupor. Look at the world religions and cults. Though vastly differing, they all contain fragments of truth, making them plausible, as well as alluring to people hungry for God. Deception distorts truth and inserts a false filter in our thinking so that truth becomes difficult to recognize.

Strongholds
The scriptures remind us in Ephesians 4:25-27 not to let the enemy get a "foothold" in our lives. This word is also translated as *place or opportunity* and literally means *space*. In other words, we are not to give the enemy an opportunity to take a place, or gain space, in our lives. If we yield this advantage to him, the enemy sets up camp and attempts to imprison us in a particular sin pattern.

- Strongholds are entrenched patterns of thought contrary to the will of God that cause us to feel powerless to change. Notice the three parts of this definition of a stronghold:
    - Entrenched patterns of thought—strongholds begin in our minds and thinking (2 Cor. 10:3-5).
    - Contrary to the will of God—we can recognize it as something not aligned to God's character, ways and Word.
    - Powerless to change—strongholds are marked by a sense of hopelessness and an inability to bring about change apart from God.

Satan tries to establish strongholds in our thinking to keep us bound in false belief systems. This can include such areas as pride, fear, poor self-esteem, and all manners of sin. Humility (acknowledging our need) and truth (rightly aligning ourselves to God and His Word) is what can free us from the strongholds of the enemy.

THOUGHTS & NOTES

An important thing to note on strongholds: from a military point of view, strongholds are built on places that are already strong (the top of a hill, the edge of a body of water, etc.). This reminds us that the devil doesn't just attack our weak spots, but also the places where we are strong. Satan may target our natural strengths causing us to rely too heavily on our own abilities, or placing our confidence in what we can do rather that what God wants to do through us.

Exploiting Relational Wounds

One of the greatest ways that the enemy tries to hinder us is through relationships. Because he recognizes that some of our greatest blessings from God come through friendship with others, the enemy will use this tool to try to bring hurt, wounds and disappointment. Some of these wounds can be so deep that they cripple our thinking and emotions. The enemy uses bad relational experiences to isolate us from others, to create a breeding ground for anger and bitterness, and to prevent us from enjoying friendships and teaming for Kingdom pursuits.

- If we have been hurt or let down by authority, this frequently causes us to move independently, making us vulnerable to the snares of the enemy.
- In Genesis 37-50, we see that Joseph had the opportunity to live the rest of his life with bitterness when his brothers threw him into a pit and sold him into slavery. He could have exercised revenge on them when he saw them in Egypt, but instead Joseph broke before God, which led to forgiveness and a cleansing of his heart that enabled him to recognize God's bigger purposes in rescuing his family.

Discouragement and Condemnation

These two missiles accuse believers and rob our joy and hope. Discouragement brings with it failure, loneliness and despair. Condemnation comes dressed in accusation, confusion and the general sense that one is not good enough.

- It is important to note the difference between conviction and condemnation. Conviction is always from God. It is clear, exposing our sin and providing a way out through humility, confession, and forgiveness. Condemnation, on the other hand, brings confusion, a sense of failure, and tends to feel like a black cloud settling over us. The way to respond in the midst of this is to ask God if there is any sin in our life. If the Holy Spirit reveals areas of sin, ask Him to forgive and cleanse you, then move on. If there is no conviction of sin, consider it condemnation and resist the enemy in the Name of Jesus.

I cannot tell how I am buffeted sometimes by temptation. I never knew how bad a heart I have. Yet I do know that I love God and love His work, and desire to serve him only and in all things. And I value above all else that precious Savior in whom alone I can be accepted.

Hudson Taylor, 1832-1905, English Missionary to China

- Elijah gives us a good biblical example (1 Kings 19:1-18) of someone caught in a place of wrestling with discouragement. After a great spiritual victory over the priests of Baal, he hides in the wilderness and asks God to take his life. God, in His love for him, sends an angel to minister to Elijah and, then, He comes Himself to speak to him. When you are discouraged, watch for messengers, in the form of people, that God sends your way to strengthen and encourage you. Listen for His voice as He draws near to you.

Distraction

Satan will attempt to shift our focus from Jesus. This can take place in many different forms, including confusion, which can rob us of our first love and fulfilling God's purposes for our lives. Busyness can rob us of time that was meant to be spent alone with God. The inappropriate pursuit of pleasure, possessions or praise from others, can lead us down a long slippery slope of misguided priorities. Relationships can also take precedence over our walk with Jesus. Even ministry can become what we are living for, instead of loving Jesus with all our heart, soul, mind and strength. Satan knows that a wrong focus can result in a shallow faith, leaving us spiritually thin and discontent. The story of Mary and Martha (Luke 10:38-42) reminds us of our true priority and who rightfully deserves the focus of our attention. Although Jesus did not condemn Martha for busying herself in service, He reminds her that there is just one thing necessary—sitting at His feet.

Called To Battle

As Christians, we encounter more than a minor struggle on Earth. Nonetheless, spiritual warfare is an image that many of us would prefer to forget. Because the Bible uses terms of warfare, it's imperative for us to adopt God's imagery to prepare for the inevitability of battle.

God has provided us with His authority, and various kinds of weaponry, to defeat the powers of darkness. Some of the strategies and weapons God gives us to fight with are unique. King Jehoshaphat sent out praise singers in front of his soldiers to confuse the enemy (2 Chr. 20); Joshua used shouting and trumpets to bring down the great city of Jericho (Jos. 6); and what better example of faith in battle than David fighting Goliath with a slingshot (1 Sam. 17). In all these events, one assurance resounds—God empowers our victory and will receive glory as we walk in obedience to Him. We war with a defeated foe (Rev. 20:10). Knowing his days are numbered, Satan is enraged and unrestrained for the lack of anything to lose. Yet, through Jesus, we possess authority to overcome him (Jude 1:9; Acts 19:14-16).

THOUGHTS & NOTES

The Spiritual Warrior's Authority

- God has all power and authority (Job 42:2; Mt. 28:18).
- God gave man authority to reveal His image and glory (Gen. 1:26); to have dominion (means to subdue, conquer, to bring into subjection) over the Earth and every living thing on the Earth (Gen. 1:28); all things are under man's feet (Ps. 8:6-8).
- Through deception, sin and disobedience, man opened the door to Satan and lost dominion (Gen. 3:1-13).
    - Satan became the ruler of this world.
    - Man suffers the consequences of sin, sickness, disease and death.
    - Apart from Jesus, Man has no authority of his own.
    - Satan has authority on the Earth to the degree that people give him access through their sin and disobedience to God.
- Jesus was sent by the Father to defeat Satan and to establish God's authority through the church.
    - Jesus defeated Satan by His life (Mt. 4:1-11) demonstrating: authority over demons (Mt. 8:28-33), authority over sin (Mt. 9:1-8), authority over sickness/disease (Mt. 8:14-17), authority over death (Mt. 9:18-26), authority over nature (Mt. 8:23-27).
    - Jesus defeated Satan by his death and resurrection (Col. 2:14-15; Heb. 2:14-15).
    - Jesus has and will ultimately defeat Satan (Rev. 20:10)
    - Following his death and resurrection, Jesus received all authority from the Father in heaven and on Earth (Mt. 28:18-20; Phil. 2:6-11).
    - Jesus has delivered believers from darkness and has brought them into His marvelous light (1 Pet. 2:9-10).
- Jesus passed His authority on to the church.
    - Jesus has given believers authority over the powers of darkness (Mt. 16:19; Lk. 10:19).
    - New Testament believers did many of the same works as Jesus: they received authority to heal sickness and diseases (Acts 3:1-10); they received authority to raise the dead (Acts 9:36-43); they received authority over demons (Acts 16:16-18); they received authority to preach the gospel so that men and women could come to Jesus (Mt. 28:18-20; Mk. 16:15-18).
    - This same authority has been given to us as believers today so that God's Kingdom might be advanced in the lives of people and in the nations of the earth (Lk. 10:19; Jn. 20:19-23; Rom. 8:31; Jam. 4:7; 1 Jn. 4:4).

Be strong! We are not here to play, to dream, to drift.
We have hard work to do, and loads to lift. Shun not the struggle, face it,
'tis God's gift. Be strong! Say not the days are evil – who's to blame?
And fold the hands and acquiesce – O shame. Stand up, speak out, and bravely,
in God's name. Be strong! It matters not how deep-entrenched the wrong, how hard the
battle goes, the day how long, Faint not, fight on! Tomorrow comes the song.

Mattie Davenport Babcock, 1858-1901, American Pastor

The Spiritual Warrior's Arsenal

A Godly Life – Eph. 4:27
- A holy life (means set apart for God) pushes back the powers of darkness on a daily basis. Humility and repentance attract the presence of God.
- The presence of Jesus in our lives threatens the enemy.
- To live godly lives requires that we deal aggressively with sin, being proactive and running from the slightest hint of temptation.
- Living a godly life recognizes that every choice either pushes back or provides an opening for the powers of darkness.
- It is essential to remember that spiritual warfare is not just praying a prayer or rebuking the devil—it is a lifestyle that we must live.

The Armor of God – Eph. 6:11-18
- Belt of Truth: resists Satanic lies and deception.
- Breastplate of Righteousness: resists false accusations of our place in Christ.
- Shoes of Preparation: enables us to stand firm and ready to share the gospel as a reconciler and peacemaker.
- Shield of Faith: enables us to stand against the arrows of unbelief.
- Helmet of Salvation: protects us against attacks on our minds.
- Sword of the Spirit: equips us with a readiness to use God's truth to bring light to the darkness.
- Spiritual warriors also "pray at all times in the Spirit" and "keep alert."

Intercession – Ez. 22:30; Dan. 10
- The enemy is defeated in the place of prayer when we "stand in the gap" before God, people and the problem, praying according to His will.
- Fasting with prayer is a powerful weapon that can defeat the powers of darkness.
- Endurance in the place of prayer is often necessary to drive out the enemy.
- Praying in accordance with God's will and in humble agreement with others can bring down strongholds.
- Prayer-walking our neighborhoods and communities is an important aspect of taking territory for the kingdom of God (Josh. 1:1-4; 6:1-21).

THOUGHTS & NOTES

The Scriptures – Heb. 4:12
- Jesus used the scriptures effectively when He was tempted by the devil (Mt. 4:1-11).
- Knowing the Word of God provides the Holy Spirit with ammunition as you pray and helps you discern God's ways in the midst of spiritual battles.
- Use the truths revealed in the scriptures to minister in the opposite spirit. Respond with generosity when there is selfishness, humility when there is pride, love when there is fear and hate, etc.

The Name of Jesus and the Blood of Jesus
- All authority resides in the Name of Jesus (Phil. 2:6-11).
- The Bible teaches that the enemy flees at the Name of Jesus (Mk. 16:17; Acts 16:16-18).
- The blood of Jesus represents the humility of Jesus displayed on the cross, which stands in stark contrast to the pride of Satan. It also reminds the enemy that our redemption was purchased by His blood (Phil. 2:6-11; Rev. 12:10-11).

Christian Unity
- God commands a blessing when His people walk together in unity (Ps. 133).
- When conflict arises it is essential to remember that our battle is not against people, but against our common enemy (Eph. 6:12).
- When enough believers in a particular place get right with God and each other, they enemy will be defeated in that place.
- Unity is simply corporate humility and the answer to all strife and division.

The Laying Down of One's Life in Obedience
- The Kingdom of God was advanced through the lives of Jesus' disciples because they were fearless, willing to lay down their lives for the gospel. They recognized that they were but aliens and strangers in this world (Heb. 11:13-16).
- A life lived in abandoned obedience to Jesus without the fear of death is a threat to the powers of darkness (Rev. 12:10-11).
- Your obedience to God allows Him to work through you, therefore pushing back the powers of darkness and advancing God's purposes.

Pray often, for prayer is a shield for the soul,
a sacrifice to God, and a scourge for Satan.

John Bunyan, 1628-1688, English Preacher and Writer

Thanksgiving, Praise and Worship
- Praise and worship directly affects things in the spiritual realm; as God is worshiped by His people His power and might are manifested (Ps. 149:6-9).
- Praise and worship creates an "atmosphere" in which God works (Ps. 22:3).
- It is a "garment" that we can put on for the spirit of heaviness (Is. 61:3).
- The story of King Jehoshaphat portrays the power of praise and worship in the midst of a battle (2 Chr. 20).

Personal Testimony
- The devil will constantly try to discredit and defame God's character and ways. Declaring the truth of who God is and what He has done defeats the enemy and his lies (Rev. 12:10-11).
- You can expose the enemy's lies as you personalize what God has done for you. In the midst of difficulties, it's good to recall how God has come through for you in past battles and to declare your confidence in Him.

Preaching the Gospel
- People can be set free when we share the good news of Jesus with them (Lk. 4:18-19).
- Preaching the gospel opens up people's eyes, turns them from darkness to light, from the power of Satan to the power of God, so they might experience forgiveness (Acts 26:18).
- When we are obedient to share Jesus where He leads us, even our physical presence in a particular place has a great effect on the powers of darkness.
- Signs and wonders and demonstrations of God's power play an important role in defeating the enemy. Remain available to the Holy Spirit as He may choose to move through you in this way to touch other's lives and to advance God's Kingdom. (Acts).

When we are obedient to share Jesus where He leads us, even our physical presence in a particular place has a great effect on the powers of darkness.

THOUGHTS & NOTES

CASTING THE NET

Take a moment and reflect on a time in your life when you experienced a spiritual conflict. What happened? What did you do? How would you handle it differently now? Record your thoughts here.

_____

_____

_____

_____

_____

_____

_____

As you reflect on your life, what schemes does the enemy tend to use with you? Review the list from this chapter and note them here.

_____

_____

_____

_____

_____

_____

_____

_____

All that is necessary for the triumph of evil is that good men do nothing.

Edmund Burke, 1729-1797, British Statesman and Philosopher

A man with God is always in the majority.

John Knox, 1505-1572, Scottish Reformer

Are you in the midst of spiritual warfare at this time? What might God be leading you to do about it? If you need to, take a moment to seek the Lord about this. Jot down here what He shows you.

_____

_____

_____

_____

_____

_____

_____

What weapons from God's arsenal have you used in the past, knowingly or unknowingly, to defeat the enemy?

_____

_____

_____

_____

_____

Is there someone you know in the midst of a spiritual battle that you could come alongside to strengthen & encourage? What do you believe God would have you do to support this person?

_____

_____

_____

_____

_____

THOUGHTS & NOTES

_____

_____

_____

_____

CATCH OF THE DAY

Chapter Summary

- We have a very real enemy in Satan who is out to steal, kill and destroy our lives.
- God is sovereign and in control, and allows the enemy to exist to develop us as believers and to reveal His character and glory as He accomplishes His purposes in the Earth.
- Satan devises schemes to accomplish his purposes. It is important for us as believers to recognize these strategies so that we might counter them, defeating the powers of darkness and advancing the kingdom of God.
- God has provided us with numerous weapons from His arsenal that can be used in humility and obedience, and in conjunction with other believers, to defeat the enemy.

What are the two or three things the Holy Spirit spoke most clearly to you through this chapter and how will you respond to Him?

I've read the last page of the Bible. It's all going to turn out all right.

Billy Graham, American Evangelist

A VIEW FROM THE SHORE

"But you will receive power when the Holy Spirit comes on you; and you will be my witnesses in Jerusalem, and in all Judea and Samaria, and to the ends of the earth".

Acts 1:8

Imagine being in Jerusalem the day the Church was birthed as recorded in the book of Acts. Only weeks after Jesus was resurrected from the dead and ascended into heaven in the presence of His disciples, it happened. They stayed in the city, as Jesus instructed, and waited until they were clothed with power, which would come to them in the person of the Holy Spirit. The disciples gathered in an upper room and spent much time in prayer, refining their relationships. Then, just as Jesus promised, Pentecost fell.

On the day of Pentecost, which referred to the Jewish Feast of Weeks celebrated on the fiftieth day after Passover, the disciples were still waiting. They began to hear a sound from heaven—maybe faint at first, but then it grew louder. Much louder! The sound resembled a mighty rushing wind and it filled the entire house where they were sitting. As they saw what appeared to be tongues of fire resting on each of them, they realized that this was the event Jesus told them to expect. And it proved worth the wait. The Holy Spirit had come and was now empowering the Church for the purposes of her destiny.

You may recall the rest of the story. God-fearing Jews from every nation, who had come to the city to celebrate Pentecost, heard the gospel message through Peter, a disciple newly empowered to lead 3,000 to salvation and baptism in faith. The infant Church grew dramatically in that single, miraculous day.

In the whirlwind of excitement, the disciples faced with eminent concerns, like *what do you do with 3,000 new believers, most of whom are visitors to the city?* They gathered the recipients of God's grace together and committed themselves to relay all that Jesus had taught them, to build relationships with these new believers, to feed them, and pray with them. There was a sense of awe as miracles occurred with regularity. People embraced sacrifice to take care of each other. The community recognized the urgent need to meet together and they continued to do so as the Lord added new believers daily to this entity called the Church.

There is much to learn about the new-born Church, fervent in passion and empowered by the Holy Spirit. The book of Acts introduces us to the person and role of the Holy Spirit—a role He continues to this day. In this chapter we will look at the church's mandate, messengers, message and mission, and we'll learn about the important place of the Holy Spirit in the lives of believers.

SETTING SAIL

In the original Greek text, the New Testament word for church is *ekklesia*, which translates as "a group called out" or an "assembly." Church, then, represents a group of people who have been *called* out of darkness and into God's light (1 Pet. 2:9-10). Scripture tells us that we are *called together* as a community of believers (Acts 2:42-47), and we are *called* for obedience to Jesus Christ (1 Pet. 1:2).

The church is both local and universal. The New Testament speaks of the local Church meeting in homes (Acts 5:42; Rom. 16:5; 1 Cor. 16:19), in the temple (Acts 2:46, 5:12, 42), in a city (Acts 8:1; 13:1), and in a region (Acts 9:31; Gal. 1:2). The universal Church, meaning global and timeless, is one (Eph. 4:4-6), holy (1 Pet. 2:9-10) and apostolic (Eph. 2:20).

To get the most out of this chapter on the church and the Holy Spirit, I want to encourage you to read through the book of Acts at the same time. This will provide the Holy Spirit with the opportunity to take these essential truths and place them deep into your heart, mind and spirit.

New Testament Portraits of the Church

The word "church" is used only twice in all the gospels (Mt. 16:18; 18:17), but this doesn't imply that the gospels do not teach us about the Church. On the contrary, Jesus had a great deal to say about the Church. He talked about His "little flock" (Lk. 12:32; Jn. 10:16), His "disciples" (Mt. 10:24-25; 14:26-27), and about the "branches" in Himself, the Vine (Jn. 15:1-8). In these and many different ways, Jesus taught His disciples what it meant to be members of His community.

The Body of Christ – Rom. 12:4-5; 1 Cor. 12:12-27; Eph. 4:11-16
- Jesus is the Head of the Church, His Body (Eph. 1:22).
- From Him, the Body grows and builds itself up in love.
- The Body is one although it consists of many members.
- Each part of the body is necessary and important and makes its own unique contribution to the Body.

THOUGHTS & NOTES

- Like joints and ligaments in the human body, the Body of Christ is connected one to another and must function together under His Headship to properly express Jesus to the world.
- Like the human body, the Body of Christ is a living organism and not an organization.

The Building of God – 1 Cor. 3:9-11; Eph. 2:19-22; 1 Pet. 2:4-6

- Jesus Christ is the chief cornerstone on which everything is built. The Church can't stand without Him.
- All believers are a dwelling in which God lives by His Spirit (1 Cor. 3:16-17).
- We are "living stones" built into a spiritual house comprised of believers from all eras of time—past, present and future, and from all the nations of the earth.

The Bride of Christ – Eph. 5:21-33; Rev. 21:9-27

- Jesus is the Bridegroom and the Church is His Bride.
- *Bride* speaks of the intimate and affectionate place that Jesus has in His heart for His church.
- Jesus has laid His life down for His Bride, the Church.
- As a bride lays aside all other loves to cling to her bridegroom, so must the Church respond to Jesus with an attitude of love, submission and obedience to Him.
- Jesus wants to build up His bride that she might reflect His glory.

The Family or People of God – Eph. 2:19; 1 Pet. 2:9-10

- God is our Father (Mt. 6:9; 2 Cor. 6:18; Eph. 4:6).
- God, as a Father, loved us enough to send His Son to die for us (Jn. 3:16).
- We have been adopted by God (Gal. 4:4-7).
- We have been called children of God (1 Jn. 3:1).
- We are brothers and sisters in Christ (Mt. 12:50; Heb. 13:1; 1 Pet. 3:8).
- The Church is to be a place of love, acceptance and forgiveness.

The Community of the Holy Spirit – The book of Acts

- The book of Acts centers on the acts of the Holy Spirit in and through the life of the Church.
- The Holy Spirit birthed, empowered, permeated and sustained the Church in Acts.
- His leadership of the Church enabled her to bring Jesus glory and advance God's Kingdom.

*The Church is the Body of Christ, and the Spirit is the Spirit of Christ.
He fills the Body, directs its movements, controls its members, inspires its wisdom,
supplies its strength. He guides into truth, sanctifies its agents, and empowers
for witnessing. The Spirit has never abdicated His authority nor relegated His power.*

Samuel Chadwick, 1860-1932, English Revivalist

The Church's Mandate

In the first chapter of Paul's letter to the Ephesians, he states three times that God's eternal plan is for His people to be to the praise of his glory (Eph. 1:6, 12, 14). Throughout the chapter, God stands as both the originator and the goal of the redemptive process. God receives glory when the church fully realizes the purpose of her existence, consciously praises God for his grace, and joyfully demonstrates God's grace by being filled with all the fullness of God (Eph. 3:19). The Church's mandates are:

To Minister to the Lord
- Ministering to the Lord in worship, prayer and obedience was a priority to the Church in Acts.
- Believers ministered to the Lord, individually and corporately, on a daily basis (Acts 2:46-47).
- The leaders heard from God as they ministered to Him (Acts 13:1-3).
- The disciples worshiped the Lord in the midst of difficult situations (Acts 16:16-34).

To Minister to One Another
- Wash one another's feet (Jn. 13:14-15)
- Love one another (Jn. 13:34)
- Be devoted to one another (Rom. 12:10)
- Honor one another (Rom. 12:10)
- Share with one another (Rom. 12:13)
- Bless, rejoice and mourn with one another (Rom. 12:14-15)
- Live in harmony with one another (Rom. 12:16, 15:5)
- Accept one another (Rom. 15:7)
- Instruct one another (Rom. 15:14)
- Greet one another (Rom. 16:16)
- Wait for one another (1 Cor. 11:33)
- Have concern for one another (1 Cor. 12:25)
- Comfort one another (2 Cor. 1:3-4)
- Serve one another (Gal. 5:13)
- Restore one another (Gal. 6:1)
- Carry one another's burdens (Gal. 6:2)
- Bear with one another (Eph. 4:2)
- Be kind and compassionate to one another (Eph. 4:32)

THOUGHTS & NOTES

- Submit yourselves to one another (Eph. 5:21)
- Consider one another better than yourself (Phil. 2:3)
- Forgive one another (Col. 3:13)
- Admonish one another (Col. 3:16)
- Allow your love to increase and overflow to one another (1 Thes. 3:12)
- Encourage and build up one another (1 Thes. 5:11)
- Be kind to one another (1 Thes. 5:15)
- Spur one another on towards love and good works (Heb. 10:24)
- Confess your sins to one another (Jam. 5:16)
- Pray for one another (Jam. 5:16)
- Offer hospitality to one another (1 Pet. 4:9)
- Walk in humility towards one another (1 Pet. 5:5)

To Minister to Unbelievers in the World
- By using opportunities that God brings our way.
- By preaching the gospel to people and nations who have not yet heard in a way they can relate to and understand.
- The disciples were called Christians ("little Christs") because they lived their lives like Jesus (Acts 11:26).

The Church's Messengers

Who are the Church's messengers? We are—you and me! To understand more fully what that means, let's look at the original twelve. We join an informal group of common folk. James, John, Peter and the others weren't particularly clever or successful. They weren't more deserving than those around them. They were ordinary. Jesus walked along the shores of Galilee and called a few fishermen, simple people who earned their keep with their hands. God saved them from their sins and made new creations of them. They emerged from the common and began taking on the extraordinary likeness and passion of Christ. Receiving their Master's message, they carried it forth. They took it to the lost while with Him, while waiting for His return, while persecuted by friends and strangers, while empowered by the Holy Spirit, while perplexed by God, man or beast. As a result, "From the days of John the Baptist until now, the kingdom of heaven has been forcefully advancing and forceful men lay hold of it" (Mt. 11:12).

Men are God's method. The church is looking for better methods;
God is looking for better men. What the church needs today is not more machinery
or better, not new organizations or more and novel methods, but men who
the Holy Spirit can use - men of prayer, men mighty in prayer.
The Holy Spirit does not come on machinery but on men.
He does not anoint plans, but men - men of prayer.

E. M. Bounds, 1835-1913, American Pastor and Man of Prayer

Names Used to Describe the Church's Messengers
- Believers described those who believed in Jesus (Acts 2:44).
- Disciples were those who learned from and had become like their teacher (Jesus) (Acts 6:2).
- Those of the Way referred to those that lived according to a special way of life (Acts 9:2).
- Christians translates as "little anointed ones" or "little Christs"(Acts 11:26).
- Saints referred to those who had been dedicated and set apart (holy) to God (Acts 26:10)

The Church's Messengers Identified With Jesus
By confessing Jesus as Lord – Rom. 10:9-10
- Because those who confessed Christ in the early Church were often persecuted, punished, imprisoned or put to death, a confession of faith in Jesus affirmed them as believers. These disciples confessed Jesus unashamedly before Jews (Acts 2:14-41), Gentiles (Acts 17:16-34), religious leaders (Acts 4:1-22) and kings (Acts 25:13-26:32).

By being baptized – Mt. 28:18-20
- By being baptized, a new believer identifies themselves with the person, death, resurrection and cause of Jesus Christ. The act of baptism testifies to the world that the new believer has been reborn into God's Kingdom and has given God their primary allegiance.
- Some examples of those baptized in Acts are: believers on the day of Pentecost (Acts 2:41), Samaritan believers (Acts 8:12), the Ethiopian (Acts 8:36-38), Saul (Acts 9:18), Lydia (Acts 16:15), the Philippian jailor and his family (Acts 16:29-34), Crispus and his household (Acts 18:8), the believers in Ephesus (Acts 19:1-5).

By receiving the Lord's Supper – Mt. 26:17-30; Acts 2:42
- The Lord's Supper is the name given to the Passover meal that Jesus celebrated with His disciples the night before He was crucified. The broken bread represents His body being broken for the sins of the world, and the wine for His blood shed for the forgiveness of sins.
- Communion, as it may be called, is a memorial to the finished work of Jesus. It is not taken to remember our sins, but to remember what Jesus did for us. It is also a reminder to look to His return when we will partake of it with Him in our Father's kingdom (Mt. 26:29).
- The celebration of the Lord's Supper is reserved for believers in Jesus. Paul instructed the Church to examine their hearts to make sure they were right with God and each other before receiving the bread and the wine (1 Cor. 11:23-34).

THOUGHTS & NOTES

The Church's Messengers Endured Persecution and Martyrdom – (Acts 5:17-42)

- The disciples encountered persecution and martyrdom (being killed for the sake of Jesus and the gospel) throughout the book of Acts: Peter & John (Acts 4:1-22), the Apostles (Acts 5:17-42), Stephen (Acts 6:8-7:60), James (Acts 12:2) and Paul (2 Cor. 11:22-33).

The traditional deaths of Jesus' disciples

- Peter was crucified upside down in Rome.
- James was beheaded in Jerusalem.
- Andrew was crucified.
- Philip died a martyr at Hierapolis.
- Bartholomew was beaten to death.
- Thomas died a martyr in India.
- Matthew died a martyr in Ethiopia.
- James (the less) was crucified in Egypt.
- Thaddaeus died a martyr in Persia.
- Simon the Zealot was crucified.
- Matthias died a martyr in Ethiopia.
- John was the only disciple to die a natural death.
- Paul was beheaded in Rome.

What Jesus and Paul Said About Persecution

- People will hate us on account of Jesus (Mt. 10:22).
- We are blessed by God when we are persecuted (Mt. 5:10-12).
- We will be persecuted for the sake of Jesus and the gospel (Mk. 10:29-30).
- We are to endure hardship as good soldiers (2 Tim. 2:3).
- Everybody who desires to live a godly life will be persecuted (2 Tim. 3:12).

How are we to respond to persecution?

- Respond accordingly in love and truth (Acts 4:18-20)
- Forgive (Acts 7:59-60)
- Look to Jesus (Acts 7:54-56)
- Follow the leadership of the Holy Spirit (Mk. 13:11)
- Love and pray (Acts 7:59,60; Mt. 5:44,45)
- Rejoice that God has made you worthy to suffer for Jesus (Acts 5:41; Mt. 5:10-12)

The Church's Message

Handed a scroll to read in a Nazarene synagogue, Jesus read the words scribed hundreds of years earlier by the prophet Isaiah—"The Spirit of the Lord is on Me, because He has anointed Me to preach good news to the poor. He has sent Me to proclaim freedom for the prisoners and recovery of sight for the blind, to release the oppressed, to proclaim the year of the Lord's favor" (Is. 61:6; Lk. 4:18-19). All eyes were upon Him as He spoke. When Jesus finished, He rolled up the scroll and handed it back to the attendant who had given it to Him. Then, to the astonishment of all who were present, He said the unthinkable, the incomprehensible, what was heresy to a staunch Pharisee of the day. The boy who grew up in their midst said—"Today this scripture is fulfilled in your hearing" (Lk. 4:20-21). In that moment, Jesus proclaimed Himself to be the long awaited Messiah, and from the ancient scripture He cited, we're told what the Messiah's ministry would be. Jesus came to preach the good news, the gospel of the Kingdom of God. Using hundreds of parables, illustrations and prophetic examples, Jesus, indeed, fulfilled the words of the prophet. The Church received His message and was to take it into all of the world (Mk. 1:14-15, Mt. 4:23, Lk. 4:43, Acts 8:12; 19:8; 28:30-31).

The Church's Message Came From First-Hand Witnesses
Because they had experienced Jesus personally in their lives, the disciples were able to testify boldly about Him to others. They couldn't help but share what they had experienced (Acts 4:20, 21:37-22:29; 1 Jn. 1:1-4).

The Message Was Motivated by Love for God and the Lost
Because of what Jesus had done for them they were compelled by love to share the gospel with those who had not yet heard (2 Cor. 5:14-21). They desired for Jesus, the Lamb of God, to receive the reward of His sufferings (Rev. 5:1-14).

The Message was All About Jesus
- Who He is (Acts 2:21,36; 9:20; 10:36-38)
- His life (Acts 2:22; 9:20; 10:37-39)
- His death and resurrection (Acts 2:22-24; 3:13-15; 3:18-26; 4:33; 10:34-43; 13:26-41; 1 Cor. 15)
- For more, take a look at some of the sermons in Acts (Acts 2:14-41; 3:11-26; 6:8-7:60; 17:16-34; 21:37-22:29)

THOUGHTS & NOTES

The Message was About God's Grace, Repentance and Faith
- It is through grace that people are saved (Acts 15:11; Eph. 2:1-10).
- Their enduring task was testifying to the gospel of God's grace (Acts 20:24).
- God confirmed the message of His grace with signs and wonders (Acts 14:3).
- Repentance and faith is the proper response of the heart to the message of God's grace (Acts 2:38; 3:19; 17:30; 20:21; 26:20).

The Message Related to All Peoples and Cultures
- They adapted the gospel message so that every person and culture could hear and understand it: Jews (Acts 13:13-42) and Gentiles (Acts 17:16-34).
- Paul became all things to all men so that some might be saved (1 Cor. 9:19-23).

The Message Told People of Their Condition Before God
- Their sin had nailed Jesus to the cross (Acts 2:22-24, 36; 3:13-15).
- All will give an account of their lives before Jesus one day (Acts 17:30, 31; 2 Cor. 5:10).
- The New Testament also teaches the reality of hell, a place for the wicked who continue in their sins rather than being saved from them by Jesus. Hell was not created for man, but for the devil and his angels (Mt. 25:41). It is described as a place of darkness (Mt. 8:12; Jude 13), eternal punishment and fire (Mt. 18:8, 25:46; Lk. 16:24), with weeping and gnashing of teeth (Mt. 8:12; 13:42), unquenchable thirst (Lk. 16:22-26), removed from the presence of the Lord (2 Thes. 1:8-9), and for those who continue in their sin (Rev. 21:5-8).
- We should only share with people about hell from a place of sincere love, compassion, and brokenness for them. It is never meant to be something that we attack unbelievers with, but rather a very real truth that should be communicated through the grace that we ourselves have received. Praying for the lost aligns our hearts with God's, allowing us to share this truth more effectively with others in an attitude of compassion and mercy.

The Message Told People How to be Made Right With God
- Repent, as a response to God's grace, for the forgiveness of sins (Acts 2:38, 3:19).
- Believe in, or put their full trust in and reliance upon, the Lord Jesus (Acts 16:31, 20:21).
- Deny yourself, take up the Cross and follow Jesus, by seeking first His kingdom (Mt. 16:24-26, 6:33).

Trying to do the Lord's work in your own strength is the most confusing, exhausting, and tedious of all work. But when you are filled with the Holy Spirit, then the ministry of Jesus just flows out of you.

Corrie ten Boom, 1892-1987, Dutch Holocaust Hero, Author of The Hiding Place

The Message was Confirmed by God Through Demonstrations of Power
- Signs and wonders were a part of the ministry of the disciples in Acts: Jesus said they would accompany them (Mk. 16:15-20), they were part of Peter's ministry (Acts 3:1-10, 9:32-43), Stephen's ministry (Acts 6:8), Philip's ministry (Acts 8:4-8) and Paul's ministry (13:6-12, 20:7-12).
- Some of the signs and wonders mentioned in Acts include:

  - The crippled, lame & paralyzed receiving healing (Acts 3:1-10, 8:7, 9:32-35, 14:8-10)
  - The death of Ananias and Sapphira (Acts 5:1-11)
  - The shadow of Peter healing some (Acts 5:12-16)
  - Demons cast out (Acts 5:16, 8:7, 16:16-18, 19:11-16)
  - Philip transported by the Spirit (Acts 8:36-40)
  - The dead raised (Acts 9:36-43, 20:7-12)
  - Angelic direction (Acts 5:17-21, 8:26, 12:1-19, 27:23,24)
  - A sorcerer made blind (Acts 13:6-12)
  - Healing and deliverance through handkerchiefs and apron (Acts 19:11,12)
  - A snakebite rendered powerless (Acts 28:3-6)

- The purpose of signs and wonders is to bear witness to Jesus, His messengers and the gospel message. In almost every case in Acts where there is a demonstration of power recorded, it either directly led to the conversion of many or it provided the disciples with an opportunity to preach the gospel (Acts 2:22; 8:5-8).
- It is important to note that God continues today to bear witness to the Lord Jesus, His messengers and the message of the gospel through signs and wonders. They are not something that can be cooked up by anyone, but are the acts of a sovereign God. Our role is to step out in faith and obedience, in the Name of Jesus, when led by the Holy Spirit. Jesus said that believers will move in signs and wonders, and will do greater things than He did in this area (Mk. 16:15-18; Jn. 14:12). If you haven't done it before, begin to regularly pray for God to confirm His message through your life with signs and wonders (Acts 4:23-31) so that Jesus will be glorified and people will come to know Him.
- Always remember that signs and wonders are to follow you – we are not to chase after them. When people are healed, it is an expression of the Kingdom of God coming upon them—a snapshot of heaven coming on Earth (Lk. 10:9). When people are not immediately healed after you have prayed for them, reassure them of your love and God's love, of His ability to heal them in His way and time, whether here on Earth now or later in heaven.

THOUGHTS & NOTES

The Church's Mission

The Church's concept of missions originated in the heart of God. A careful study of Scripture reveals His consistent, purposeful, and merciful desire to see all peoples come into fellowship with Him. "Here is a trustworthy saying that deserves full acceptance: Christ Jesus came into the world to save sinners" (1 Tim. 1:15). The Church is to tell of the good news of salvation in Jesus Christ to every person "to the ends of the earth" (Acts 1:8). His purpose, then, becomes our mission, in order that all men might know and enjoy Him forever.

To Preach the Gospel to All Nations
- Jesus told the disciples to take the gospel everywhere to everyone (Mk. 16:15-20).
- Jesus commissioned His disciples to make disciples of every nation (people groupings) (Mt. 28:18-20).

The Progression of the Gospel in Acts
- To Jerusalem (local) (Acts 1-7)
- To Judea and Samaria (regional/national) (Acts 8-12)
- To the ends of the earth (international) (Acts 13-28)

Nothing could stop the advancement of the gospel in Acts
- Not hatred, jealousy or prejudices (Acts 5:40-42)
- Not lies (Acts 5:1-11)
- Not threats (Acts 4:18-20, 31)
- Not persecution (Acts 8:1-4, 9:1-19)
- Not trials or imprisonment (Acts 24-26; Acts 5:17-21; Acts 12:1-18)
- Not stonings or martyrdom (Acts 7:54-8:4; Acts 12:1,2,24; 14:19-21)
- Not riots (Acts 19)
- Not geography (Acts 9:31)
- Not scatterings (Acts 8:1-4)
- Not storms or shipwrecks (Acts 27:42-28:10)
- Not false brothers or false teaching (Acts 15:1-19)
- Not religious leaders (Acts 5:40-42)
- Not kings (Acts 12)
- Not those who refuse to hear the gospel (Acts 28:23-31)

We need a baptism of clear seeing. We desperately need seers who can see through the mist--Christian leaders with prophetic vision. Unless they come soon it will be too late for this generation. And if they do come we will no doubt crucify a few of them in the name of our worldly orthodoxy.

A.W. Tozer, 1897-1963, American Pastor and Writer

God provides the church with godly leaders to steer the church towards its mission
- Biblical leadership is about serving people towards God's way and purposes (Mt. 20:20-28).
- Biblical leadership is something that one is called to by God, and is a stewarding of God's people and purposes (Acts 20:28).
- The qualifications of biblical leadership are based upon godly character and spiritual maturity (Acts 6:1-7; 1 Tim. 3:1-13; Titus 1:5-9).
- Biblical leadership is usually expressed by teams of leaders. Someone will serve as "chief among them," yet the leadership is really shared as each leader on the team yields to the Holy Spirit's direction as He emphasizes certain gifts in various situations and seasons (Acts 13:1-3, 14:23). Note the relationship of Paul and Barnabas. Barnabas begins as the lead person but shortly yields to Paul's gifts and placement by the Holy Spirit (Acts 9-15).
- Some of the responsibilities of leaders in the church include:
    - To seek God in prayer (Acts 1:14,24, 6:2-4, 10:9-48, 14:23, 20:25-38)
    - Shepherding the flock (Acts 20:28; 1 Pet. 5:1-4)
    - Teaching, discipling and preparing God's people for works of service (1 Tim. 3:2; Titus 1:9; Mt. 28:19,20; Eph. 4:11-16)
    - Releasing people into their gifts and ministries (Acts 6:1-7; Acts 13:1-3; 1 Tim. 4:14)
    - Watching for false teachers and false doctrine (Acts 20:28-31; Titus 1:9),
    - Administration of practical needs (Acts 6:1-7; Acts 11:27-30).

Deeper waters

As stated earlier, the book of Acts is about the acts of the Holy Spirit in and through the newborn Church. This third-person of the Godhead not only played an important role in the birth, life and expansion of the Church then, but He continues today, as well. Let's take a look at what Scripture teaches about the Holy Spirit.

Although you cannot see the Holy Spirit, you know He is there because you see the effect of His presence on the things He touches

THOUGHTS & NOTES ————

Indwelled by the Holy Spirit

limited by the finite, man can explain things only in the context of his physical world. Because we experience the concreteness of family, we understand God as Father, and we identify with God as Son. The Holy Spirit, however, is slightly beyond our grasp. Nothing in the material world can help us by drawing comparisons. The Bible uses a material analogy just once to help us understand. In John 3:8, Jesus said, "The wind blows wherever it pleases. You hear its sound, but you cannot tell where it comes from or where it is going. So it is with everyone born of the Spirit." He was saying that although you cannot see the Holy Spirit, you know He is there because you see the effect of His presence on the things He touches. Jesus also told us that the presence of the Holy Spirit would be greater than His own (Jn. 16:7). Restricted by physical form, Jesus could be in just one place at a time. But the Holy Spirit would come and indwell all believers, at all times. In other words, men walked with Jesus, separated, perhaps in times of need, by occasions such as sleep. Through the coming of His Spirit, however, none of us in relationship with Christ would know separation again. By His indwelling Spirit, we would walk with Jesus without interruption.

Who Is The Holy Spirit?
- He is the third person of the Godhead, the Trinity (2 Cor. 13:14; Mt. 28:19).
- He has the very same attributes as the Father and the Son (Jesus).
- He is spirit (Jn. 4:24).
- He is all-knowing (Omniscient) (1 Cor. 2:10-11).
- He is all-powerful (Omnipotent) (Job 33:4; Acts 2:1-4).
- He is all-present (Omnipresent) (Ps. 139:7).
- He is eternal (Heb. 9:14).
- He is holy (Ps. 51:11; Is. 63:10), wise (Dan. 4:8,9,18), and good (Neh. 9:20; Ps. 143:10).
- He has the attributes of personality: mind (Rom. 8:27); will (1 Cor. 12:11); love (Rom. 15:30); thought, knowledge and words (1 Cor. 2:6-16); He can be quenched (1 Thes. 5:19) and grieved (Eph. 4:30).
- He is sent to us by the Father and the Son (Jesus) (Jn. 14:16, 15:26).
- He always bears witness of Jesus and glorifies Him (Jn. 15:26, 16:12-15).

Some Symbols of the Holy Spirit
- *Breath or wind* — He is invisible, life-sustaining and all-powerful (Jn. 3:8, 20:22; Acts 2:1-4).
- *Dove* — He is gentle and pure (Mt. 3:16).
- *Oil* — He anoints us for service (1 Sam. 16:13; Lk. 4:18).

If we think of the Holy Spirit only as an impersonal power or influence, then our thought will constantly be, how can I get hold of and use the Holy Spirit; but if we think of Him in the biblical way as a divine Person, infinitely wise, infinitely holy, infinitely tender, then our thought will constantly be, "How can the Holy Spirit get hold of and use me?".

R.A. Torrey, 1856-1928, American Pastor, Evangelist and Educator

- *Fire* — His presence purifies, illuminates, and welds together God's people (Mt. 3:11-12; Acts 2:3-4).
- *Living Water* — He brings life, refreshment, and quenches thirst (Jn. 4:14, 7:38,39).
- *Deposit* — of what God has in store for us (2 Cor. 1:21, 22; Eph. 1:13, 14).

The Works of the Holy Spirit

The Holy Spirit indwells the believer forever (Jn. 14:16-20). He was promised to us by Jesus, who said, "But the Counselor, the Holy Spirit, whom the Father will send in My name, will teach you all things and will remind you of everything I have said to you" (Jn. 14-26). Jesus reaffirmed His promise, saying, "When the Counselor comes, whom I will send to you from the Father, the Spirit of truth, who goes out from the Father, He will testify about Me..." (Jn. 15:26).

The Holy Spirit brings to mind God's truth. As if we were walking arm-in-arm with a close Friend, the Holy Spirit speaks to us, reminding us of things we have forgotten, reminding us of God's Word and applying it to our situations (Jn. 14:26). His work in the believer produces an intimate love relationship with God. He is our Comforter, Encourager, and Helper who comes to our aid. Some of the Holy Spirit's works include:

Bringing the Presence of Jesus into Our Lives
- He was sent to us by Jesus so that we would not be orphans (Jn. 14:18).
- He baptizes us into the Body of Christ (1 Cor. 12:13).
- He fills us and lives within us (Eph. 5:18; Rom. 8:9).
- He gives us the certainty of being children of God (Rom. 8:15-16).
- He comes as our helper, comforter and counselor (Jn. 14:16,26, 16:7)

Bringing the Likeness of Jesus into Our Lives
- He guides us into all truth and brings it to our remembrance (Jn. 14:26, 16:13).
- He creates within us a spiritual disposition (Rom. 8:5).
- He convicts us of sin and righteousness (Jn. 16:8-11).
- He puts sin to death in our lives as we yield to Him (Rom. 8:13-14).
- He sanctifies us, allowing us to become more like Jesus (2 Thes. 2:13-15).
- He brings forth the fruit of the Spirit in our lives (Gal. 5:22-23).

THOUGHTS & NOTES

Bringing the Power of Jesus into and through Our Lives
- He helps us in our weakness, especially in prayer (Rom. 8:26-27).
- He gives us the power to overcome sin in our lives (Gal. 5:16-26).
- He gives us the ability to know God's will and the power to do it (Rom. 8:14; Acts 13:1-3).
- He empowers us with spiritual gifts and anoints us to use them to advance His kingdom (1 Cor. 12:7-11).
- He empowers us to be witnesses of Jesus (Acts 1:8).

The Disciple's Relationship with the Holy Spirit
- Disciples are born-again by the Spirit (Jn. 3:5-8).
- Disciples are baptized into God's family by the Spirit (1 Cor. 12:13).
- Disciples are empowered by the Holy Spirit (Acts 1:8, 2:38, 39).
- Disciples are to be constantly refilled by the Spirit (Eph. 5:18).
- Disciples are to live by the Spirit (Gal. 5:16).
- Disciples are to keep in step with the Spirit (Gal. 5:25).
- Disciples are to be led by the Spirit (Rom. 8:14).
- Disciples are to bear the fruit of the Spirit in their lives (Gal. 5:22-23).
- Disciples are empowered by the Spirit to function in their gifts (1 Cor. 12:4-11).
- Disciples are not to quench (say no when He says yes) or grieve (say yes when He says no) the Holy Spirit (1 Thes. 5:19; Eph. 4:30).

The Empowerment of the Holy Spirit
- Our heavenly Father desires to give us the Holy Spirit when we ask (Lk. 11:13).
- God commands us to be filled with the Spirit (Eph. 5:18).
- The disciples needed to be empowered by the Holy Spirit to become effective witnesses (Lk. 24:49; Acts 1:4-8).
- Repentance of sin and commitment to the Lordship of Jesus preceded the empowerment of the Spirit in the lives of Jesus' disciples (Acts 2:38).
- The Holy Spirit was promised not only to the disciples in Acts, but to us today (Acts 2:38-39).
- A study of the life of Peter, before and after being empowered by the Holy Spirit, reveals the significance of this empowerment in one's life. (Compare him in the gospels accounts to Acts 2-15, after receiving the Holy Spirit.)
- The evidence of the Holy Spirit's empowerment in the lives of believers is power (Acts 1:8). This power was manifested in many ways in the book of Acts, including loving others, being obedient to God, praying with power, becoming bold witnesses, functioning in spiritual gifts, moving in signs and wonders, and ministering to others.

Breath in me, O Holy Spirit, that my thoughts may all be holy.
Act in me, O Holy Spirit, that my work, too, may be holy.
Draw my heart, O Holy Spirit, that I love but what is holy.
Strengthen me, O Holy Spirit, to defend all that is holy.
Guard me, then, O Holy Spirit, that I always may be holy.

St. Augustine of Hippo, 354-430, Church Father

- Another expression that can occur with the empowering of the Holy Spirit is speaking in tongues. This occurred a number of times in the book of Acts (Acts 2:1-4, 10:44-46, 19:1-7). This expression of tongues is used for personal edification and as a prayer language. This seems to be different than the gift of tongues, which is accompanied by the gift of interpretation of tongues (1 Cor. 12:10) and is used in public settings to bless the Body and be a sign for unbelievers. See 1 Cor. 14 for Paul's teaching on this topic.
- When we become Christians, the Holy Spirit comes and dwells within us making us children of God (Jn. 3:5-8; Rom. 8:13-17; 1 Cor. 12:13). The empowerment of the Holy Spirit might be pictured as the Holy Spirit coming upon a believer to empower them for God's service.

Abiding in the Holy Spirit

(John 15:1-17) The secret of the Christian life is found in John 15:5. Jesus told his disciples, "I am the vine, you are the branches: If a man remains in Me, and I in him, he will bear much fruit; for apart from Me you can do nothing." This abiding in Christ, and Christ abiding in us, and the coming of the Holy Spirit are intimately related. You cannot abide in Christ without walking in the Spirit.

Abiding Speaks of Complete Dependence
- A branch's whole existence depends on the vine.
- Without the vine a branch withers and dies.
- Just like the branch, disciples must realize that without a daily dependence on the Holy Spirit their spiritual lives will wither and die.

Abiding Speaks of Deep Trust and Rest
- A branch does not show signs of anxiety, but rests completely in the vine.
- Though other branches may grow bigger and taller, even bear more fruit, the branch never competes.
- Just like the branch, disciples must trust and rest in the Holy Spirit's leading in their lives.

Abiding Speaks of Close Communion
- A branch has constant, unbroken communion with the vine.
- A branch recognizes that its close communion is the key to its life and that without the nurturing flow of sap, there is no way it can be a healthy, growing, fruit-bearing tree.
- Just like the branch, disciples must walk in constant fellowship daily with the Holy Spirit if they intend to be healthy, growing, fruit-bearing believers.

THOUGHTS & NOTES

Abiding Speaks of Bearing Fruit
- A branch does no work whatsoever to bear fruit, but remains yielded to the vine for its flow to bear fruit.
- The vine does all the work, while the branch remains available to be used by the vine to bear fruit.
- Just like the branch, disciples not need to strive to bear fruit, but live yielded to the Holy Spirit and allow Him to move through them to bear fruit—fruit that will last.

Abiding Speaks of Total Surrender
- A branch is totally given to the vine and is at its disposal.
- All that the branch has and is can be used by the vine as the vine chooses.
- Just like the branch, disciples must totally surrender to the Holy Spirit, allowing Him to choose how He would like to flow through them for God's glory.

CASTING THE NET

What has been your perception of the church? After catching a glimpse of it now through the book of Acts, how has it changed? In light of these truths what are you doing to contribute to your local church?

_____

_____

_____

_____

_____

_____

_____

_____

_____

_____

The branch of the vine does not worry, and toil, and rush here to seek for sunshine, and
there to find rain. No; it rests in union and communion with the vine;
and at the right time, and in the right way, is the right fruit found on it.
Let us so abide in the Lord Jesus.

Hudson Taylor, 1832-1905, English Missionary to China

Is your life aligned to the three mandates of the Church—ministering first to the Lord? Ministering to one another? Ministering to the unbelievers that God has placed around you in the world? Where might the Holy Spirit lead you to make adjustments in these areas ?

_____

_____

_____

_____

_____

_____

_____

_____

What spoke to you the most about the Church's messengers? What about the Church's message? Are you praying for God to confirm the message of Jesus with demonstrations of power? What are you actively doing to participate in helping the Church fulfill its mission?

_____

_____

_____

_____

_____

_____

_____

_____

_____

THOUGHTS & NOTES

_____

_____

_____

_____

What did you believe about the Holy Spirit before studying this chapter? What did you learn most about Him and His relationship with you? Did you read through the book of Acts yet?

_____

_____

_____

_____

_____

_____

_____

_____

Do you sense the need to be empowered by God to enable you to better serve Him? Ask Jesus to empower you with the Holy Spirit. Visit with your pastor, or another spiritual leader friend, should you want to talk to someone more about this. Invite them to pray with you.

_____

_____

_____

_____

_____

_____

_____

_____

_____

_____

_____

_____

CATCH OF THE DAY

Chapter Summary

- Jesus loves His Church and portrays her through the Scriptures to us as His Body, His Building, His Bride, His Family and the Community of the Holy Spirit.
- The Church's mandate is to minister to Jesus, minister to one another, and to minister to unbelievers in the world around us.
- The Church's messengers identified themselves completely with Jesus and endured persecution as a result.
- The Church's message and mission is to reveal Jesus to those who don't yet know Him, both locally and globally, in words and actions, and in demonstrations of power.
- The Holy Spirit is the third member of the Godhead and is to be active in our lives as believers. The empowering of the Holy Spirit by Jesus is for the effective service of believers.

What are the two or three things the Holy Spirit spoke most clearly to you through this chapter and how will you respond to Him?

_____

_____

_____

_____

_____

_____

_____

_____

_____

THOUGHTS & NOTES

_____

_____

_____

CHAPTER 10

ADVANCING THE KINGDOM

A VIEW FROM THE SHORE

"And this gospel of Kingdom will be preached in the whole world
as a testimony to all nations, and then the end will come."
Matthew 24:14

"Then Jesus came to them and said, 'All authority in heaven
and on earth has been given to me. Therefore go and make disciples
of all nations, baptizing them in the name of the Father
and of the Son and of the Holy Spirit, and teaching them
to obey everything I have commanded you.
And surely I am with you always, to the very end of the age.'"
Matthew 28:18-20

We see the Kingdom of God preached throughout the New Testament. It speaks of God's dominion, the sphere where Jesus reigns as Lord, where His character is displayed, where His ways are exalted, where His Word exists as the foundation of truth—where His will is done. The Kingdom of God is the eternal arena believers enter as they give their lives to Jesus.

Jesus taught extensively about God's Kingdom. His parables provide insights about its nature, for the Kingdom of God differs from the kingdom of this world (Mt. 13:1-52). While instructing believers to seek first the Kingdom, Jesus promised that His Father would tend their cares (Mt. 6:33). He directed His disciples to turn their hearts to His purposes and pray that the Kingdom of God would manifest on Earth, just as it does in heaven (Mt. 6:9-10). He shared with His disciples the keys to the Kingdom (Mt. 16:19), telling them how to become great within it (Mt. 18:1-4). When people were healed, Jesus said that the Kingdom had come near them (Lk. 10:9).

Our Savior revealed to us that the Kingdom of God is displayed on Earth in and through the Church. He commissioned His disciples to advance His Kingdom, declaring its good news that every tribe, language, people, and nation may know Him and that His will may be done in the Earth (Rev. 5:9,10, 11:15). Jesus wants believers to model the values of the Kingdom so the world will recognize their King and be drawn to His presence. He desires the heartbeat of the Kingdom—bringing glory to God—to beat within every disciple (1 Cor. 10:31).

Like a multifaceted gemstone, the truths of the Kingdom are spectacular and enumerable (Mt. 5:7). Among them is the truth that the coming of God's Kingdom defeats Satan. Much is taught in the scriptures about what the Kingdom of God means in our lives, not only in regard to eternity, but concerning our everyday lives.

In this chapter we will explore the Kingdom by becoming acquainted with its scope, characteristics, values and essence. We'll look at ways the Kingdom can be advanced in the Earth through missions and evangelism, as well as how to discern truth from error by learning about the triad of truth from the writings of the disciple John.

SETTING SAIL

All are invited. People from every country, class and social background are welcome to enter the Kingdom of God. No admission will be denied for lack of material wealth, worldly wisdom, or physical beauty (Mt. 8:11; 19:23-24; 21:31, Lk. 18:16-17, 1 Tim. 2:3-4). The Kingdom of God—or the Kingdom of heaven, as it is also referred to in Scripture—is an everlasting kingdom which spans the mighty Universe. Currently invisible to the human eye and unheard of by a vast number of people, the Kingdom of God is, nevertheless, more real and abiding than all the earthly kingdoms and empires this world has ever known.

God's Kingdom is a spiritual realm, which only those born of the Spirit may enter. These come through one divine portal—through faith in Jesus Christ. Bestowed rare privileges, citizens transform from creations born of dust to children embraced by a loving and attentive Father God (1Jn. 3:1-2). Those who accept His offer of salvation also become heirs of the Kingdom—"joint heirs with Christ" (Mt. 25:34; 1 Cor. 6:9-10; 15:50; Gal. 5:21). Scripture tells us we will govern with him throughout eternity (Rom. 8:16-18, Jam. 2:5, Lk. 12:32; 22:29-30, Dan. 7:27).

The Importance of the Kingdom of God

The prophet Isaiah wrote, "For to us a child is born, to us a Son is given, and the government will be on His shoulders. And He will be called Wonderful Counselor, Mighty God, Everlasting Father, Prince of Peace. Of the increase of His government and peace, there will be no end. He will reign on David's throne and over his kingdom, establishing and upholding it with justice and righteousness from that time on and forever" (Is. 9:6-7).

Jesus compared the Kingdom's value to a pearl that a person sells everything he owns to obtain (Mt. 13:44-45). We're told, "...seek first His kingdom and His righteousness, and all these things will be given to you as well (Mt. 6:33). The role of the Kingdom of God in Scripture is all-encompassing and God desires for us to understand it and participate as a part of it.

THOUGHTS & NOTES

In the Scriptures

- The Kingdom of God encompasses God's redemptive work seen throughout the scriptures and in history. It can be considered the central theme of the Bible.
- The biblical vision of the Kingdom of God is the greatest vision anyone can possess. It allows men and women to engage in a purpose, calling and destiny that are full of hope, eternal in scope, and worth giving their lives for.
- It is the single truth that unifies and empowers the people of God in every generation to include every tribe, language, people and nation.
- The Scripture speaks of the Kingdom in three stages:
    - *Past*, in the coming of Jesus
    - *Present*, now with us
    - *Future*, fully revealed in Jesus' coming when "every knee shall bow"
- The *Kingdom of God* or the *Kingdom of Heaven* appears over 100 times in the Gospels, with over 90 of those expressions coming from Jesus Himself. Matthew refers to the Kingdom as the Kingdom of Heaven so as to not offend a primarily Jewish audience who revere the Name of God.
- We also see the Kingdom theme continue throughout the book of Acts, in Paul's writings and in the book of Revelation.

In the Life and Ministry of Jesus

- With Jesus came the Kingdom of God—it is inextricably linked with Jesus Himself (Mt. 4:17, 23).
- The Kingdom of God was the central passionate message of Jesus while He walked on the Earth. In reading through the Gospels, it becomes apparent that the Kingdom theme is expressed throughout the life and ministry of Jesus, in His teaching, works, and even in His death.
- Jesus used many parables to teach truths about the Kingdom (Mt. 13:1-52).
- Even after His resurrection Jesus appeared to His disciples over a period of 40 days, speaking with them about the Kingdom of God (Acts 1:6).

The biblical vision of the Kingdom of God... allows men and women to engage in a purpose, calling and destiny that are full of hope, eternal in scope, and worth giving their lives for.

Do all the good you can
By all the means you can
In all the ways you can
In all the places you can
To all the people you can
As long as ever you can

John Wesley, 1703-1791, Anglican Clergyman, Evangelist, and Co-founder of Methodist Church

In the Lives and Ministries of Disciples of Jesus

` When the original disciples finally understood that the Kingdom was not about the current realization of Jesus' earthly kingship as it was about a heavenly rule with worldwide, generational and eternal purposes, they, too, proclaimed the message of the Kingdom.

- Through the book of Acts, the good news of the Kingdom was preached, argued, taught, explained and declared (Acts 1:6, 8:12, 14:22, 19:8, 28:23,31).
- Paul also wrote about the King and His Kingdom (1 Cor. 4:20, 6:9,10; 15:24; Eph. 5:5; Col. 1:12,13).
- The last book of the Bible, Revelation, as authored by John, a disciple of Jesus, speaks a number of times about the Kingdom (Rev. 1:6, 5:10, 11:15, 12:10).
- It is important to note that although the Kingdom theme continues throughout the New Testament, an even greater emphasis is placed by its writers on the King of the Kingdom, the Lord Jesus Christ.

Defining the Kingdom of God

How do you briefly sum up something that was, that is, and that is to come? In His entire ministry, Jesus never defined the Kingdom in concise, straightforward terminology. Instead, He explained its nature by a variety of images, metaphors, and parables. The Kingdom is like a mustard seed that grows into a tree, like a pearl buried in a field, like a net that gathers fish, like a landowner who rents his vineyard to evil men, like a king who prepared a wedding banquet for his son, like yeast that a woman mixes into a large amount of flour, like the owner of a house who brings out of his storeroom new treasures as well as old.... none of these metaphors, images, or parables exhausts the meaning of God's Kingdom. Instead, Jesus' teaching provides a variety of different perspectives on it. He shows us that the Kingdom centers on the forgiveness of sins (Mt. 18:21-35), repentance and faith (Mt. 4:17), righteous living (Mt. 5:3; 5:17-20), and new birth (Jn. 3:5).

Every Kingdom Has Four Components
- A king who rules.
- Citizens or people over whom the king rules.
- Laws and a government to administer its laws.
- A territory over which the king rules.

THOUGHTS & NOTES

- In the Kingdom of God, Jesus is the ruler and King. Those who submit to His Lordship become the citizens of the Kingdom, and God's character, ways, word and will form the foundation of it. The territory of God's Kingdom is every part of creation that is yielded to His Lordship.
- Jesus gave us a picture of the Kingdom when He taught His disciples to pray, *"Thy Kingdom come, Thy will be done on Earth as it is in heaven"* (Mt. 6:10).
  - In heaven, God's character is on display, His ways are honored, His word is obeyed and His will is done. God desires the happenings of Earth to be likewise.
  - Because God loves us and wants the best for our lives, He desires us to walk according to His character, ways, Word and will. This means basing all truth upon who He is. It means growing in the working knowledge of His ways, and intentionally applying His Word to our lives and obediently following His lead.
- The Kingdom of God can thus be simply defined as the arena where Jesus rules and His will is being done.

Kingdom Influence

God desires His kingdom to influence every tier of our lives.

- *The Individual* – Believers must come to know the King (Jesus) and His ways, obediently follow His Word and His will. We must adopt the values of the Kingdom as our own. And we must pursue God's purposes in a manner appropriate with our spheres of influence, gifts and callings.
- *The Family* – The family is the primary social building block of society. Therefore, as hearts and minds transform to Kingdom realities, the family should begin to function as a micro-cosm of the Kingdom. Husbands should lay down their lives for their wives, wives should submit to their husbands, children should honor and obey their parents.
- *The Church* – The Church is the community of those who accept the kingly rule of Jesus and find themselves bound together in common allegiance to Him. The Church is the embassy of God's ambassadors who, together, pursue their mission to advance God's Kingdom.
- *The World* – Believers are to take God's Kingdom into all segments of society, influencing them towards God's ways and purposes. Along with family and the church, this includes the spheres of government, education, the arts, entertainment and sports, media and business.

It is the duty of every Christian to be Christ to his neighbor.

Martin Luther, 1483-1546, German Theologian and Reformer

We must win rulers; political, economic, scientific, artistic personalities.
They are the engineers of souls. They mold the souls of men.
Winning them, you win the people they lead and influence.

Richard Wurmbrand, 1909-2001, Persecuted Romanian Minister

Characteristics of the Kingdom of God

The Kingdom of God is a kingdom of benevolence, holiness, and power. God's power flows through His Kingdom, at once, like a gentle stream and a forceful tidal front that overcomes darkness, deception and death. God's Kingdom pulsates with life-giving, soul-cleansing refreshment for the peoples of the Earth.

The prophet Habakkuk foretold that "the Earth will be filled with the glory of the Lord, as the waters cover the sea" (Hab. 2:14). That is the crowning feature of God's Kingdom. The Psalmist echoed this truth, saying, "All You have made will praise You, O Lord; Your saints will extol You. They will tell of the glory of Your Kingdom and speak of Your might, so that all men may know of Your mighty acts and the glorious splendor of Your Kingdom. Your Kingdom is an everlasting Kingdom, and Your dominion endures through all generations" (Ps. 145:10-13).

The Scope of the Kingdom
- The scope of God's Kingdom is to reconcile all things to Himself (Col. 1:19-20).
    - This includes all of creation (Rom. 8:18-23).
    - This includes all of mankind (2 Cor. 5:17-21).
    - This includes all of our relationships (Eph. 2:11-22).
- The scope of God's Kingdom includes bringing all the world's kingdoms under the Lordship of Christ (Rev. 11:15).
- Every tribe, language, people and nation (Rev. 5:9-14; 7:9-12).
- Every king bringing their nation's splendor before King Jesus in worship (Rev. 21:24-26). What a day it will be when we see the fulfillment of this truth in heaven as the nations of the Earth offer their glory and honor to Jesus in a heavenly procession!

The Values of the Kingdom – Mt. 5-7
Everyone upholds a set of values, whether we deliberately choose to or not. Values represent the things that are most important to us and they are seen in our attitudes, choices and behavior. Surpassing what we say or believe is important, our values depict what we cling to in the deepest places of our hearts.
- Our allegiances, affections and loyalties—our heart attachments—are an overflow of what we genuinely value.
- Our values are reflected in how we spend our time, energy and resources.

THOUGHTS & NOTES

- We are most willing to sacrifice for what we most value. For example—
    - If someone says they value the scriptures, but don't invest time in them, they don't really value them as much as they thought.
    - If someone says they value their relationship with their spouse or children, but isn't willing to spend quality time and energy developing and deepening those relationships, they don't really value them as much as they thought.
    - If someone believes in advancing God's Kingdom but is not willing to sacrifice their time, energy or resources to do so, they don't value it as much as they thought.
- Kingdom values are revealed in God's character, His ways, His Word and His will.
- Kingdom values often stand in stark contrast to those of the world around us. According to Scripture, we must die to live and become poor to be rich, giving is better than receiving and we must serve to become great (Lk. 9:23-26; Mt. 5:3; Acts 20:35; Mk. 10:42-45).
- Jesus is our model and the embodiment of Kingdom values and attitudes. It all starts with Him as the King who came in humility to serve and to lay His life down for others (Phil. 2:5-11; Jn. 15:13).
- A thorough reading and reflection on Jesus' Sermon on the Mount will reveal His foundational teaching on life in the Kingdom. Consider some of the Kingdom values and their blessings, recorded in this passage of Scripture (Mt. 5:1-12).
    - *Blessed are the poor in spirit*—those who are spiritually and emotionally in need of God's help in their lives, compared to those who are self-reliant and not needy of anything or anyone. *Theirs is the kingdom of heaven.*
    - *Blessed are those who mourn*—those who experience the pain of loss, compared to those who are unable to live honestly from their hearts. *They shall be comforted.*
    - *Blessed are those who are meek*—those who are slow to speak, quick to listen and, in gentleness, support the growth of others, compared to those who aggressively assert themselves over others to advance their agendas. *They will inherit the Earth.*
    - *Blessed are those who hunger and thirst for righteousness*—those who desire to walk rightly before God and see justice triumph over injustice, compared to those who seek pleasure, satisfaction and fulfillment for themselves. *They will be filled.*
    - *Blessed are the merciful*—those who demonstrate forgiveness and kindness to the undeserving, compared to those who execute vengeance and judgment by taking things into their own hands. *They will be shown mercy.*
    - *Blessed are the pure in heart*—those whose hearts reflect their sincere love and loyalty to God in who they are and what they do, compared to those committed to pursuing the self-serving intentions of their hearts. *They shall see God.*

The world is my parish.

John Wesley, 1703-1791, Anglican Clergyman, Evangelist, and Co-founder of Methodism

- *Blessed are the peacemakers*—those who work with God in the reconciling of relationships, compared to those who hold grudges and act in an aggressive manner towards others. *They will be called sons of God.*
- *Blessed are those who are persecuted because of righteousness*—those who are insulted, punished, or are falsely accused on account of Jesus, compared to those who seek the establishment of their own kingdoms over the establishment of His. *They will receive the kingdom of heaven and will receive great reward in heaven.*

• As Kingdom citizens, believers need to align their values with God. Doing so allows us to become more like Jesus in our attitudes, choices and behaviors.
- This is why knowing God's character, ways, Word and will is so important.
- This is why cultivating an ability to hear and obey God's voice and following the lead of the Holy Spirit is essential.

• Walking in Kingdom values and attitudes lets us reflect Jesus and His Kingdom to the world, allowing them to see a more accurate picture of who He really is and what the Kingdom is like.

The Heartbeat of the Kingdom – The Glory of God

The heartbeat of the Kingdom is the pursuit of giving God glory. In the Old Testament, the Hebrew word for glory, *kabod*, means "honor, weight, reputation, splendor." This speaks of the weightiness of God's presence (Is. 6:1-8; Dan. 10:2-19; Rev. 1:12-20). In the New Testament, the Greek word, *doxa*, in earlier history, referred to one's reputation, or one's "good name."

• Glorifying God allows His presence to come and rule as King (Ps. 24:7-10).
• Glorifying God declares His name among the nations and peoples of the Earth (Ps. 96:1-13).
• As Jesus was exalted God was glorified (Phil. 2:6-11).
• When Moses asked God to show him His glory, God revealed His character to Him (Ex. 33:18-34:7).
• To *glorify* can also mean to *enhance God's reputation*. While no one can improve who God is, often His reputation does not measure up to the reality of who He is because of the way His people have lived their lives.
• Glorifying God involves living our lives in such a way that people see and are drawn to the beauty and wonder of His character, ways, works and will (Mt. 5:14-16).
• Throughout Scripture, God's people are seen doing acts in the Name of God to bring Him glory. Here are a few examples:
- Abraham (Gen. 12:1-3, 7-8)
- Moses (Ex. 9:13-16; 15:1-18)
- David (1 Ch. 16:1-36; Psalms)

THOUGHTS & NOTES

- Solomon (1 Ki. 5:3-5, 10:1-13, 23-24)
- Jesus (Mt. 28:18-20; Jn. 17:4)
- Disciples of Jesus – prayed and ministered in the Name of Jesus (Acts 2:21,38, 3:1-10,16; 4:7-12, 27-31; 5:40,41; 8:12; 10:43-48; 16:16-18; 19:17-20; 21:12-14)
- Paul (Acts 9:10-16; 22:14-16; Rom. 1:5, 10:13; Col. 3:17; 2 Thes. 1:11-12)
- The book of Revelation also speaks of the glory of God (Rev. 1:6, 4:9-11, 5:12-14, 7:9-12, 14:6,7, 15:1-8, 19:1-8, 21:9-14, 22-27)

How does the glory of God impact our lives?

- Our Value—The life of Jesus and His hope reveals God's glory through us. We are living temples for the revealing of His glory (Col. 1:27).
- Our Purpose in Life—The Westminster Shorter Catechism states, "The chief end of man is to glorify God and enjoy Him forever".
- Our Vision—That the whole Earth will be covered with the glory of the Lord (Ps. 72:19)
- Our Prayer Life—By praying as the Holy Spirit leads in the Name of Jesus, He gets all the glory when our prayers are answered (Jn. 16:23-24).
- Our Service and Sacrifice—We are willing to do whatever He asks so that His Name is glorified (Jn. 12:23-26).
- Our Relationships— God's glory is at stake in the righteous display of our relationships, which is why we encourage, serve and correct each other.
- God's Call—We must finish the work God has given us to do for His glory (Jn. 17:4).
- Unity—A corporate passion for giving God glory will produce unity in the Church (Jn. 17:20-23).
- Evangelism—The primary purpose of evangelism is to reconcile people to God so that they may bring God glory by knowing Him and fulfilling His purposes in and through their lives.
- Our Reference Point—In everything we do, we must do it for the glory and honor of God (1 Cor. 10:31).

The heartbeat of the Kingdom is the pursuit of giving God glory.

Lord, make me see thy glory in every place.

Michelangelo, 1475-1564, Renaissance Artist

Deeper waters

To establish His Kingdom, God desires to restore man's identity and his purpose for being. Scripture tells us, "For we are God's workmanship, created in Christ Jesus to do good works, which God prepared in advance for us to do" (Eph. 2:10). The Lord's mission is clear—that all peoples should know Him, as it is written—"This mystery is that through the gospel the Gentiles are heirs together with Israel, members together of one body, and sharers together in the promise in Christ Jesus" (Eph. 3:6). The God of the Universe has entrusted to us the advancement of His Kingdom, a mission expressed by Paul—"Although I am less than the least of all God's people, this grace was given me: to preach to the Gentiles the unsearchable riches of Christ, and to make plain to everyone the administration of this mystery, which for ages past was kept hidden in God, who created all things" (Eph. 3:8-9).

God's Heart for the Nations

Since the fall of man, God has been interested in redeeming all peoples to Himself. The Christian church is to tell of the good news of salvation in Jesus Christ to every person "to the ends of the earth" (Acts 1:8). The starting point is to understand and respond to the Biblical mandate and, by God's grace, to develop His heart for the "lost" who are perishing.

Every Tribe, Language, People and Nation – Rev. 5:9-14, 7:9-12
- God desires the advancement of His Kingdom so that every tribe, language, people and nation might have the opportunity to know Him.
- Matthew 28 states, "Go into all the world and make disciples of all nations." The Greek word for nations was *ethnos*, which refers to a grouping of people based on commonalties.
  - A people may be connected through common historical or family roots.
  - A people may be connected by a specific culture.
  - A people may be connected through language.
  - A people may be connected through shared values and beliefs.
  - A people may be connected through interests, experiences, etc.
- An unreached people group may be defined as *a grouping of people that has no Christian community and witness within itself.*
- God desires an expression of the Kingdom among every people group.

THOUGHTS & NOTES

- God wants all the peoples of the Earth to know Him and be discipled (Mt. 28:18-20).
- God wants every people represented before His throne (Rev. 7:9-12).

Our God is a Missionary God
- We see God reaching out to nations as early as the book of Genesis, through Abraham, as God intended to bless Abraham, and through him, bless all peoples on Earth (Gen. 12:1-3).
- God used Israel to reveal Himself and to point the nations to Him. A few examples:
  - God revealed His power and might to Pharaoh and Egypt (Ex. 4-15).
  - He gave His commands and decrees so that the nations might see Him through Israel (Dt. 4:5-8).
  - He showed Himself to the Philistines through a shepherd boy (1 Sam. 17:45-47).
  - Daniel's rescue in the lion's den caused the king of Babylon to honor God (Dan. 6:25-28).
- The Psalmist declares God's glory in the nations (Ps. 96).
- A glimpse of the heart of God is seen in Isaiah related to the failure of the nations to come into God's house (Is. 26:17-18).
- God revealed His heart through the coming of Jesus, the Messiah.
  - He came to set the captives free (Lk. 4:18-19).
  - He came that people might be born into His Kingdom (Jn. 3:16).
  - He came to express His love to all nations (Mk. 11:17).
  - Jesus consistently reached out to people of all nations (Lk. 7:1-10; Jn. 4:1-42).
  - His final commission to His disciples to preach the good news to all creation and make disciples of all nations (Mt. 28:18-20; Mk. 16:15-20; Acts 1:8).

God's Thumbprint Among the Nations
- God made the nations of the Earth and set them in place throughout generations (Acts 17:24-28).
- Within every people group God has deposited redemptive clues on how they may be reached for Him and His purposes. He has set eternity in the hearts of men (Eccl. 3:11).

The God of the Universe has entrusted to us the advancement of His Kingdom.

Evangelism is not a professional job for a few trained men, but is instead the unrelenting responsibility of every person who belongs to the company of Jesus.

Elton Trueblood, 1900-1994, Quaker Educator, Philosopher and Theologian

I care not where I go, or how I live, or what I endure so that I may save souls. When I sleep I dream of them; when I awake they are first in my thoughts... no amount of scholastic attainment, of able and profound exposition of brilliant and stirring eloquence can atone for the absence of a deep impassioned sympathetic love for human souls.

David Brainerd, 1718-1747, Missionary to the American Indians

Evangelism

Evangelism is nothing more than God's deliberate work through believers empowered by the Holy Spirit to take the Gospel of the Kingdom into every household, hamlet and hut in the world for the purpose of persuading the lost to come to salvation.

Our Responsibility to Evangelism
- We involve ourselves in evangelism to bring God glory as the nations worship before His throne (Rev. 5:9-14, 7:9-12).
- We involve ourselves in evangelism because Jesus has asked us to (Mt. 28:18-20; Mk. 16:15-20; Acts 1:8).
- We involve ourselves in evangelism because the need of the world is so great (Is. 53:6).
- We involve ourselves in evangelism because Jesus longs for everyone to come to repentance and to know Him (1 Tim. 2:4; 2 Pet. 3:9).
- We involve ourselves in evangelism because the cry from hell is so great (Lk. 16:19-31).
- We involve ourselves in evangelism because reaching our generation is our responsibility (Ez. 33:1-9).
- We involve ourselves in evangelism because it will bring back the King (Mt. 24:14).

Called As Witnesses – Lk. 24:45-49; Acts 1:8
- A witness testifies to what they have seen, heard, and experienced for themselves (Acts 4:20).
- Every disciple of Jesus is a witness to what God has done in his or her life.
- Being a witness is not something we turn on and off. Our witness is the total package of who we are—our values, character, attitudes and actions.
- We will always convey to people around us what is most important in our lives. We must examine ourselves—are we conveying Jesus and His impact on our lives or something else? You are a witness to everyone around you of what stands foremost in your life.
- Our words and life are inextricably linked and will convey to those around us what we most live for.
- If we claim to belong to Jesus but our lives don't back it up, we deceive ourselves, and we may cause others to reject Him, the gospel and the Church because of our actions (1Jn. 2:4).
- We are witnesses all the time and do not need to wait for a special call from God to become one.
- Let your light shine so that others will experience Jesus (Mt. 5:14-16).

THOUGHTS & NOTES

Foundational Truths

- All people outside of Jesus are eternally lost (Jn. 3:16-18).
    - Lost people are not our enemies, but enslaved people needing Jesus.
- Jesus is the only way to God (Jn. 14:6; Acts 4:12).
- The Bible is the Word of God (2 Tim 3:16-17).
- We have been given the ministry and message to reconcile people to God (2 Cor. 5:18-19).
- We are Christ's ambassadors (2 Cor. 5:20).
- We are to reflect the heart of Jesus by actively reaching out to the poor and needy
(Lk. 4:18,19; Lk. 10:25-37; Acts 9:36-43; Gal. 2:7-10; Jam. 1:27)
- We have been given authority to make disciples of Jesus (Mt. 28:18-20).
- The Church is to work together as a team to reach the lost (1 Cor. 3:6-9).
- The Holy Spirit will go ahead of us to prepare the hearts of those to whom we will minister
(Acts 8:26-40).

Introducing Jesus
- The vast majority of people who receive Jesus do so through relationship.
    - Peter came to Jesus through Andrew (Jn. 1:40-42).
    - Nathaniel came to Jesus through Philip (Jn. 1:44-51).
    - The people at the wedding in Cana encountered Jesus through Mary (Jn. 2:1-11).
    - The Samaritan women brought people in her village to Jesus (Jn. 4:28, 39-42).
    - Matthew introduced his friends to Jesus at a party in his home (Mt. 9:10-13).
    - Friends lowered a paralytic through the roof to get a touch from Jesus (Mk. 2:1-12).
- Most people come to Jesus through family, friends, co-workers and neighbors who express
genuine care and interest in their lives, and serve them well.
- Ministering relationally, heart-to-heart, is the most natural and effective way to lead
people to Jesus.

Our Spheres of Relationships

- None of us is able to impact the world with the gospel by ourselves. But we can be
intentional about reaching those God has put in our sphere of relationships.
- Who, within your sphere of relationships, does not know Jesus? This is your starting place –
begin to pray for them regularly.
- You will find some within your sphere of relationships are not open to the gospel message,
but they are open to you.
    - Pray for them.
    - Love and serve them.
    - Continue to build your friendship with them.

Always seek peace between your heart and God, but in this world,
always be careful to remain ever-restless, never satisfied,
and always abounding in the work of the Lord.

Jim Elliot, 1927-1956, American Missionary to Ecuador, Martyr

True spirituality is the Lordship of Jesus Christ in the whole of life.

Francis Schaeffer, 1912-1984, Christian Philosopher and Apologist

- Others are open to you and are receptive to the gospel message.
  - Pray for them.
  - Love and serve them.
  - Present Jesus to them in a way they can understand and relate to

Opportunities for Impact

Jesus told His disciples, "In the same way, let your light shine before men, that they may see your good deeds and praise your Father in heaven" (Mt. 5:16). He understood that our redeemed souls are the primary exhibit of God's grace. As our transforming lives radiate glory in a dark world, we become His display of wisdom and power on Earth and in spiritual realms (Eph. 3:10). And while we are not informed about every conflict in the struggle between the kingdoms of light and of darkness, God depends on us to demonstrate his goodness, mercy, and love.

Actively Serve People
- Jesus laid His life down to serve the lost that they might know Him (Mt. 20:28; Phil. 2:5-11).
- Serving is a bridge across which Jesus can walk from your life to touch the life of another.
- Serve those who don't know Jesus as a family and as a Christian community.
- Impact someone's life by acts of kindness that simply go one step beyond the cultural norm (what people would expect).

Befriend Others
- Express your genuine interest and care for people.
- Be a good listener and a faithful friend that others can count on.
- Share your life with others. Invite them to participate with you in special and everyday activities. Let them observe the life of Jesus in you.
- Treat others with honor and kindness.

Cooperate with the Holy Spirit in Ministry
- Pray for the lost as the Holy Spirit leads you.
  - Pray for open doors (Col. 4:3).
  - Pray for boldness (Acts 4:29).
  - Pray for wisdom (Jam. 1:5).
  - Pray to be harmless (Mt. 10:16).

THOUGHTS & NOTES

- Pray for open hearts (Acts 16:14).
- Pray for conviction of sin (Jn. 16:8).
- Pray that the Holy Spirit will reveal Jesus to them (Jn. 15:26; 2 Cor. 4:4).
- Pray for demonstrations of power, signs and wonders (Acts 14:3).
- Pray for their salvation (2 Pet. 3:9).
- Listen to the Holy Spirit as you minister to people.
- Be obedient to things the Holy Spirit asks you to do (Acts 8:26-40).
- Be available to the Holy Spirit should He choose to operate in signs and wonders through you (read the book of Acts to see demonstrations of this truth).

Sharing Your Faith

God is the initiator, as well as the means, of our salvation. He is the One who gives a desire for spiritual knowledge and draws people closer to receiving Jesus and giving their lives to Him. This process may take a few minutes or a lifetime. But we need not fear sharing our faith. Evangelism will naturally flow from our life-changing relationships with God as we seek to unite our hearts with His. Through the power of the Holy Spirit, we will possess everything we need to communicate to those in our lives how they, too, can experience the regenerating power of God.

Sharing Your Testimony
What's your story? Share with others how you came to know Jesus.
- Life before you came to know Jesus.
    - What were you like before giving your life to Jesus?
- Events that led to your salvation.
    - Share the circumstances of your life that led you to respond to Jesus.
- The day you encountered Jesus.
    - How did you actually come to Jesus?
- Life changes since knowing Jesus.
    - How has Jesus changed your life? Where are you still growing?

> # Evangelism will naturally flow from our life-changing relationship with God as we seek to unite our hearts with His.

Every man is a missionary, now and forever, for good or for evil, whether he intends or designs it or not. He may be a blot radiating his dark influence outward to the very circumference of society, or he may be a blessing spreading benediction over the length and breadth of the world. But a blank he cannot be: there are no moral blanks; there are no neutral characters.

Thomas Chalmers, 1780-1847, Scottish Preacher and Professor

An Example of a Basic Presentation of the Gospel Message

- You are uniquely created by God.
    - God desires that we walk in relationship with Him (Ex. 33:11; Jer. 9:23-24).
    - God desires that we enjoy meaningful relationships in our life (1Jn. 4:7-8).
    - God desires that we fulfill His destiny for us (Jer .1:4,5; Phil. 3:7-11)
- What went wrong?
    - All of us have sinned (Rom. 3:23-24, 6:23).
    - We've each pursued our own ways out of a heart of selfishness (Is. 53:6).
    - We have been separated from God (Is. 59:2).
- God's Plan of Reconciliation
    - God came to Earth in the person of Jesus Christ (Jn. 1; Phil. 2:6-11).
    - Jesus lived a perfect, sinless life and died in our place, so that the sin of mankind would be atoned for (2 Cor. 5:17-21; 1 Pet. 3:18).
    - Jesus rose from the dead and is alive today, desiring relationship with us (Acts 2:24, 32; Rom. 8:34-39; 2 Pet. 3:9).
- How to Reconcile With God
    - Repentance (turning away from your sin towards God) (Acts 2:37-39).
    - Believe (or putting one's full trust) in Jesus (Jn. 3:16; Rom. 10:9-10).
    - Forsake all and follow Jesus with your whole heart (Lk. 9:23-26).
- Promises for Those Who Follow Jesus
    - All who call on the Lord will be saved (Acts 2:21).
    - If we confess our sins God will forgive us (1Jn. 1:9).
    - We have been created to fulfill a God-given destiny (Eph. 2:10).

Practical Steps to Impact Neighborhoods & Nations

The Apostle Paul pleaded for prayer for his own personal witness. He said, "Pray also for me, that whenever I open my mouth, words may be given me so that I will fearlessly make known the mystery of the gospel, for which I am an ambassador in chains. Pray that I may declare it fearlessly, as I should" (Eph. 6:19-20).

God invites us to set our sights on Kingdom advancement by praying for our families, neighbors, cities and nations.

THOUGHTS & NOTES

"Ask of Me" – Ps. 2:8; Ez. 22:30
- It all begins in the place of prayer. History belongs to those who pray!
- God invites us to set our sites on Kingdom advancement by praying for our families, neighbors, cities and nations.
- As you seek God in prayer, He will lead and guide you.
- Pray with faith as He shows you how to pray (Mt. 17:20; 1Jn. 5:14-15).

Dream God's Dreams – Mt. 6:10; Rev. 11:15
- God desires for His will to be done on Earth as it is in heaven.
- God wants the lost to come to know Him and prodigals to return.
- God longs for His bride, the Church, to function together as a Body for His glory.
- God desires that you catch His heart for your family, neighbors, community and world.

Victory Enforced – Lk. 10:19; Rev. 12:11
- We must remember that we serve a God who makes war against the enemy (Rev. 19:11-16).
- Jesus has already defeated Satan. It is the Church's job to bring its application on Earth.
- Jesus has given the Church authority over the powers of darkness (Lk. 10:19).
- We must be aware of the devil's schemes so that we can defeat him (2 Cor. 2:11; Eph. 6:11).

Acting Prophetically – Jn. 5:19
- Acting prophetically means viewing people and situations with divine eyes and insight and acting accordingly.
- How can we respond to the people and circumstances in our lives with Jesus' heart, hands and power?
- To function this way we must completely yield to God and be willing to obey His voice.
- To obey God may mean stepping outside of one's comfort zone.

Need Each Other – Rom. 12:3-5; 1 Cor. 12:21
- Jesus serves as the Head of the Church.
- We are a Body, therefore, we desperately need to team with each other to advance the Kingdom.
- Each member of the team has a role to play. We must find our roles, grow in them, and honor all the roles of the team.
- As we team together, let's remember to walk rightly under the authority of those God has put over us as leaders.

Revival comes from heaven when heroic souls enter the conflict
determined to win or die – or if need be, to win and die!

Charles Finney, 1792-1875, American Preacher and Revivalist

I have but one passion – it is He, it is He alone.
The world is the field and the field is the world; and henceforth that country
shall be my home where I can be most used in winning souls for Christ.

Count Zinzendorf, 1700-1760, Founder of Herrnhut, Moravian Leader

Christ Jesus and the Cross – 1 Cor. 2:2; Lk. 9:23

- The world desperately needs to see Jesus through our lives.
- The power of the cross needs to be demonstrated through us as we lay down our lives for others.
- This means dying to our rights and investing in the lives of others.
- The cross is our message, that Jesus died for our sins and invites us to follow Him.

Influencing Culture – Mt. 5:13-16; 2 Cor. 5:19-20

- God has called us to be salt and light in the world around us.
- As a Christian there is no difference between secular and sacred. Whatever God calls us to is a sacred calling.
- We are called to serve, bless and impact others via the 'Dozen Domains' of culture:
  - Family – shaping marriages and raising children according to the ways of God.
  - Church & Missions – equipping and mobilizing people to fulfill God's purposes for their lives.
  - Government/Law/Nation-Security – leading with a heart of benevolence, justice and wisdom.
  - Education & Students – teaching students character and truths revealed in the Scriptures.
  - Media – influencing the communication of truth via electronic, print and digital media.
  - Arts/Entertainment/Sports – revealing God's glory through creativity, performance and teaming.
  - Business – managing and distributing resources with integrity for the advancement of God's Kingdom.
  - Science & Technology – using current discoveries and tools to benefit people worldwide.
  - Health/Medicine/Wholeness – sharing resources that aid in people's physical, mental and emotional health.
  - Environment/Agriculture/Zoology – stewarding God's creation for the benefit of current and future generations.
  - Non-Profits & Service Organizations – meeting the practical needs of people via justice, mercy and hope.
  - Peoples – serving people groupings who have an affinity based on God-given distinctives of culture and calling.
- As we serve where God has called us, we will impact spheres of society with Kingdom truths, so that the demonstration of God's character, ways, and will can be demonstrated and multiplied.

THOUGHTS & NOTES

Neighborhoods and Nations – Mt. 22:39; Rev. 7:9

- As Christians we must act local while thinking global.
- Advancing the Kingdom involves reaching those in our present sphere of relationship for Jesus.
- It also means that we need to be praying for God's work in the nations of the Earth.
- Support missions and go to the nations when given the opportunity.

Glorifying Jesus – Jn. 15:8, 17:4; 1 Cor. 10:31; Rev. 4:11

- Glorifying Jesus is the heartbeat of everything we do as believers. It is about Him receiving the glory due His Name.
- Glorifying Jesus is enhancing His reputation in the eyes of others—meaning that the way we live our lives causes others to catch a glimpse of who God really is and what His Kingdom is all about.
- Remember, the primary purpose of evangelism is to reconcile people to God so that they may bring God glory by knowing Him and fulfilling His purposes in their lives.

Discerning the Messenger and the Message

As we invest ourselves to advance God's Kingdom, we must be aware of Satan's strategy to blind the minds of the unbelieving so that they might not see the light of the gospel (2 Cor. 4:1-6). A myriad of worldviews represented in false religious structures have thrived since Satan first began his deception in the Garden of Eden. Various world religions, primitive cults, distorted sects of purported Christianity, atheistic philosophies, blended beliefs and the occult have been erected by Satan to rob God of His glory. Each worldview mixes just enough truth in its web of falsehoods to lead people astray from a personal, lifesaving relationship with Jesus.

About half of the books of the New Testament were written to confront and correct false teachers and teachings. The religious background of the New Testament included such things as Jewish, Samaritan, Greek and Roman religious practices, folk religions, mystery religions, various blended beliefs such as Gnosticism, the Judaizers, and what is known as the Colossian Heresy. These represented everything from religious zealots, to mythology, to emperor worship, to magic and astrology, to the worshiping of angels and distortions about Jesus Christ.

The disciple, John, authored several books of the Bible to counter false teachings. He provides disciples of Jesus today with a triad of truth to discern whether a messenger and their message align with Jesus and the Kingdom of God (1Jn. 4:1-6).

If sinners be dammed, at least let them leap to Hell over our bodies.
If they will perish, let them perish with our arms about their knees.
Let no one go there unwarned and unprayed for.

Charles Spurgeon, 1834-1892, English Preacher and Author

Some wish to live within the sound of a chapel bell,
I want to run a rescue shop within a yard of Hell.

C.T. Studd, British Cricket Player and Missionary to China, India, Africa

What do they believe about Jesus?
- Who do they say Jesus Is? Does their representation of Jesus align with Scripture? (1Jn. 2:21-23, 4:1-3; Jn. 14:6)
- Do they agree with the following about Jesus:
    - Jesus is the unique and pre-existent Son of God, who in love and obedience to His Father became a human being who lived on this Earth and died a substitutionary death for the sins of all mankind, after which He rose from the dead for the salvation of mankind. Jesus lives today, interceding for the peoples of the Earth. He is the only way to God—the way, the truth and the life.
- Do they agree with the historical Apostle's Creed (which first appeared as a baptismal confession in second-century Rome) and Nicene Creed (which was approved at the Council of Nicea in 325 A.D. to counter heresy)? See the text of both these creeds on the next page.

Do they walk in the light and truth of Scripture?
1Jn. 1:5-10, 2:3-6; Jn. 3:19-21, 8:31-32
- Do they view Scripture as the inspired and infallible Word of God? 2 Tim. 3:16,17
- Do they view Scripture as the final word of authority related to faith, teaching and practice?
- Does their life and teaching align with the Word of God?

Do they love fellow believers?
1Jn. 2:9-11, 3:14-18, 4:7-12, 4:19-21; Jn. 13:34-35, 15:12, 13, 17
- Those who are born of God have a sincere and genuine love and affection for other Christians.
- Believers possess a willingness to lay their lives down for fellow Christians.

A myriad of worldviews represented in false religious structures...have been erected by Satan to rob God of His glory by keeping people bound in dead-end hopes as they worship false idols and gods.

THOUGHTS & NOTES

The Apostle's Creed

I believe in God, the Father Almighty, Creator of heaven and earth.

I believe in Jesus Christ, God's only Son, our Lord, who was conceived by the Holy Spirit, born of the Virgin Mary, suffered under Pontius Pilate, was crucified, dead, and buried; he descended into hell. On the third day he rose again; he ascended into heaven, he is seated at the right hand of the Father, and he will come again to judge the living and the dead.

I believe in the Holy Spirit, the holy catholic church, the communion of saints, the forgiveness of sins, the resurrection of the body, and the life everlasting. Amen.

The Nicene Creed

I believe in one God the Father Almighty; Maker of heaven and earth, and of all things visible and invisible.

And in one Lord Jesus Christ, the only-begotten Son of God, begotten of the Father before all worlds. God of God, Light of Light, very God of very God, begotten, not made, being of one substance with the Father; by whom all things were made; who, for us men and for our salvation, came down from heaven, and was incarnate by the Holy Ghost of the virgin Mary, and was made man; and was crucified also for us under Pontius Pilate; he suffered and was buried; and the third day he rose again, according to the Scriptures; and ascended into heaven, and sitteth on the right hand of the Father; and he shall come again, with glory, to judge both the quick and the dead; whose kingdom shall have no end.

And I believe in the Holy Ghost, the Lord and Giver of Life; who proceedeth from the Father and the Son; who with the Father and the Son together is worshiped and glorified; who spake by the Prophets. And I believe in one Holy Catholic and Apostolic Church. I acknowledge one Baptism for the remission of sins; and I look for the resurrection of the dead, and the life of the world to come. Amen.

There are three stages in the work of God: impossible, difficult, done.

Hudson Taylor, 1832-1905, English Missionary to China

Could a mariner sit idle if he heard the drowning cry?
Could a doctor sit in comfort and just let his patients die?
Could a fireman sit idle, let men burn and give no hand?
Can you sit at ease in Zion with the world around you damned?

Leonard Ravenhill, 1907-1994, English Evangelist and Revivalist

CASTING THE NET

What are three or four things that have you learned about the Kingdom of God?

_____

_____

_____

_____

_____

_____

_____

As of now, what are two or three areas of your value system that you see need to be rightly aligned to Kingdom values? Consider where you currently invest your time, energy and resources.

_____

_____

_____

_____

_____

_____

_____

_____

_____

THOUGHTS & NOTES

_____

_____

_____

Consider for a moment the heartbeat of the Kingdom, which is the glory of God. How might you live to better glorify Jesus? Do you have God's heart for the nations? If not, consider asking him for it now.

_____

_____

_____

_____

_____

When was the last time that you intentionally shared Jesus with someone who doesn't know Him? Is there a family member or friend that comes to your mind as you consider this? Take a moment and pray for them now that God's Kingdom will be advanced in their life as they come to know Jesus.

_____

_____

_____

_____

_____

_____

_____

What are the three parts of the *Triad of Truth?*

_____

_____

_____

'Not called!' did you say? 'Not heard the call,' I think you should say.
Put your ear down to the Bible, and hear him bid you go and pull sinners
out of the fire of sin. Put your ear down to the burdened, agonized heart
of humanity, and listen to its pitiful wail for help. Go stand by the gates of hell,
and hear the damned entreat you to go to their father's house and bid
their brothers and sisters, and servants and masters not to come there.
And then look Christ in the face, whose mercy you have professed to obey,
and tell him whether you will join heart and soul and body and circumstances
in the march to publish his mercy to the world.

William Booth, 1829-1912, Salvation Army Founder

CATCH OF THE DAY

Chapter Summary

- The Kingdom of God is "the arena where Jesus rules and His will is being done."
- God desires us to align our lives to the values of His Kingdom.
- The heartbeat of the Kingdom is to bring God glory in all that we are and all that we do.
- We can advance the Kingdom of God in the nations of the Earth by sharing our faith and teaming with others to impact our world.
- As we advance the Kingdom, we can trust the Lord to help us discern the messengers and messages of world religions and cults that would try to sway us or others from God's truth.

What are the two or three things the Holy Spirit spoke most clearly to you through this chapter and how will you respond to Him?

_____

_____

_____

_____

_____

_____

_____

_____

_____

THOUGHTS & NOTES

_____

_____

_____

_____

A VIEW FROM THE SHORE

"For you formed my inward parts; you knitted me together
in my mother's womb. I praise you, for I am fearfully and wonderfully made.
Wonderful are your works; my soul knows it very well."

Psalm 139:3-4

Have you ever considered how uniquely intricate and wonderfully God created you? He gave you a distinct set of eyes, fingerprints, DNA, each of which paints a brush stroke of your likeness on the canvas that solely reflects *you*.

When we were still in our mother's womb, God determined our physical makeup and our physical heritage. He chose our sex, our facial and body features, our intellect and aptitudes. In doing so, He chose our social heritage—our race, culture and language, our family and environment. He chose whether we would view His creation from three feet or seven feet tall, that we would see in color, have the ability to hear sounds and enjoy touch and smell. His hand was in the complete formation of our being and its legacy—even to the extent of redeeming the ugly effects of sin in our lives. His purpose was—*and is*—divine.

These truths remind us that each of us has a destiny. God created us, not as pre-programmed robots, but as individuals called to fulfill His purposes as we walk in friendship with Him in our generation. My life and your life have purpose, a divine destiny birthed in the heart of God before we were born. Our physical attributes, our personality, and everything we've experienced and received are intended for His glory.

Have you ever noticed that more often

than not a person's life purpose emerges, not when he launches out on his own, but when he invests in the lives of others? As Christians, the fulfillment of God's purposes for our lives comes in the context of our relationship with others. Though our purposes are unique and special, they will always be others-oriented. God uses people to shape our call, to team with us, and to remain involved in the end result of our calling. The fruit of our obedience to Him is lives impacted and Jesus glorified.

Biblical characters such as Jeremiah (Jer. 1:6-10), David (1 Sam. 16:1-13, Acts 13:36), John the Baptist (Lk. 1:1-45), Jesus (Jn. 17:1-5) and Paul (Acts 9:1-19, Gal. 1:13-17) knew they were called by God to fulfill His purposes. Perhaps, you, too, have a similar *knowing*. You sense God has called you to some task or service. Perhaps you've identified this purpose, or maybe you've glimpsed pieces of it. Maybe you're just now realizing that you have unique God-given gifts and abilities. Have you questioned whether God has a specific role that He is calling you to in His Kingdom?

In this chapter we will examine some biblical principles related to God's purposes for your life, assist you in uncovering what you are passionate about, and help you in the discovery of your giftedness.

SETTING SAIL

When we become followers of Jesus we are inducted as members of His team. This teaming can be expressed locally and globally as we belong to the worldwide Body of Christ. On an athletic team, in a band or business, we recognize the importance of positioning people to tap into their unique abilities. When people are strategically positioned, personal fulfillment, corporate success, and overall fruitfulness and effectiveness result. Of course, the converse is equally true—when people are poorly positioned, quality and contentment plummet.

It's important for us as Christians to discover our positions on the Lord's team. As we mature as His disciples, our roles likewise mature, equipping us to identify more readily our life's purpose, as well as our passions, and the areas where He has gifted us. Let's embark on this discovery by first looking at *purpose*.

Purpose

Some people think that life unravels perchance and that a given moment is about nothing more than a temporal exchange of ideas and events. The Bible tells us differently, though, promising that everything in our lives works towards a higher good or purpose (Rom. 5:3-5; 8:28). It also teaches us that God has planned a life replete with purpose and that we have a responsibility to discover and lend ourselves to it (Pr. 16:9; Jer. 29: 11-13; Eph. 2:10). We can begin the process of identifying our purpose in Jesus by studying Scripture to gain a fuller understanding of God's methods and agenda.

Jesus Lived with Purpose
Jesus lived His life out of a deliberate sense of purpose and vision. He knew who He was and why He had come (Jn. 13:3), and set His heart to be obedient to complete what God had given Him to do.
- "You are to give Him the name Jesus, because He will save His people from their sins... and they will call Him Immanuel which means 'God with us'" (Mt. 1:21-23).
- "For I have come down from heaven not to do my own will but to do the will of Him who sent me" (Jn. 6:38).

THOUGHTS & NOTES

- "I have brought you glory on earth by completing the work you gave me to do" (Jn. 17:4).
- "For the Son of Man came to seek and save what was lost" (Lk. 19:10).
- "For God did not send His Son into the world to condemn the world, but to save the world through Him" (Jn. 3:17).
- "I have come that they may have life, and have it to the full" (Jn. 10:10).
- "In fact, for this reason I was born, and for this I came into the world, to testify to the truth" (Jn. 18:37).
- He came to show us the Father – "Anyone who has seen me has seen the Father" (Jn. 14:9).
- "The reason the Son of God appeared was to destroy the devil's work" (1Jn. 3:8).

How Does God Reveal Life Purpose?

When we seek God with our whole heart, and seek wisdom from godly people and leaders in our lives, our life's purpose becomes clear. A study of how God revealed a sense of purpose and destiny to people in the Scriptures helps to discover one's life purpose.

- *Call from Birth*: There are times when God may speak to a child's parents or other godly people to disclose His intentions for that child's life. Jeremiah and John the Baptist illustrate this (Jer. 1:4-10; Lk. 1:5-80).
- *Heavenly Call*: God imparts a vision of purpose by intervening in a person's life in an awe-inspiring way, such as His audible voice, an angelic visitation, a deeply moving dream or vision, etc. Examples include Moses at the burning bush, Mary and the angel Gabriel, Paul on the road to Damascus, and Peter's vision (Ex. 3; Lk. 1:26-38; Acts 9:1-31; Acts 10).
- *Providential Circumstances*: While journeying through life, God may open doors of opportunity that result in His purposes being accomplished. The lives of Esther and Daniel illustrate this.
- Growing *Awareness* : A gradual revelation of life purpose commonly follows consistent obedience over the years. God's presence in the midst of one's service can also confirm an individual's life purpose. The story of Joseph in Genesis 37-50 provides a wonderful portrait of how God reveals His purposes while developing the character necessary to fulfill His call.
- *Prophetic Confirmation*: Along with revealing His intentions to the individual, God may also choose to use others to confirm that a person is moving towards God-given purposes. This particular expression often serves as a confirmation of what God has already spoken to that person. Read 1 Samuel 16:1-13 to see how God used this expression to establish David's life purpose.

Keep a clear eye towards life's end. Do not forget your purpose and destiny as God's creature. What you are in His sight is what you are and nothing more. Remember that when you leave this earth, you can take nothing that you have received...but only what you have given; a full heart enriched by honest service, love, sacrifice and courage.

Francis of Assisi, 1182-1226, Founder of the Franciscan Order

Unique Workmanship

Life purpose is an extension of the way God uniquely made us. It overflows from inner ingredients such as those listed below.

- *Natural Talents*: What natural abilities have you demonstrated since childhood?
- *Acquired Skills*: What skills have you learned over the years of your life?
- *Spiritual Gifts*: What is your primary spiritual gift(s)?
- *Inward Desires*: What do you really want to do?
- *Fruitfulness*: What do you do that produces growing, lasting, multiplying fruit?
- *Affirmation*: What do other people and leaders who know you best affirm in you?
- *Convictions*: What are you stirred or compelled to do for the glory of God?
- *Passion*: What particular groups of people, nations, tasks, or needs stir passion in you?
- *Fulfillment*: What do you deeply enjoy doing – feeling like you were born for this?
- *Circumstances*: What opportunities has God put right in front of you now?

Life Purpose Reference Points

- *God's Purposes*: Our personal life's purpose must reference God's larger purposes of fulfilling the Great Commission to "Go and make disciples of all nations, baptizing them in the name of the Father and of the Son and of the Holy Spirit, and teaching them to obey everything I have commanded you" (Mt. 28:19-20). In the big picture, this is the purpose every believer is called to, and it is our joint intention as a body of believers in Jesus.
- *Be Who You Are*: It is important to be true to who God has made you to be. You have a unique and valuable contribution to offer, so don't waste your time comparing yourself to others or wishing you had someone else's gifts and calling.
- *Teaming*: To fulfill our life purpose, God will team us with others of different personalities and gifts. Pay close attention to those whom God may be calling you to join for His purposes.
- *Serving*: It all begins here. Your life's purpose will revolve around serving people. Often, as you support others to fulfill their life's purposes, yours will emerge.
- *For God's Glory*: The ultimate end—what we live and give ourselves for—is God's glory. Our greatest purpose is to make known the character and ways of Jesus so that others will give Him the glory that He is due.

THOUGHTS & NOTES

Passion

As a part of discovering the purpose for which we have been born, we must consider the area of passion. Passion is that part of us that has to do with our deepest desires. It speaks of strong emotions, our likes and loves. It can cause excitement and motivation that enables us to sacrifice to accomplish our purposes. Some of our passions pertain with the things God has created within us for the refreshment of our beings, whether physically, mentally emotionally, or socially. Others relate to our calling and life purpose.

Passion Evaluation

Passion can demonstrate a God-given desire that compels us to make a difference in a particular area. To help you discover your passions, set aside an extended period of time and consider the following questions. Answer them as honestly as you can. Record your insights for future reference.

- What makes life worth living for you?
- If you knew that you would succeed, what would you like to accomplish?
- What makes you laugh and cry? Why?
- At the end of your life, where would you like to know that you made a real difference?
- When your name is mentioned to friends what do they say you are passionate about?
- What topics of conversation keep you up talking and dreaming late into the night?
- If you could have anyone's job whose would it be and why?
- For what would you be willing to be persecuted?
- What do you enjoy doing most for others?
- What do you find yourself doing with excellence, while at the same time being deeply fulfilled?
- What verses or portions of Scripture speak most loudly and consistently to you?
- What consistent patterns or themes seem to reoccur in your life?
- Is there a particular group of people that you find your heart consistently going out to?
- Are there certain needs or concerns that you repeatedly find yourself involved with?
- What does it seem that God most anoints you to do?

God loves with a great love the man
whose heart is bursting with a passion for the impossible.

William Booth, 1829-1912, Salvation Army Founder

Deeper Waters

The scriptures teach that every believer has an instrumental role in building up the Body of Christ. 1 Corinthians 12:7 says, "Now to each one the manifestation of the Spirit is given for the common good." Spiritual gifts—divine abilities through which God's Spirit pours His love, mercy, and power into the lives of others—advance God's Kingdom and bring glory to God.

The Spiritual Gifts

Paul tells us, "Now about spiritual gifts, brothers, I do not want you to be ignorant (1 Cor. 12:1). The Greek word he used for "spiritual gifts" was *pneumatikon*, which literally means "spirituals." The context shows that such "spirituals" were gifts and abilities given to Christians by the Lord and energized by His Holy Spirit. The Greek word typically used for spiritual gifts was *charismata*, from the root word, *charis*, which means "grace." In other words, spiritual gifts are "grace-gifts" that God bestows on us for the building up of His Body.

An Introduction to Spiritual Gifts
- God is the one who gifts us (Rom. 12:6; 1 Cor. 12:11; Eph. 4:7).
- Although there are other passages that address spiritual gifts, the three primary passages that deal with this subject are Romans 12, 1 Corinthians 12 and Ephesians 4. Gifts are discussed in Scripture in the context of the Body and are provided for the building up of others, not the promotion of ourselves.
    - The context of Romans 12 promotes unity.
    - The context of 1 Corinthians 12 is worship gatherings.
    - The context of Ephesians 4 is gifts of leadership given to the Body.
- Each member of the Body of Christ is given gifts to build it up quantitatively and qualitatively (Eph. 4:11-16).
- It is the Holy Spirit's role to put each member where He wants them to function (1 Cor. 12:11).
- Gifts are not earned or learned, but rather God-given extensions of His grace given for His purposes. We can become skillful in the usage of our gifts by yielding to the Holy Spirit. We can also grow in the effective use of our gifts as we use them and observe their usage in the lives of similarly gifted people.

THOUGHTS & NOTES

- When we submit our lives to Jesus, the entirety of who we are must be set apart for His use, including our giftedness. All that we are, including our personalities, can become vessels through which our gifts flow. However, to be used by the Lord, requires a breaking of (crucifying, dying to) our independence so we may function under the Lordship of Jesus.
- Just because God has gifted us in a particular area does not mean we should feel compelled to function in our gifts every time an opportunity presents itself. Even this area must be subject to walking in obedience to Jesus!
- It is essential to grow in godly character and allow Jesus to mend past hurts so we can function from a platform of greater wholeness. Character deficiencies and our lack of wholeness can hinder others from receiving from the Lord through us.
- At times it may seem difficult to distinguish between our natural abilities, acquired skills and spiritual gifts. Because we are God's workmanship He'll use everything that He has given us for His purposes.
- God seems to give "measures of grace" related to gifts on a periodic and permanent basis.
- There also appears to be various "measures of grace" related to spheres or breadth of influence related to gifts and calling.
- Many people, especially leaders, have a gift-mix with one gift serving as the primary and the others functioning in tandem with it.
- Is it possible that God doesn't give us gifts as much as He operates gifts through us? We must remember that ultimately Jesus desires to express His character, ways and power through our lives to impact others.
- The following indicators help us to discern if we are functioning in our gifts:
    - *Acknowledgement* — by those whom you walk with as well as those on the receiving end of your gifts.
    - *Consistency* — over a period of time and in various settings.
    - *Fruitfulness* — the observation of tangible fruit as a direct result of operating in your gift(s).
    - *Sense of Destiny* — when there is an inner sense that you are fulfilling what you were born to do.

Spiritual gifts are divine abilities through which God's Spirit pours His love, mercy and power into the lives of others.

Defining Spiritual Gifts

As we've seen, God gives us spiritual gifts for the purpose of building up others in a life of faith. Often times, these gifts override our natural deficits. Ancient and contemporary examples abound of people who lacked training or necessary qualifications, but supernaturally benefited the Church and the world as the Holy Spirit empowered them. God takes pleasure in turning the tables on the expected (1 Cor. 1:26-31), which is why He chose Moses, a stutterer, to lead His people from Egypt, or why He picked a slight shepherd boy—David— to defeat a giant. Our spiritual gifts may coincide or contrast with our natural make-up, but it is the same Lord of hosts who give us talents, aptitudes, gifts and skills. Through Paul we learn in Romans, "We have different gifts according to the grace given us" (Rom. 12:6).

- Spiritual gifts are special abilities given by God to believers for the building up of the Body of Christ and for the advancement of God's kingdom. Spiritual gifts contain a very real supernatural dynamic to them.
- The scriptures give us a representation of spiritual gifts. There may be others not directly labeled as gifts in Scripture, yet are confirmed by Scripture. For example: intercession, worship leading, craftsmanship, etc.
- Some spiritual gifts can be defined with more certainty than others because there is more information about them in Scripture. Because of the challenge of defining spiritual gifts, it is important not to get too bogged down in the process of definition. Instead, simply use what God has given you in the opportunities currently before you for His glory and the process of identification will become much clearer.
- There is a wide range of positions in the Body of Christ on how many spiritual gifts there are. Because the scriptures don't identify a specific number of gifts, we must do our best in being true to Scripture and in observing the work of the Holy Spirit through the lives of believers.
- The intention of the accompanied list of spiritual gifts, and their definitions, is to provide you with a means to discover how the Holy Spirit may choose to work in and through your life for His purposes.
- The *core meaning* in the following gift summaries represents words that are used to describe the gift in the original Hebrew (OT) or Greek (NT) language. The *observations* come from numerous resources and the author's years of ministry and are simply meant to help you better discover and understand the gift. *Cautions* serve as reminders of potential weaknesses or warnings to be aware of related to the gift. The *possible biblical examples* reveal people and/or situations from scripture that may provide a picture of that gift in action.

THOUGHTS & NOTES

The following list of spiritual gifts appear in the order that they are found in the New Testament, particularly in the gift portions of Romans 12, Ephesians 4 and 1 Corinthians 12. Many of these gifts, and the others that are identified in this roster of spiritual gifts, can also be evidenced in the lives of people in the Old Testament.

Prophetic Ministry – Rom. 12:6; 1 Cor. 12:10, 28; Eph .4:11
- *Core Meaning*: a foreteller, prophesy, to show or make known one's thoughts, luminousness
- *Definition*: A supernatural ability given by God to reveal and proclaim truth in a relevant manner for the purpose of strengthening, encouraging and comfort.

  Note: This profile simply represents a general overview of the gift of prophecy (inspirational, general aim of strengthening, encouraging and comforting), ministering in the prophetic (more specific and revelational words, providing God's perspective), and the role of the Prophet (God's mouthpiece to churches, cities, regions, and nations, foretelling His purposes).

- *Observations*:
    - Ability to quickly discern the character, motives, and attitudes of people or a group.
    - Are dependent on the scriptures and the Spirit to validate the authority of their words; are not afraid to speak publicly or take stands on important issues.
    - When sharing words from God it often results in conviction, repentance, holiness and realignment with God's Word and purposes.
    - May often "hear from God" by "seeing" things from Him (visions, mental images).
- *Caution*: A clear conscience and brokenness is required, otherwise they will appear critical, harsh and judgmental, instead of loving, causing listeners to reject their message. Also, remember that all prophecy is imperfect (due to the vessels that receive and give it) and needs to be subject to spiritual leaders for judgment and application.
- *Possible Biblical Examples*:
    - The 17 Old Testament Prophetic Books
    - Agabus in Acts 11:27-30

Spiritual gifts are special abilities given by God to believers for the building up of the Body of Christ and for the advancement of God's Kingdom.

There is no work better than to please God; to pour water, to wash dishes, to be a cobbler, or an apostle, all are one; to wash dishes and to preach are all one, as touching the deed, to please God.

William Tyndale, 1494-1536, English Translator and Martyr

Serving – Rom. 12:7

- *Core Meaning*: attendance as a waiter, aid, service
- *Definition*: A supernatural ability given by God to demonstrate love and support by seeing and meeting practical needs.
- *Observations*:
    - Has the ability to detect and meet tangible, practical needs; motivated to meet practical needs as quickly as possible.
    - Will often use practical needs as the determining factor in their guidance; enjoys fulfilling short-term goals.
    - Demonstrates great energy and strength in their work, determined to finish the task; are the invaluable "worker bees" of the Body of Christ.
    - Has a desire to serve without fanfare, yet needs to be appreciated and affirmed and to see the vital role they play on the team.
- *Caution*: The focus and effort of meeting practical needs may be viewed as a lack of interest in a person's spiritual needs, which is usually not the case. Also, the story of Mary and Martha is a reminder that in the midst of serving it is still essential to take time away from busyness to sit at the feet of Jesus.
- *Possible Biblical Examples*:
    - Martha in Lk. 10:38-42
    - Waiting on tables in Acts 6:1-7 (note the fruit in vs. 7)

Teaching – Rom. 12:7; 1 Cor. 12:28-29; Eph. 4:11

- *Core Meaning*: to teach, instruct, an instructor, teacher, master
- *Definition*: A supernatural ability given by God to teach God's truths in such a way as to enable others to understand and apply it to their lives.
- *Observations*:
    - Has a tremendous drive to understand God's truth and looks for effective ways to explain it to others so they can apply it to their lives.
    - Communicates biblical truths to inspire greater obedience to God and His Word; is frustrated when Scripture is taken out of context by others.
    - Desires to share the whole counsel of God to develop mature disciples.
    - Believe that truth needs to be tethered to the scriptures, then validated by human experiences.
- *Caution*: True teaching is not complete until the learner understands what the teacher has taught and knows how it applies to their life.
- *Possible Biblical Examples*:
    - See Jesus in the Gospels as a Teacher (i.e. The Sermon on the Mount in Mt. 5-7)
    - Paul – Acts, Pauline Letters

THOUGHTS & NOTES

Exhortation – Rom. 12:8

- *Core Meaning*: to call near, come alongside, incite by word, comfort, exhort
- *Definition*: A supernatural ability given by God to stimulate faith and growth in others through encouragement, comfort and urging one to action.
- *Observations*:
    - They tend to be optimistic and full of hope; people like being around them because of their upbeat attitude.
    - They freely give their advice to others with the aim of seeing them grow.
    - They enjoy relating real life experiences to others, along with God's truths, with the aim of encouraging, comforting and consoling.
    - They do not easily give up on people.
- *Caution*: The sense of urgency to meet the need right away must be tempered by following the Holy Spirit's lead. Can appear pushy when giving steps of action as they expect people to start doing what they have suggested immediately.
- *Possible Biblical Example*:
    - Barnabas, the Son of Encouragement – Acts 4:36; 11:22-26; 15:22-35

Giving – Rom. 12:8

- *Core Meaning*: to give, to give over
- *Definition*: A supernatural ability given by God to acquire and contribute resources for the extension of God's kingdom.
- *Observations*:
    - Has a capacity to make money and give resources to others.
    - Manages resources and lifestyle in order to give as much as they can.
    - Sees wise investments, and gives towards organizations and projects that multiply themselves.
    - Tends to have a view of God more as their business partner; responds more to logic than emotional appeals.
- *Caution*: Remember that the church's direction is determined by its leaders as they follow Jesus, not by the giver. This gift also needs to recognize that their obedience in giving is a spiritual contribution to the advancement of the Kingdom, not just a material one.
- *Possible Biblical Examples*:
    - Joseph of Arimathea in the burial of Jesus – Mt. 27:57-61
    - The Church in Jerusalem in Acts 4:34-37

The world does not need more Christian writers –
it needs more good writers and composers who are Christians.

C.S. Lewis, 1898-1963, English Intellectual Giant, Writer

Leadership (Ruling) – Rom. 12:8

- *Core Meaning*: to stand before, to preside, be over, rule
- *Definition*: A supernatural ability given by God to lead a group of people towards accomplishing God's purposes together.
- *Observations*:
    - Ability to see ahead where others don't and lead accordingly.
    - Vision-casting, providing direction, and creating structures for the accomplishing of various tasks are all expressions of this gift.
    - Demonstrates leadership by positioning people rightly to attain common objectives.
    - Defines godly leadership as serving people towards God's ways and purposes.
- *Caution*: Needs to realize that relational credibility takes time and is crucial for effective leadership. Also, as the leader, they must be ready and willing to endure personal reactions from others as they accomplish God's purposes.
- *Possible Biblical Examples*:
    - The life of Moses in Exodus
    - The life of Jesus in the Gospels

Mercy – Rom. 12:8

- *Core Meaning*: compassionate by word or deed, have compassion, have mercy on
- *Definition*: A supernatural ability given by God to relieve people's suffering by practical expressions of compassion.
- *Observations*:
    - Attracted to and attracts hurting people.
    - Is able to quickly identify with people's feelings and empathize with them.
    - Has an unusual desire to express love in tangible ways to helpless people.
    - Focus is on alleviating the pain or discomfort of people, particularly their emotional or physical suffering.
- *Caution*: Needs to be aware that rescuing people from their difficulties could be hindering what God is trying to do in them. Moving with God in obedience to His promptings for people, rather than out of emotions alone, allows God to express His compassion in power through the mercy gifted person.
- *Possible Biblical Examples*:
    - The Life of Jesus in the Gospels, especially when it comes to healing
    - The Good Samaritan in Lk. 10:25-37

THOUGHTS & NOTES

Word of Wisdom – 1 Cor. 12:8

- *Core Meaning*: wisdom, something said, utterance of wisdom
- *Definition*: A supernatural ability given by God to receive impressions of wisdom, which otherwise may not have been known, to apply to a person or situation for God's purposes.
- *Observations*:
    - Sensitive to the Holy Spirit's promptings, they are enabled to recognize insights God may infuse to a particular situation or person.
    - May grasp certain situations intuitively seeing God's solution for it almost simultaneously.
    - Receives wisdom that provides solutions in the midst of conflict and confusion.
    - Because it is a word of wisdom, it is something God gives to be shared with others.
- *Caution*: As with every gift, not everyone functions in this, therefore it is important to be patient. It is also necessary to be grounded in Scripture and to walk in the fear of the Lord.
- *Possible Biblical Examples*:
    - Solomon in 1 Ki. 3:16-28 is an Old Testament example that offers a picture of this gift.
    - James during the Jerusalem Council in Acts 15:1-36

Word of Knowledge – 1 Cor. 12:8

- *Core Meaning*: knowing, something said, utterance of knowledge
- *Definition*: A supernatural ability given by God to receive impressions of knowledge, which otherwise may not have been known, to apply to a person or situation for God's purposes.
- *Observations*:
    - Recognizes in certain situations that the Holy Spirit wants to do something and they position themselves before God to receive knowledge that could not originate with them.
    - May receive impressions from God in a variety of ways, including an inner knowing, seeing with the mind's eye, inner pictures or visions, feeling physical pain, etc.
    - When shared and acted on, it releases the activity of God into the person or situation.
    - Because it is a word of knowledge it is something God gives to be shared with others.
- *Caution*: Needs to be sensitive to when and how this word is shared with others.
- *Possible Biblical Examples*:
    - Jesus with the woman at the well in Jn. 4
    - Peter with Ananias and Sapphira in Acts 5:1-11

*The idea that the service to God should have only to do
with a church altar, singing, reading, sacrifice, and the like is without doubt
but the worst trick of the devil. How could the devil have led us more effectively
astray than by the narrow conception that service to God takes place
only in a church and by the works done therein...
The whole world could abound with the services to the Lord –
not only in churches but also in the home, kitchen, workshop, field.*

Martin Luther, 1483-1546, German Theologian and Reformer

Faith – 1 Cor. 12:9
- *Core Meaning*: persuasion, convince, rely
- *Definition*: A supernatural ability given by God to recognize in a given situation what God intends to do and to trust Him for it until it comes to pass.
- *Observations*:
    - Has immovable faith for what God wants to do when others around them don't.
    - Moves in complete confidence of God's ability to overcome huge obstacles.
    - Because they can see things "already done" they have faith when others won't.
    - God often intervenes supernaturally on their behalf.
- *Caution*: In the midst of trusting what God has said, it is important to listen to and receive the wise counsel of others around them.
- *Possible Biblical Examples*:
    - Daniel in the Den of Lions – Daniel 6
    - The Heroes of Faith in Hebrews 11

Healings – 1 Cor. 12:9,28,30
- *Core Meaning*: to heal, to cure, make whole
- *Definition*: A supernatural ability given by God to restore health and wholeness to a person.
- *Observations*:
    - The word used here is plural, "healings", which seems to indicate that various kinds of healings are available through this gift including physical, emotional and spiritual.
    - They operate out of a compassion and desire to see people made well.
    - They have an unusual ability to sense the presence of God when He is present to heal and God often demonstrates His power through them.
    - Healing may occur in a number of ways, including through prayer, touch, or words spoken.
- *Caution*: Like every other gift, following the lead of the Holy Spirit in obedience – both in direction and timing – is essential.
- *Possible Biblical Examples*:
    - Jesus in Mk. 2:1-12
    - Peter and John in Acts 3:1-16

THOUGHTS & NOTES

Working of Miracles – 1 Cor. 12:10,28
- *Core Meaning*: operation, force, working, miraculous power, mighty deed, powerful workings
- *Definition*: A supernatural ability given by God to perform miracles in the Name of Jesus.
- *Observations*:
    - These workings of power are often used by God to authenticate and validate the gospel message and its messengers; signs and wonders point to Jesus.
    - A person with this gift is often put in situations by God where His power needs to be demonstrated; this may also include deliverance from demonic strongholds.
    - They move in faith and obedience to God becoming vessels through which His supernatural power and miraculous intervention is released and experienced by others.
    - Sees spiritual realities and discerns imminent power encounters.
- *Caution*: Remember that miracles are initiated by God and are for His purposes. Follow His lead and He will be glorified through His workings of power.
- *Possible Biblical Examples*:
    - The Miracles of Jesus throughout the Gospels
    - The Disciples in the Book of Acts: 3:1-10, 8:5-8, 9:32-43, 13:6-12, 19:11-12, 28:3-6

Discerning of Spirits – 1 Cor. 12:10
- *Core Meaning*: to separate thoroughly, discriminate, distinguish, to try, to decide
- *Definition*: A supernatural ability given by God to perceive whether behavior or activity is from God, man or the demonic realm.
- *Observations*:
    - Heightened sensitivity and intuitive grasp of people and situations.
    - Able to identify deception or inconsistencies in other's lives or teachings.
    - Has the ability to see "behind-the-scenes" spiritually; can sense the presence of evil.
    - Can be bent towards trying to figure out what is wrong with something.
- *Caution*: Needs to seek confirmation before speaking what they are sensing; can have a tendency to be critical and judgmental if their lives are not backed up by prayer and godly character.
- *Possible Biblical Examples*:
    - Jesus and Peter in Mt. 16:21-23
    - Peter with Simon the Sorcerer in Acts 8:9-25

Tongues – 1 Cor. 12:10, 28-30; 1 Cor. 14
- *Core Meaning*: tongue, kind, a language
- *Definition*: A supernatural ability given by God to utter divinely inspired words in a language they have never learned.

Note: There seems to be a difference between tongues that may accompany the baptism of the Holy Spirit and is used as a prayer language, with the Gift of Tongues for public and corporate use that is interpreted by the gift of interpreting tongues (Read Acts 2:1-11 and 1 Cor. 14).

- *Observations*:
    - Utters spontaneous messages by the Spirit in a language unfamiliar to the gifted person.
    - In public meetings there is to be order when the gift of tongues is in operation; only a few messages are to be given and they are to be given one at a time.
    - When the gift is used there should be time given for the interpretation so that all present may be edified.
    - Suggestions have been made that this gift may also include the ability by some to learn many languages; although that appears to be something different than described as tongues in the scriptures.
- *Caution*: Tongues as a spontaneous message should not be given unless there is someone present with the gift of interpretation of tongues.
- *Possible Biblical Example*:
    - The Day of Pentecost in Acts 2:1-11

Interpretation of Tongues – 1 Cor. 12:10, 28-30; 1 Cor. 14
- *Core Meaning*: to translate or interpret
- *Definition*: A supernatural ability given by God to make known the spontaneous message given by the one with the Gift of Tongues.
- *Observations*:
    - Used in tandem with the Gift of Tongues.
    - Responds to a message given in tongues by providing interpretation for the hearers.
    - Edifies the Body by translating this message from God.
    - Demonstrates God's power through this miraculous manifestation.
- *Caution*: This gift should be exercised in conjunction with the gift of tongues and in an orderly manner. The message interpreted should align to the ways and will of God.
- *Possible Biblical Examples*:
    - The Day of Pentecost in Acts 2:1-11

THOUGHTS & NOTES ━━━━━━━

Apostolic Ministry – 1 Cor. 12:28-29; Eph. 4:11,12
- *Core Meaning*: set apart, sent out, a delegate, ambassador
- *Definition*: A supernatural ability given by God to pioneer, establish and oversee new works for the advancement of God's kingdom.
- *Observations*:
    - Authority to found and establish new works and the structures that go with it.
    - Tends to be trans-local in their thinking and in their sphere of influence.
    - Can operate within one's culture or cross-culturally.
    - In Scripture, apostolically gifted people moved in signs and wonders.
    - Note: While the office of the original twelve apostles was unique to them, the role of apostolic ministry continues today.
- *Caution*: For their own protection, they must be walking with and submitted to a group of leaders (elders in a local church or some kind of relational team), and they must recognize that a misuse of their authority can quench the Spirit and wound people.
- *Possible Biblical Examples*:
    - The Disciples of Jesus
    - Paul in Acts; Paul's Letters

Helps – 1 Cor. 12:28
- *Core Meaning*: relief, to take, to help
- *Definition*: A supernatural ability given by God to unselfishly relieve others of necessary duties freeing them to use their gifts more effectively for God's purposes.
- *Observations*:
    - They have a unique ability to see how others may be helped.
    - They desire to help others accomplish tasks in practical ways; a willingness to do little jobs, that, if not done, may actually hinder the Body.
    - Their practical service releases others to operate more fully in their gifts.
    - They often come alongside leaders to relieve them of loads, allowing the leader to give their full attention to the matters at hand.
- *Caution*: Their quickness in meeting needs may cause them to miss spiritual lessons that God is trying to teach them or those to whom they are rendering aid.
- *Possible Biblical Examples*:
    - Elisha ministered to Elijah as his attendant – 1 Ki. 19:19-21
    - Phoebe in Rom. 16:1,2

Wherever you are, be all there. Live to the hilt every situation
you believe to be the will of God.

Jim Elliot, 1927-1956, American Missionary to Ecuador, Martyr

Administration – 1 Cor. 12:28

- *Core Meaning*: to steer, pilot, directorship
- *Definition*: A supernatural ability given by God to organize and guide towards God-given purposes.
- *Observations*:
  - Has a knack for organizing, planning, developing strategies; helps units of the Body organize to reach their goals.
  - Likes to standardize methods and procedures for doing things.
  - Doesn't mind managing things initiated by others.
  - Identifies with the words efficient and effective.
- *Caution*: Because this gift tends to come alongside a leader, they need to be open to adjusting their plans to better serve the leader they are teamed with.
- *Possible Biblical Examples*:
  - Jethro in Ex. 18
  - Disciples in Acts 6:1-7

Evangelism – Eph. 4:11

- *Core Meaning*: messenger, preacher of the gospel, to bring good news
- *Definition*: A supernatural ability given by God to communicate the gospel message to unbelievers so that they become followers of Jesus.
- *Observations*:
  - They proclaim the gospel in an authoritative way that draws others to Jesus and are able to adapt their presentation to connect with their audience.
  - They tend to have an ability to influence people, to easily converse with strangers, and to freely insert spiritual truths into normal conversation with unbelievers.
  - They carry an intense unrest with the thought of unsaved and eternally lost people.
  - This gift, in context of Ephesians 4, also implies an ability to equip others to naturally and powerfully share their faith.
- *Caution*: Avoid becoming critical of others not as actively sharing their faith as you are, recognizing that all are called by Jesus to be witnesses, but not all are gifted in evangelism.
- *Possible Biblical Examples*:
  - Jesus and Zacchaeus in Lk. 19:1-10
  - Philip and the Ethiopian in Acts 8:26-40

THOUGHTS & NOTES

Pastor – Eph. 4:11-12
- *Core Meaning*: to shepherd a flock
- *Definition*: A supernatural ability given by God to tend and guide a group of people towards spiritual maturity and God's purposes.
- *Observations*:
  - Oversees and guides a group of God's people.
  - Expresses care for their flock, nurtures and grows people into the likeness of Jesus.
  - Models spiritual maturity, helps flock digest truth, and protects them from error.
  - Desires to see each member of their flock fulfill God's purposes for their life.
- *Caution*: The Scripture teaches in Ezekiel 34 that God will deal with those who neglect or abuse their pastoral oversight responsibilities. Pastors must be ready to bless and release those who grow beyond them, allowing them to follow God into the next leg of their spiritual journey.
- *Possible Biblical Examples*:
  - Jesus, the Good Shepherd in Jn. 10:1-18 and 1 Pet. 5:1-4
  - Timothy—read Paul's instructions to this young pastor in 1 and 2 Timothy.

Hospitality – 1 Pet. 4:9-10; Rom. 12:13
- *Core Meaning*: fond of guests, foreign (strangers), a friend
- *Definition*: A supernatural ability given by God to express care and friendliness to guests by providing relationship, food and a place to stay.
- *Observations*:
  - Creates an environment where people feel cared for and honored.
  - Embraces visitors and guests, quickly making them feel at home.
  - An ability to set people at ease in their home.
  - Creates a safe and comfortable setting for relationships to flourish.
- *Caution*: This is more than simply entertaining in one's home, although that, too, can be an expression of a hospitality gift. They must be sensitive to other family members when inviting others in to the home.
- *Possible Biblical Example*:
  - Lydia in Acts 16:13-15

Gifts are not earned or learned, but rather, are God-given extensions of His grace given for His purposes.

If a commission by an earthly king is considered an honour,
how can a commission by a Heavenly King be considered a sacrifice?

David Livingstone, 1813-1873, Scottish Missionary and African Explorer

Intercession – Ez. 22:30; Rom. 8:26-27; Jn. 17:9-26; 1 Tim. 2:1,2
- *Core Meaning*: to plead on behalf of someone, stand in the gap, intercede
- *Definition*: A supernatural ability given by God to intercede in the place of prayer on behalf of others to the point of breakthrough.
- *Observations*:
  - Compelled by the Spirit of God to earnestly pray regarding something on God's heart.
  - Is aware of the spiritual battles being waged daily and prays and acts accordingly.
  - Prays in response to the leading of the Holy Spirit, whether they understand or not.
  - Convinced that God moves in direct response to prayer (and fasting).
- *Caution*: Due to extended times in the presence of the Lord and having, at times, subjective supernatural experiences, it is important to be grounded in the Scriptures. It is also very important to know when, and with whom, to share what the Lord has shown you and when to remain silent.
- *Possible Biblical Examples*:
  - Abraham in regards to Sodom and Gomorrah in Gen. 18:16-33
  - Moses with Israel in Ex. 32:7-14
  - Daniel in Dan. 9,10

Craftsmanship – Ex. 31:3-5, 31-35; 35:38-36:1
- *Core Meaning*: workmanship, ministry
- *Definition*: A supernatural ability given by God to creatively form or build hand-crafted items to be used for God's purposes.
- *Observations*:
  - Has an ability to work well with their hands.
  - Utilizes various tools with skill to create or build.
  - Familiarity with and usage of all kinds of materials: wood, cloth, metal, paint, etc.
  - Their workmanship can look big and bold or practical and tangible.
- *Caution*: People with this gift often fail to see the reality of how they are making a contribution to the advancement of the kingdom.
- *Possible Biblical Examples*:
  - 2 Ki. 22:3-7
  - Dorcas in Acts 9:36-43

THOUGHTS & NOTES

Artistic Communication – 1 Chron. 15:12,19,22; Ps. 150:3-5
- *Core Meaning*: minstrel, song, proclaim, instruction
- *Definition*: A supernatural ability given by God to communicate God's character, ways and truths through various artistic expressions.
- *Observations*:
  - Music: singing, playing instruments, songwriting, leading worship.
  - Includes artistic expressions such as drama, mime, dance, art, writing, fine arts, etc.
  - Uses various art forms to uniquely communicate God's truths to others in a fresh way.
  - Uses creativity to captivate people causing them to follow/obey Jesus.
- *Caution*: It's important to remember that art is for the glory of God and to build up others. Those blessed with this gift also need to see input from others as constructive (not criticism). They also need to resist becoming overly independent.
- *Possible Biblical Examples*:
  - David dancing before the Lord – 2 Sam. 6:14-15
  - Jesus teaching through Parables

More gifts?
- Because 1 Corinthians 13 follows Paul's comments and instructions on spiritual gifts in chapter 12, some believe that such things as voluntary poverty and martyrdom, mentioned in 13:3, should also be identified as spiritual gifts. Others in the Body of Christ recognize things like celibacy, being a missionary, and the interpretation of dreams as spiritual gifts.

Discovering Your Spiritual Gifts

When our gifts fit the tasks to which we are called, we serve more effectively and joyfully. By understanding how God has created us, what passions burn within us, and the spiritual gifts we've received from the Holy Spirit, God can confirm our calling and set us on the path of His plan for using our lives to glorify Him in service and ministry. Here are a few practical gifts to help you discover your gifts:

- *Seek God* – Ask God to show you where He has gifted you for His purposes.
- *Walk in humility* – Be true to who God has made you and don't try to be somebody else.
- *Look for opportunities to serve* – Most people discover their gifts as they use them. As you take advantage of opportunities to serve right where you are with a right heart attitude, you will discover, over time, where God has called you to invest in the long-term.
- *Be obedient to God* – Step out when God leads you and watch what He does through you.

Let us live as though Christ were crucified yesterday,
risen today, and coming tomorrow!

Martin Luther, 1483-1546, German Theologian and Reformer

- *Gift attraction* — People with similar gifts often are attracted to each other – notice where those that you have an affinity with are gifted.
- *Through others* — Ask about a half dozen people who know you best what they think your gifts are.
- *Through your spiritual leaders* — Because God gives our leaders wisdom and insight for our lives they will be able to help us identify some of our spiritual gifts.

Ministry Modifiers

As we discover our life purpose, it is important to recognize God's timing in our lives. These five ministry modifiers are seasoned principles intended to help you determine where you currently are in your life as it relates to your purpose, passion and giftedness.

- *Seasons of Life* — What "season of life" does God presently have you in? What is He speaking to you about? Is it one of internal healing? Is God dealing with issues of the heart and rightly aligning you to His Word and Spirit? Is it a time to focus and invest in your marriage and family life? A time to learn? A time to serve diligently? A time to graduate to a new level in your gifts? Whatever the season, once you understand it, you will have an understanding of how and with whom to spend your time.
- *A Servant Attitude* — No matter what God calls us to, or who He calls us to serve, we need to be ready to express our servant's heart by jumping in and meeting the needs of others, even when it is off-center of our passions and gifts.
- *On the Altar* — Unless we place our life's purpose, passions, and gifts on the altar before the Lord, we may find that we are driven to accomplish them in our own strength and in our own time. Once we have fully yielded them to Jesus, He will be able to guide us into His purposes for our lives.
- *Obeying God* — Are you asking God to bless you as you actively pursue your own agenda? Or are you joining God where He is working? The easiest way to get involved in God's purposes is to observe where God is working and then join Him in it. Regardless of our gifts, it is important that we learn to let God operate them through us in obedience and relationship with Him, not according to man-based needs or desires.
- *Living in Balance* — There is wisdom to a balanced life. Along with discovering and living in your life purpose, passions and gifts, don't forget to pursue other key ingredients in your walk with Jesus. Worship, prayer, knowing God's Word, listening to and obeying His voice, developing godly character, pursuing personal wholeness, tending your relationships, walking under authority, and growing in the ways of God are examples of areas we can grow in.

THOUGHTS & NOTES

CASTING THE NET

What has God shown you regarding His unique purpose for your life? With whom, what, where, when and how does it involve you?

_____

_____

_____

_____

_____

_____

_____

_____

What are you passionate about?

_____

_____

_____

_____

What do you believe are your spiritual gifts?

_____

_____

_____

_____

_____

_____

_____

_____

*Truly, at the day of judgment we shall not be examined by what we have read,
but what we have done; not how well we have spoken,
but how religiously we have lived.*

Thomas A'Kempis, 1380–1471, German Mystic and Author

What is something you can do now to try an discover more about your gifts?

_____

_____

_____

_____

_____

_____

_____

Which Ministry Modifier spoke most loudly to you?

_____

_____

_____

_____

_____

_____

_____

_____

THOUGHTS & NOTES

_____

_____

_____

_____

CATCH OF THE DAY

Chapter Summary

- God has a unique purpose in life for each one us. We can discover our life's purpose as we walk with Him and recognize how He has created us.
- What we are passionate about can point us towards what God is calling us to do, thus directing us to fulfill our life's purpose.
- God is the one who gifts us, and it is our responsibility to walk with Him in the discovery and development of these gifts for His purposes and glory.
- Every believer has at least one spiritual gift, and often those called to leadership have a primary gift that is supported by one or more secondary gifts.

What are the two or three things the Holy Spirit spoke most clearly to you about through this chapter and how will you respond to Him?

_____

_____

_____

_____

_____

_____

_____

_____

_____

_____

_____

_____

_____

_____

CHAPTER 12
MENTORING & MAKING DISCIPLES

 # A VIEW FROM THE SHORE

"Then Jesus came to them and said, 'All authority in heaven and on earth has been given to me. Therefore go and make disciples of all nations, baptizing them in the name of the Father and of the Son and of the Holy Spirit, and teaching them to obey everything I have commanded you. And surely I am with you always, to the very end of the age."

Matthew 28:18-20

At the end of His time on earth, Jesus commissions His disciples to go into all the world and relay to others what He had given to them. This commission, stated in the above verse, was more than a good suggestion about what to do when He left them. It was a mandate from heaven.

The concept of making disciples (and mentoring) was laid out by God and communicated through Jesus for the purpose of expanding God's Kingdom in the Earth. The formula was simple—pass on to others what Jesus has passed on to us. This is a chief principle of the Kingdom. In a number of forms, we are encouraged to invest in the lives of others from the wealth we have received. We see this modeled throughout Scripture depicted in the lifestyles chosen by biblical greats. Moses invested in Joshua, Jonathan peer-parented David, Elizabeth mentored Mary, and Paul spoke into the life of young Timothy.

When we observe the life of Jesus we notice several things. First, He was obedient to His Father, even to the point of death on the cross. Second, He loved, ministered to, and taught the multitudes. Third, he invested three years of His life discipling twelve people. Pause for a moment and consider the effects of this third point. Because of His commitment and focus on investing His life

into people—twelve men, to be exact—every generation since has had the opportunity to hear the gospel message and walk with Jesus, including ours today! What incredible ramifications!

As we begin this final chapter, I want to challenge you to learn more about disciple-making and mentoring—and to find some for your life and to become one for others. Making disciples is the relational method God created to demonstrate and multiply His character and His ways in the lives of others. As we become His hands and His feet and stand in His stead, allowing the Holy Spirit to replicate His likeness in our lives, the truths of the Kingdom are passed on to the lives and generations of those behind us.

Look around you. Begin with your own family and then extend outward to your neighbors, friends, and those you work with. Whom do you walk closely with in the Kingdom? Now consider the things God has taught you that you can pass on to them. You don't have to be an expert in an area to be a mentor – just simply a couple of steps ahead.

Are you up for the challenge of investing in others? If so, the pages that follow will begin a new chapter in your life, one through which God's Kingdom can be advanced and where Jesus is glorified.

SETTING SAIL

Discipleship not only involves being with Jesus, becoming like Jesus, and following Jesus, it also means that it becomes our aim to disciple others to do the same. God has taught us many things, blessing us with knowledge, wisdom, gifts, and experiences that should be replicated in the lives of others. In Matthew 28:18-20 Jesus specifically asked His disciples to 'make disciples'.

Disciple-making is reproducing the character, ways and mission of Jesus in those around us expecting them to multiply the same in others. It is grounding followers of Jesus in core truths from the Scriptures so they can experience His Presence in their daily lives. It is teaching them how to hear from God and obey Him. It is helping them to become good relaters out of a spirit of humility and honoring those around them. It's walking alongside them in discovering, developing and deploying their gifts. It's helping them catch God's vision to touch the world around them. And, in the end, it's asking them to multiply the same in others. Who are you discipling right now?

Jesus commands us to make disciples. Mentoring is a method that can help produce that result as one person walks alongside others imparting to them things they may need in their lives, relationships or profession. Others may use the method of coaching people towards the things of God by asking purposeful questions that help guide people to discover things on their own. However we get there, the key here is being deliberate and intentional in obeying the command of Jesus to make disciples.

Let's begin by taking a look at Jesus as disciple-maker and then discover some principles that will help you to become an effective disciple-maker and mentor.

Observations & Principles from the Life of Jesus

Jesus has summoned us to His side, but not simply to put us to work. His summoning is a call to follow Him (Matt 4:19) and to enjoy Him in an intimate relationship (1 Cor. 1:9). This is foremost. If the disciples had lost interest in Jesus as a person and friend, they would have ceased walking with Him. In the context of a deepening intimacy with the Master, they began to think, feel, and act like the Master (2 Cor. 3:18). It is the same with us. Jesus' call to discipleship is an all-or-nothing summons, reaching into all the areas of our lives. His call requires that we give Him preeminence over our closest relationships and our dreams and desires. It means that we become His servants in the world. Jesus promises us that when we give up that which we cannot keep, we gain that which we cannot lose (Mt. 16:25). He calls us for a supreme purpose—"Come follow me, and I will make you fishers of men" (Mt. 4:19; Mk. 1:17).

THOUGHTS & NOTES

Observations on Disciple Making—Matthew 28:18-20
- Jesus has been given all authority in heaven and on earth.
- In light of that authority, He commands His disciples to go and make disciples.
- Jesus provides His disciples with all the authority they need to make disciples.
- Disciples of Jesus are to be made from every nation (every people).
- Entire nations and peoples can be impacted through the process of disciple making.
- New disciples are baptized in the Name of the Father, Son and Holy Spirit.
- Further-along disciples are to teach new disciples to obey what Jesus had passed on to them.
- Jesus promises that His presence will be with those who are making disciples.
- The imperative in Mt. 28 is "make," which translates from the original language to—as you are going make disciples. In other words, as you are going about the ordinary activities of your life, be intentional about making disciples for Jesus.

Observations from Mark 3:13-19 on Disciple Making
- Jesus called those He wanted (Lk. 6:12 tells us that Jesus did this after a night of prayer).
- They came to Him.
- He appointed 12 to be with Him:
    - so that He might send them out to preach.
    - so that they might have authority to drive out demons.
- Jesus replicated in them His commission from the Father to preach good news and demonstrate God's authority and power.

The Rabbinic Model
- As a Rabbi, or Jewish teacher, Jesus would have anticipated that His life and mission would be replicated by His followers. Teacher-disciple relationships at the time of the New Testament were characterized by the concept of *mimesis*, or imitation. This meant that the teacher's lifestyle would be discernable in the life of their students.
- Note the rabbinic feel in Jesus' comments, like the one found in Jn. 13:34, "As I...so you" (also see Lk. 6:40; Jn. 17:18,23; 20:21)
- We see this same feel in 1 Cor. 11:1 when Paul says, "Imitate me even as I imitate Christ."

The Disciple Making Pattern
- *Called*: Jesus called them to become fishers of men (Mt. 4:18-20).
- *Committed*: They left all and followed Him (Mt. 4:21-22).
- *Molded*: He taught them His ways (Mt. 5-7).
- *Modeled*: He provided them with experiences to show them how and what to do (Mt. 8-9).
- *Mobilized*: He sent them out to apply what they had learned by ministering to others (Mt. 10).
- *Multiplied*: He commissioned them to pass on to others what He had passed on to them (Mt. 28:18-20).

Discipleship Legacy
- The fruit of Jesus' investment in the lives of His disciples is far-reaching; it can be seen in the book of Acts and beyond.
- In Acts we observe disciples who were praying, obeying, sharing Jesus, teaching, healing, and moving in the same kind of authority as Jesus.
- The kingdom was advanced so much so that the Book of Acts refers to Paul and his team as those who turned the world upside down (Acts 17:6).
- All the disciples, except for John (who died a natural death), literally laid down their lives for Jesus and the gospel.
- Jesus' disciples multiplied their lives into others, creating a seven-generation "mentoring chain": Jesus – His Disciples – Barnabas – Paul – Timothy – Faithful Men – Others (2 Tim. 2:2).
- Jesus mentored the original twelve in such a wonderful way that the gospel message has continued to spread throughout the generations – right up to today!

Mentoring

There are wonderful illustrations of mentoring in Scripture. The following five along with Jesus and His disciples provide key insights into the truths of mentoring. Please note that although one person may be the mentor and the other the mentee, there may be times when the roles reverse. The principle is to remain open to receive from the Lord through each other.

THOUGHTS & NOTES

Biblical Examples of Mentoring

- Moses & Joshua (Exodus-Deuteronomy)
- Elijah & Elisha (1 Ki. 19:19-21; 2 Ki. 1-2)
- Jonathan & David (1 & 2 Sam.)
- Elizabeth & Mary (Lk. 1)
- Paul & Timothy/Titus (Acts; 1 & 2 Tim.; Titus)

Mentoring Defined

Mentoring is a relational experience through which one person deliberately passes along to another person what God has given them.

- Mentoring is a relational experience.
    - Jesus called the twelve, first and foremost, to be with Him.
    - Mentoring begins with relationship; before we can speak into someone's life there must be a level of love and trust.
- Mentoring is deliberate.
    - Mentoring that is intentional, where both parties (the mentor and mentee) are aware of the mentoring commitment, will be the most effective and bear the best fruit.
- Mentoring involves a mentor.
    - To mentor others does not require that one is perfect, but rather that a person be a step or two ahead in the area(s) they will pass on to others.
    - A mentor must be able to bring some expertise and experience in the area(s) where you would like to grow.
    - When looking for a mentor, find someone that you honor and respect, and whose wisdom and input you value.
- Mentoring involves a mentee.
    - Jesus spent a whole night in prayer before choosing His twelve disciples; if He spent that much time praying about who He was to invest in so should we – Lk. 6:12-16
    - If you have to choose between a person with tremendous skills and a horrible character and attitude, and a person with less skills but with great character and attitude, choose the latter.

Jesus mentored the original twelve in such a wonderful way that the gospel message has continued to spread throughout the generations.

More time with less people equals greater impact for the Kingdom.

Attributed to Dawson Trotman, 1906-1956, Founder of the Navigators

- Mentoring is about giving to others what God has given you.
  - God has provided each of us with a multitude of resources, including knowledge, wisdom, gifts, skills and experiences that we can employ to mentor others.
  - Areas in which to mentor may include things related to your spiritual development such as how to pray, study the scriptures, share your faith, lead worship, etc.
  - It also includes all kinds of other things like how to use a computer, how to bake, how to be a better leader, how to play an instrument, how to play a sport, etc.
  - Remember, everything God has given us is to be yielded to Him for His purposes and glory. We may never know, for instance, when a language we've learned is needed by someone who is called by God to serve a people group that speaks it.

 # Deeper waters

From within our personal communities, we can pursue discipleship through three types of mentoring relationships, each with unique qualities and opportunities for growth. To receive all that God has for us through each other's lives, we should prayerfully seek to remain active in Upward Mentoring, Downward Mentoring and Side-by-Side Mentoring.

Upward Mentoring
- Upward Mentoring is participating in the mentoring relationship as a mentee. It involves receiving from someone who has more experience and has gone before us in a particular area. The mentor provides perspective, wisdom, direction and accountability as they show us the way.
- Upward Mentoring challenges us to grow and become everything God desires us to be. It also guards the wells of our lives from becoming empty as fresh input pours in from others.

Downward Mentoring
- Downward Mentoring assumes the role of the mentor; supporting, raising up, discipling those who are coming up behind us. It is the primary means of developing the capacity, commitment and values that will enable the next generation to serve God faithfully.
- When we mentor others we will grow with the ones we're training. Mentoring tends to shake our complacency, renew our convictions, and challenge us to go deeper in areas of our own lives.

THOUGHTS & NOTES

Side-by-Side Mentoring

- Side-by-Side Mentoring refers to our peers/friends who we naturally engage because of age, job, common life circumstances, etc. They are "peer-parenting" relationships, where investments in each other's lives compel growth and accountability. Side-by-Side mentors really know each other, love each other, identify with each other and walk with each other in the midst of daily life. These relationships provide a fount of support and encouragement.
- There are two kinds of peer mentoring relationships. In-Side Mentors form within the context of mutual participation in a group or organization. These mentors share the same information and provide a safe place for confidentiality as only members of the same group can. Out-Side Mentors refers to those peer relationships with others outside of a group or organization. These mentors provide objective perspective that keep in check tendencies towards narrowness often held by a group. Both of these relationships are needed in our lives for balance and wisdom.

Eight Kinds of Mentors

One stop shopping—Wouldn't it be nice to find a seasoned person to mentor us in every area of our lives? Unfortunately, one such flesh-and-bone human being does not exist. In God's glorious economy, each of us has strengths and weaknesses. The youngest among us has something to offer the oldest and vice-versa. In other words, we're all capable of mentoring and we're all in need of mentoring. The key to the latter is finding someone with a higher level of expertise and experience to mentor us in that area. This means it is possible we might have several mentors at the same time, each challenging us differently. And, of course, the reverse is true. We might find ourselves simultaneously investing in several people, each of whom is learning something different.

According to Dr. Robert Clinton*, there are eight kinds of mentors . The first three are Active Mentors, noted by a deliberate commitment on the part of the mentor and mentee; the next three are Periodic Mentors who involve themselves on occasion as needed; and the last two are Indirect Mentors, those whose influence is more oblique. It's important to recognize the kinds of mentors we may need in our lives, as well as the type of mentoring roles we can play in other's lives. This understanding provides both parties with the opportunity for maximum impact.

would like to acknowledge Dr. J. Robert Clinton, whose material from The Mentor's Handbook, *has helped shape my understanding of ·ntoring. I have gleaned from his material on this subject and it is used here with his expressed permission.*

The Foundation-Layer

- *Role*: This kind of mentor facilitates the establishment of solid foundations and godly habits in the lives of new Christians, enabling them to faithfully follow Jesus and fulfill their God-given destiny.
- *Focus*: The focus of the Foundation-Layer is to come alongside and help root new believers in the things of God. This should include such things as building their involvement in Scripture, prayer, walking in the community of a local church, sharing their faith, serving and giving, discovering spiritual gifts, etc.
- *Helpful Tip*: Unlike all the other kinds of mentoring relationships that we will look at where the mentee should pursue the mentor, The Foundation-Layer needs to pursue the new believer. These first steps of maturing in God's ways are critical to their future growth and fulfillment of God's call on their lives.

The Guide

- *Role*: This kind of mentor facilitates a person's development by helping them to evaluate where they are and provide them with a sense of perspective, direction and wisdom related to on-going growth and maturity.
- *Focus*: These mentors are good at assessing and evaluating spirituality. Their primary contributions are godly perspective, insights concerning growth and maturity, and providing the accountability needed to see change and development.
- *Helpful Tip*: Those functioning in this role need to continue their growth in knowing God and His Word. They should be people who have walked with God long enough to understand the challenges, to have persevered through difficulty, humbled themselves when blessed, and pursued the will of God in the midst of diverse life circumstances.

The Coach

- *Role*: This kind of mentor provides motivation and skills that are needed for a task or challenge.
- *Focus*: The Coach is particularly important when it's time to step into a new responsibility or develop a new skill. They have the ability to impart specific skills that are needed for the task, and they impart confidence and understanding in the use of those skills.
- *Helpful Tip*: Identify skills that merit passing on to others. Consider how you will impart these skills. Model what you teach.

THOUGHTS & NOTES

The Counselor
- *Role*: This kind of mentor provides timely advice and impartial perspective on one's self, others, circumstances, and life choices.
- *Focus*: The Counselor serves as encouragement, a sounding board, a link to resources, as one who brings perspective to the big picture and gives advice for specific situations.
- *Helpful Tip*: Recognize the difference between those you may serve in this capacity periodically, compared to those God calls you to provide counsel to on a longer term basis.

The Teacher
- *Role*: This kind of mentor provides knowledge and understanding on a particular subject.
- *Focus*: The Teacher empowers the mentee by knowing what resources are needed and providing them. They also organize and impart knowledge on a subject, helping to apply that knowledge to the mentee's situation.
- *Helpful Tip*: If you are gifted as a teacher, consider the value of channeling your teaching skills into mentoring relationships. Identify the major subjects you can teach and tailor them to work with an individual or small group.

The Sponsor
- *Role*: This kind of mentor, having positional or spiritual authority within an organization or sphere of relationships, serves as a resource and counsel in areas of career and ministry development.
- *Focus*: The emphasis of The Sponsor is to provide guidance and wisdom as the mentee moves within an organization or sphere of influence, insuring that they receive encouragement and developmental support as they discover the most effective service. Most Sponsors hold senior leadership roles or have widespread credibility with people of influence allowing them to serve as a bridge on behalf of those they sponsor.
- *Helpful Hint*: As The Sponsor, seek the Lord about who you are to come alongside to mentor. The fact that you are in a role of influence carries with it the responsibility of stewarding it judiciously. Integrity and competence is essential to maintain credibility. The mentee should be advised to concentrate on developing his or her full potential, and when choosing career opportunities, choose to work with an organization that believes in and practices mentoring.

Few things help an individual more than to place responsibility upon him, and to let him know you trust him.

Booker T. Washington, 1856-1915, America's Foremost Black Educator of the Early 20th Century

The Contemporary Model
- *Role*: This kind of mentor is a living example from which to glean values, principles, attitudes, and skills. They serve the mentee as a model, or standard of what they would like to become in an area(s) of their life.
- *Focus*: There is less intentionality with the Contemporary Model than in the other kinds of mentoring because it is primarily the mentee's observations that influence their growth. Values, principles, attitudes, and even various skills can be caught through this indirect style of mentoring. The Contemporary Model will probably be unaware that they are playing a significant role in the life of another.
- *Helpful Tip*: The mentee should spend as much time as possible in settings that will allow them to observe the mentor. Identify the positive values and principles from their lives and seek to emulate them. Remember, no one is perfect, so don't fail to desire the good things that are evident because of failings and shortcomings.

The Historical Model
- *Role*: This kind of mentor is one from whom inspiration, hope and principles for fulfilling God's purposes for our lives can be drawn.
- *Focus*: The Historical Model represents men and women from previous eras whose biographies instill values, principles, and skills. They are heroes of the past whose lives we are able to glimpse from beginning to end, providing us with any understanding of seasons and imparting timeless qualities of perspective and valor.
- *Helpful Tip*: The mentee can begin today by selecting a Historical Model and researching his or her life in search of key truths that God may wish to impart through.

Five Points for Finding a Mentor

Mentors don't often knock on our doors and offer their services, so how do we go about choosing and acquiring a mentor? I suggest that you begin by asking yourself the following questions.

Where do I want to grow?
- The first step is identifying an area in our lives where we desire to grow. It can be anything. What has God been speaking to you about? He knows our needs and understands better than us that we could use some help in our growth.

THOUGHTS & NOTES

Who can I learn from?

- Wonderful mentoring resources surround us. Most of us, though, fail to look at the people in our lives through a mentoring grid. But look around you, ask yourselves—and ask God— who might be able to serve you in an upward mentoring relationship. Consider what kind of a mentor you need in light of your personality, the areas you'd like to grow in, and the style of training you think might prove most effective. Do you need a guide, a coach, a counselor?
- Who has some level of expertise and experience in the area you want to grow in? Do you honor them in your heart? Are you able to receive from them?
- If you think you may have found a possible mentor, ask if you could meet with them at a convenient time in their schedule. You don't necessarily need to declare your interest in establishing a mentor relationship right away, but take time to build a level of friendship and relational comfort.
- Is there a sense of naturalness in the relationship? Is there a good chemistry between you? Do they take a sincere interest in your life? Do you feel honored and encouraged by them when you are with them?
- As you get to know them, do you find yourself drawn to them? As you talk together, do you find that they have the expertise and experience in the area you desire to cultivate?
- If the answer to these questions is yes, prayerfully consider asking if they might be willing to spend some time with you so you could learn from them.

What's the agenda and what works best for the mentor?

- If the mentor agrees to a mentoring relationship, schedule a time when the two of you can meet to talk about what your times together will look like. Is there a certain book to read or a project to work on together? How often will you meet and for how long? This is a time to lay out expectations and to set goals for what will be accomplished.
- Arrange your schedule around the mentor. Find out what works best for them and accommodate the demands of their lives. They are giving up their time for you so do all you can to work with them.

How do I receive the most from a mentor?

- Come to your times together prepared. Ask questions. Listen intently. Write down what they teach you and look for ways to apply it in your life. Invite them to hold you accountable.
- Remember, you've asked them to help you. It is always the mentee's responsibility to pursue the mentor, not vice-versa. The fastest way to end a mentoring relationship is neglecting to show up for an appointment, or to not invest yourself in what has been taught.

What happens next?

- Continue to be diligent through the length of the commitment. When the pre-established concluding point arrives, you can agree to continue for another period of time or celebrate together and move on. If you are interested in another mentor to help you along the next leg of your journey, your present mentor may have counsel or a resource to connect you with. Seek their advice and remember to honor them for the time and investment they have made in your life.

Five Points for Mentoring Others

Mentoring is not an assembly-line—we are not striving to make die-cast replicas of ourselves. On the contrary, as disciples of Jesus we desire to impart Christlikeness, while prayerfully nourishing beliefs that breathe life into the mind, heart and soul of those we mentor. A good mentor always aims to reproduce assets in others while valuing the differences each person brings to the process. Because our heavenly Father is the giver of gifts, the wise mentor celebrates the mentee's God-ordained uniqueness and comes alongside them to develop them further.

Examine Yourself

- Along with catching Jesus' heart to invest in others, there are some practical considerations before launching into mentoring. You must examine your values and priorities, and look at how you spend your time so you will be able to give yourself to coming alongside others in the mentoring relationship.

Recognize What Kind(s) of Mentor You Are

- Earlier in this chapter, we looked at eight kinds of mentors. It is not unusual to find yourself able to function comfortably in more than one category. Generally, though, one or two kinds of mentoring will come more naturally. Of the eight kinds of mentors, which one or two do you most identify yourself with?
- It is important to acknowledge the kind(s) of mentor you are. This will help you determine if you're a good match for someone who asks you to mentor them. If, for example, someone needs a coach to provide them with worship leading skills, and you're not a worship leader, nor are you a coach, then you know someone else is better suited for their needs.

THOUGHTS & NOTES

Choosing Mentees

- Prayerfully ask God to show you who you are to invest in. Jesus prayed about it ahead of time (Lk. 6:12-16); so should we.
- If someone approaches you about mentoring them, the first question you need to ask is, "In what area?" Where do they need your help? Ask them to be specific. This immediately allows you to evaluate whether their need matches your skill set and whether your kind of mentoring would meet their desired end. In other words, if they need a Counselor and you're a Foundation-Layer, you know that someone else is better suited for the relationship.
- When you are considering mentoring someone, a comfortable relational connect is very important. If there is not a natural relational chemistry, this may not be someone you are to invest your life in.
- Qualities to look for in a potential mentee include humility, faithfulness, commitment, a good attitude, teachability, a servant's heart, and the Fear of the Lord. These seven virtues will fuel a positive, productive time together.
- When considering a possible mentee, you don't need to tell them you are going to mentor them. Just begin relationally and see where God takes it. Love them, honor them, and serve them. Speak into their lives to the degree they allow you. If both of you determine that it is emerging into a mentoring relationship, just take it from there.
- One thing I have noted in my years of mentoring is that like-gifted people are attracted to each other. For example, because I am a leader, I attract other leaders, and what begins as friendship may develop into a mentoring relationship. Pay attention to like-gifted people around you and listen to what the Lord may say to you.

Because our heavenly Father is the giver of gifts, the wise mentor celebrates the mentee's God-ordained uniqueness and comes alongside them to develop them further.

Men, where are your men? Ladies, where are your women?
With whom are you investing your life?

Dawson Trotman, 1906-1956, Founder of the Navigators

Determine the Agenda

- Once you know from the Lord who you are to mentor, you must also determine the agenda, boundaries that need to be set in place, expectations and/ or requirements, when and where you will meet, resources to be used, and what the end result in the mentee should look like. These factors should be established on the front end.
- Mentoring can take place one-on-one, in a small group, or in larger group settings. I enjoy groups of a dozen or so that have the same developmental need. When mentoring in this fashion, I remain available to them for one-on-one meetings as necessary to help them process and apply what we are learning more personally.
- The mentor should use a combination of instruction, demonstration, experiences and accountability to help the mentee grow. I personally like the Jesus model: (1) Jesus did it and the disciples watched; (2) Jesus did it and the disciples helped; (3) The disciples did it and Jesus coached and encouraged; (4) The disciples did it and Jesus left.

Commit to Complete and Celebrate

- Stay committed to the *people* you mentor, during the *process* of working with them, and remain faithful to the *purpose* for which you began.
- Finish what you started. As far as time is concerned, I recommend about 3 months for the first go around. You can always re-up if the desire is there for both parties to continue.
- Part of the completion process is making sure the mentee is prepared to multiply their life into the lives of others. Ultimately, multiplication is a key goal.
- Just as Paul passed by his mentor, Barnabas, be prepared to allow mentees that are more gifted than you to pass you by. Be their greatest encouragement and look for ways to promote them before and to others.
- Once the season of mentoring comes to an end, celebrate together what God has done. Go out to eat, have a party, or do something fun together. Pray over the mentee and release them to follow God into the next part of their journey with Him.

The mentor should use a combination of instruction, demonstration, experiences and accountability to help the mentee grow.

THOUGHTS & NOTES

CASTING THE NET

What are a couple of key principles you observed from the life of Jesus as disciple-maker that you can implement in your life?

_____

_____

_____

_____

_____

_____

_____

Consider some areas of expertise and experience that you may be able to pass on to others. Think first about the issues of your life spiritually, and then broader areas of your life. Write them down here.

_____

_____

_____

_____

_____

_____

_____

_____

_____

_____

_____

_____

Sow an act and you reap a habit. Sow a habit and you reap a character.
Sow a character and you reap a destiny.

Charles Reade, 1814–84, English Novelist and Dramatist

Think of your spheres of mentoring. Who is in your life that may be an upward mentor? Who would be a side-by-side mentor in your life? What about downward mentoring? Who might you be able to invest in for the sake of the kingdom?

_____

_____

_____

_____

_____

_____

_____

What kind of mentor do you need in your life right now?

_____

_____

_____

_____

What kind(s) of mentor are you?

_____

_____

_____

_____

_____

THOUGHTS & NOTES ━━━━━━━

_____

_____

_____

CATCH OF THE DAY

Chapter Summary

- Jesus has modeled for us the principle of mentoring and given us the mandate and authority to make disciples.
- Mentoring is defined as a relational experience through which one person deliberately gives to another person what God has given them.
- There are three spheres of mentoring relationships: Upward Mentoring, Downward Mentoring and Side-by-Side Mentoring.
- There are eight kinds of mentors:

    - The Foundation-Layer   - The Teacher
    - The Guide   - The Sponsor
    - The Coach   - The Contemporary Model
    - The Counselor   - The Historical Model

- God has provided us with many wonderful people in our lives from whom we can receive mentoring and to whom we can invest ourselves for God's purposes as He leads.

What are the two or three things the Holy Spirit spoke most clearly to you about through this chapter and how will you respond to Him?

_____

_____

_____

_____

_____

_____

*If you read history you will find that the Christians who did most
for the present world were those who thought most of the next.
The apostles themselves, who set out on foot to convert the Roman Empire,
the great men who built up the Middle Ages, the English evangelicals
who abolished the slave trade, all left their mark on earth, precisely because
their minds were occupied with Heaven. It is since Christians have largely ceased
to think of the other world that they have become so ineffective in this one.
Aim at Heaven and you will get earth "thrown in."
Aim at earth and you will get neither.*

C.S. Lewis, 1898-1963, English Intellectual Giant, Writer

REFLECTIONS
on the Character of God

A VIEW FROM THE SHORE

"This is what the Lord says: 'Let not the wise man boast of his wisdom
or the strong man boast of his strength or the rich man boast in his riches,
but let him who boasts boast about this: that he knows and understands me,
that I am the Lord, who exercises kindness, justice and righteousness
on the earth, for in these I delight,' declares the Lord."

Jeremiah 9:23-24

The primary purpose of our Christian life is the pursuit of knowing God. God reveals Himself in Scripture through His character. To help you draw closer to God, you will find 52 names, titles and attributes that depict His nature. The idea is to reflect on one per week throughout the year to allow the Holy Spirit to renew your heart and mind and to convey who God is and what He's really like.

Each aspect of God's character has two parts to it: *Reflection* and *Life Response*. The *Reflection* section will provide you with five scriptures that pertain to a certain aspect of God's character. Take one passage per day and reflect on it in the context you find it. You have been provided with space to note insights given to you by the Holy Spirit.

The *Life Response* section provides you with two additional verses to ponder. These two passages relate to your response to that particular name, title or attribute of God. It may be in thanks or praise, or by walking in obedience to become more like Jesus in an area of your life. These verses also demonstrate how that particular aspect of God's

character applies to your life and relationships so the world may have a more accurate picture of who God is through your life. Use the space provided to record what God may ask you to do to become more like Him in your character.

Feel free to go through the list in order, or jump around depending on what is going on in your life. Once you have completed the 52 traits that have been provided, you will find over 170 other names, titles and attributes of God to pursue in Scripture.

As you begin this journey to know God more, keep these two thoughts close to your heart and mind: first, as David said in Psalm 27:4, *"One thing I ask of the Lord, this is what I seek: that I may dwell in the house of the Lord all the days of my life, to gaze upon the beauty of the Lord and to seek Him in His temple."* Second, that *"the chief end of man is to glorify God and enjoy Him forever"* (Westminster Catechism).

Set your heart on dwelling in God's presence all the days of your life. As you do, you'll find yourself gazing upon His beauty and enjoying Him forever.

God Almighty

- **Reflection**
  Job 11:7-9; Isaiah 6:1-8; Revelation 4:1-11; Revelation 11:15-19; Revelation 15:1-4

_____

_____

_____

_____

_____

_____

_____

_____

- **Life Response**
  Genesis 17:1; Amos 5:14

_____

_____

_____

God's Anger

- **Reflection**
  Exodus 32:1-4; Numbers 11:1-3; Numbers 12:1-16; Psalm 145:8; John 2:13-17

_____

_____

_____

_____

_____

_____

_____

- **Life Response**
  Ephesians 4:26,27; James 1:19-21

_____

_____

_____

Comforter •

- **Reflection**
  Psalm 23:4; Psalm 71:19-21 / 94:17-19; Psalm 119:50,52,76; Isaiah 12:1,2; Isaiah 66:12,13

_____

_____

_____

_____

_____

_____

_____

_____

- **Life Response**
  Isaiah 40:1; 2 Corinthians 1:3-7

_____

_____

_____

God's Compassion •

- **Reflection**
  Psalm 103:13; Psalm 116:5; Matthew 9:35-38; Matthew 15:29-38; James 5:11

_____

_____

_____

_____

_____

_____

_____

- **Life Response**
  Ephesians 4:32; 1 Peter 3:8,9

_____

_____

_____

Creator

- **Reflection**
  Genesis 1:1-2:25; Nehemiah 9:6; Colossians 1:15-17; Hebrews 11:3; Revelation 4:9-11

  _____

  _____

  _____

  _____

  _____

  _____

  _____

  _____

- **Life Response**
  Ephesians 2:10; Ecclesiastes 12:1

  _____

  _____

  _____

Deliverer

- **Reflection**
  Exodus 14:5-31; Daniel 3:1-30; Daniel 6:1-28; Psalm 34:4-7; Acts 12:1-19

  _____

  _____

  _____

  _____

  _____

  _____

  _____

- **Life Response**
  2 Corinthians 1:10; 2 Timothy 4:16-18

  _____

  _____

  _____

REFLECTIONS ON THE CHARACTER OF GOD

The Eternal God

- **Reflection**
  Psalm 135:13; Psalm 145:13; 1 Timothy 1:17; 2 Peter 3:8; Revelation 1:8

- **Life Response**
  John 3:16; 2 Corinthians 5:1

God's Faithfulness

- **Reflection**
  Deuteronomy 7:9; Psalm 145:13; Lam. 3:23; 1 Corinthians 10:13; 1 Thess. 5:23,24 5:23,24

- **Life Response**
  Matthew 25:21-23; Revelation 2:10

Father

- **Reflection**

Isaiah 9:6; Isaiah 64:8; Matthew 6:25-34; 2 Corinthians 6:18; 1 John 3:1

_____

_____

_____

_____

_____

_____

_____

_____

- **Life Response**

Romans 8:15-17; Galatians 4:4-7

_____

_____

_____

God's Forgiveness

- **Reflection**

Psalm 103:2-5; Matthew 6:9-15; John 8:1-11; Ephesians 1:7,8; 1 John 1:9

_____

_____

_____

_____

_____

_____

_____

- **Life Response**

Matthew 18:21-35; Colossians 3:13

_____

_____

_____

————————————————————————————— *Friend* ●

- **Reflection**
  Exodus 33:7-11; Proverbs 18:24; Matthew 11:19; Luke 19:1-10; James 2:23

_____

_____

_____

_____

_____

_____

_____

_____

- **Life Response**
  1 Samuel 18:1-4; John 15:13-15

_____

_____

_____

————————————————————————— *God's Gentleness* ●

- **Reflection**
  1 Kings 19:11-13; Isaiah 40:11; Matthew 11:28-30; Matthew 21:1-5; 2 Corinthians 10:1

_____

_____

_____

_____

_____

_____

_____

_____

- **Life Response**
  Ephesians 4:2; 1 Peter 3:15,16

_____

_____

_____

God's Glory

- **Reflection**
  Exodus 33:18-34:7; Psalm 19:1-6; Isaiah 6:1-8; Revelation 4:9-11; Revelation 21:22-27

  _____

  _____

  _____

  _____

  _____

  _____

  _____

  _____

- **Life Response**
  Psalm 96:1-13; 1 Corinthians 10:31

  _____

  _____

  _____

God's Goodness

- **Reflection**
  Psalm 25:8; Psalm 34:8; Psalm 86:5; Nahum 1:7; Acts 10:38

  _____

  _____

  _____

  _____

  _____

  _____

  _____

  _____

- **Life Response**
  Psalm 37:3,4; 1 Peter 2:1-3, 11-12

  _____

  _____

  _____

God's Grace

- **Reflection**
  John 1:14-17; Romans 3:23,24; Ephesians 2:5-10; Titus 2:11-14; James 4:6

_____

_____

_____

_____

_____

_____

_____

- **Life Response**
  2 Corinthians 12:7-10; Hebrews 4-14-16

_____

_____

_____

God's Greatness

- **Reflection**
  Deuteronomy 3:24; 10:17-22; 1 Chronicles 29:10-13; Psalm 145:3 1 John 3:19,20

_____

_____

_____

_____

_____

- **Life Response**
  Psalm 150; Matthew 20:25-28

_____

_____

_____

Head of the Church

- **Reflection**
  Ephesians 1:22,23; Ephesians 4:15,16; Ephesians 5:23; Colossians 1:17-20; Colossians 2:19

  _____

  _____

  _____

  _____

  _____

  _____

  _____

- **Life Response**
  Romans 12:4–8; 1 Corinthians 12:12-27

  _____

  _____

  _____

Healer

- **Reflection**
  Exodus 15:26; Psalm 147:3; Isaiah 53:4,5; Matthew 8:1-3; Mark 10:46-52

  _____

  _____

  _____

  _____

  _____

  _____

  _____

- **Life Response**
  2 Chronicles 7:14; Mark 16:15-18

  _____

  _____

REFLECTIONS ON THE CHARACTER OF GOD

God's Holiness

- **Reflection**
  Exodus 15:11; Psalm 99:1-9; Isaiah 6:1-8; Revelation 4:8; Revelation 15:3,4

- **Life Response**
  Hebrews 12:14; 1 Peter 1:15

God's Humility

- **Reflection**
  Matthew 11:28-30; Luke 2:6,7; John 13:3-15; 2 Corinthians 8:9; Philippians 2:5-11

- **Life Response**
  Philippians 2:3; James 4:10

Intercessor

- **Reflection**
  Isaiah 53:12; John 17:1-26; Romans 8:26,27; Romans 8:34; Hebrews 7:25

_____

_____

_____

_____

_____

_____

_____

- **Life Response**
  Ezekiel 22:30; 1 Timothy 2:1-4

_____

_____

_____

God's Jealousy

- **Reflection**
  Exodus 20:4-6; Exodus 34:14; Deuteronomy 4:23,24; Deuteronomy 32:21; Zechariah 8:1-5

_____

_____

_____

_____

_____

_____

_____

- **Life Response**
  2 Corinthians 11:1-3; Galatians 5:19-21

_____

_____

_____

God's Joy

- **Reflection**
  Zephaniah 3:17; Luke 10:21; Luke 15:3-7; Romans 14:17; Hebrews 12:2

- **Life Response**
  Matthew 5:11,12; Philippians 4:4

Judge

- **Reflection**
  Psalm 58:11; Psalm 96:13; Matthew 16:27; Matthew 25:31-46; Revelation 20:11-15

- **Life Response**
  2 Corinthians 5:9,10; 1 Peter 1:17

God's Justice

- **Reflection**
  Psalm 103:6; Isaiah 61:8; John 5:28-30; 1 John 1:9; Revelation 15:1-4

  _____

  _____

  _____

  _____

  _____

  _____

  _____

  _____

- **Life Response**
  Psalm 106:3; Micah 6:8

  _____

  _____

  _____

God's Kindness

- **Reflection**
  Psalm 18:50; Jeremiah 9:24; Luke 6:32-36; Romans 2:1-4; Ephesians 2:6,7

  _____

  _____

  _____

  _____

  _____

  _____

  _____

  _____

- **Life Response**
  Ephesians 4:32; 1 Thessalonians 5:15

  _____

  _____

  _____

King

- **Reflection**
  Psalm 24:7-10; 1 Timothy 1:17; 1 Timothy 6:11-16; Revelation 17:14; Revelation 19:11-16

- **Life Response**
  Matthew 25:34-40; Revelation 15:1-4

Lamb of God

- **Reflection**
  Exodus 12:21-30; Isaiah 53:4-12; John 1:29-42; 1 Corinthians 5:7; Revelation 5:6-14

- **Life Response**
  Revelation 12:7-12; Revelation 21:22-22:5

Light

- **Reflection**
  Psalm 27:1; Psalm 104:1-3; John 1:1-13; John 8:12; 1 John 1:5-7

_____

_____

_____

_____

_____

_____

_____

_____

- **Life Response**
  Matthew 5:14-16; Ephesians 5:9-20

_____

_____

_____

Lord

- **Reflection**
  Deut. 10:12-22; Acts 2:36-39; 1 Corinthians 8:4-6; Philippians 2:6-11; Rev. 19:11-16

_____

_____

_____

_____

_____

_____

_____

_____

- **Life Response**
  Psalm 95:6-9; Psalm 100:1-5

_____

_____

_____

God's Love

- **Reflection**
  John 3:16; John 17:20-23; Romans 5:8; Romans 8:35-39; 1 John 3:1

_____

_____

_____

_____

_____

_____

_____

- **Life Response**
  Mark 12:28-31; 1 Corinthians 13:1-8

_____

_____

_____

God's Mercy

- **Reflection**
  Lamentations 3:22,23; Micah 6:8, 7:18-20; Ephesians 2:1-5; Titus 3:3-7; James 2:12,13

_____

_____

_____

_____

_____

_____

_____

- **Life Response**
  Matthew 5:7; Luke 6:27-36

_____

_____

_____

Messiah (Christ)

- **Reflection**
  Matthew 16:13-20; 26:62-64; John 4:13-26; Acts 2:29-41; 5:42, 9:22, 18:28, 26:19-23

_____

_____

_____

_____

_____

_____

_____

- **Life Response**
  2 Corinthians 5:17–21; 1 John 5:1

_____

_____

_____

God's Patience

- **Reflection**
  Nehemiah 9:28-31; Romans 2:3,4; 1 Timothy 1:15-17; 1 Peter 3:18-22; 2 Peter 3:8,9

_____

_____

_____

_____

_____

_____

- **Life Response**
  Psalm 40:1-3; 1 Thessalonians 5:14

_____

_____

_____

God's Power ●

- **Reflection**
  2 Chronicles 25:7,8; Psalm 147:1-6; Mark 4:35-41; Mark 5:21-43; Romans 1:16,17

- **Life Response**
  Luke 10:19; Acts 1:8

God's Presence ●

- **Reflection**
  Genesis 28:10-17; Exodus 33:12-23; Psalm 139:1-18; Psalm 145:17-20; Isaiah 43:1-7

- **Life Response**
  Matthew 18:19,20; Matthew 28:18-20

Prince of Peace

- **Reflection**
  Isaiah 9:6,7; John 14:25-27; Ephesians 2:14-22; Philippians 4:4-7; Colossians 1:15-20

_____

_____

_____

_____

_____

_____

_____

_____

- **Life Response**
  Romans 12:17-21; Colossians 3:15-17

_____

_____

_____

Protector

- **Reflection**
  Exodus 14:5-31; 2 Kings 6:8-23; Psalm 34:7; Psalm 91:1-16; Psalm 125:1,2

_____

_____

_____

_____

_____

_____

_____

_____

- **Life Response**
  John 17:6-19; 2 Thessalonians 3:1-3

_____

_____

_____

Provider

- **Reflection**
  Genesis 22:1-14; Psalm 37:25,26; Malachi 3:6-12; Matthew 14:13-21; Philippians 4:19

_____

_____

_____

_____

_____

_____

_____

_____

- **Life Response**
  Matthew 10:5-10; John 14:1-3

_____

_____

_____

Redeemer

- **Reflection**
  Job 19:25; Galatians 3:10-14; Colossians 1:9-14; 1 Peter 1:18-21; Revelation 5:9,10

_____

_____

_____

_____

_____

_____

_____

- **Life Response**
  Psalm 34:22; Hebrews 9:11-15

_____

_____

_____

Resurrection

- **Reflection**
  Luke 24:1-49; John 11:17-44; Acts 2:22-24; Romans 4:18-25; 1 Corinthians 15:1-8

_____

_____

_____

_____

_____

_____

_____

- **Life Response**
  John 6:35-40; 1 Corinthians 15:50-58

_____

_____

_____

God's Righteousness

- **Reflection**
  Psalm 71:19; Psalm 89:14; Psalm 145:17; Jeremiah 23:5,6; Romans 3:21-24

_____

_____

_____

_____

_____

_____

_____

- **Life Response**
  1 Timothy 6:11; 2 Timothy 4:6-8

_____

_____

_____

The Rock

- **Reflection**
  Genesis 49:22-25; Deuteronomy 32:3,4; Psalm 18:1-3; Psalm 19:14; Isaiah 26:3,4

_____

_____

_____

_____

_____

_____

_____

- **Life Response**
  Matthew 7:24-27; Matthew 16:13-19

_____

_____

_____

Savior

- **Reflection**
  Matthew 1:18-21; John 3:16,17; 1 Timothy 4:9,10; Titus 3:4-7; 1 John 4:13-16

_____

_____

_____

_____

_____

_____

- **Life Response**
  Acts 2:21; 1 Timothy 2:1-6

_____

_____

_____

Servant

- **Reflection**
  Matthew 20:20-28; Luke 22:24-27; John 13:1-5; 2 Corinthians 6:3–10; Philippians 2:5-11

  _____

  _____

  _____

  _____

  _____

  _____

  _____

- **Life Response**
  John 13:12-17; Ephesians 6:5-8

  _____

  _____

  _____

Shepherd

- **Reflection**
  Psalm 23:1-6; Isaiah 40:11; John 10:11-15; Hebrews 13:20,21; 1 Peter 2:25

  _____

  _____

  _____

  _____

  _____

  _____

  _____

- **Life Response**
  John 10:3-5, 27; 1 Peter 5:2-4

  _____

  _____

  _____

God's Sovereignty

- **Reflection**
  Job 9:10-12; Psalm 135:5-7; Isaiah 40:10-26; Daniel 4:35; Romans 9:19-21

  _____

  _____

  _____

  _____

  _____

  _____

  _____

  _____

- **Life Response**
  Deuteronomy 4:39,40; Matthew 19:26

  _____

  _____

  _____

The Truth

- **Reflection**
  John 1:14; John 14:6; John 14: 16,17; John 18:37; Hebrews 6:18

  _____

  _____

  _____

  _____

  _____

  _____

  _____

  _____

- **Life Response**
  John 8:31,32; 16:13; Ephesians 4:15

  _____

  _____

  _____

God's Unchangeableness

- **Reflection**
  Psalm 33:6-11; Psalm 102:27; Malachi 3:6; Hebrews 13:8; James 1:17

  _____

  _____

  _____

  _____

  _____

  _____

  _____

  _____

- **Life Response**
  1 Corinthians 15:58; James 1:6,7

  _____

  _____

  _____

God's Unsearchableness

- **Reflection**
  Job 5:8-16; Job 11:7-9; Ecclesiastes 3:11; Isaiah 40:12-31; 1 Corinthians 2:9-16

  _____

  _____

  _____

  _____

  _____

  _____

  _____

- **Life Response**
  Psalm 139:23,23; Jeremiah 29:11-13

  _____

  _____

  _____

The Victor

- **Reflection**
  John 16:33; 1 Corinthians 15:53-58; Colossians 2:13-15; Revelation 19:11-21; 20:1-15

_____

_____

_____

_____

_____

_____

_____

- **Life Response**
  Romans 8:37; Revelation 2:7, 2:11, 2:17, 2:26-28, 3:5, 3:12, 3:21

_____

_____

_____

God's Wisdom

- **Reflection**
  Psalm 104:24; Daniel 2:20-23; Romans 11:33-36; 1 Corinthians 1:18-25; Colossians 2:2,3

_____

_____

_____

_____

_____

_____

_____

- **Life Response**
  Proverbs 9:10; James 1:5

_____

_____

_____

Other Names, Titles, and Attributes of God

Here is a list of more aspects of God's character that can be discovered and reflected upon from the Scriptures. Always remember that the primary way that God reveals Himself to us is through His Names, Titles and Attributes. Seek out God's character as you read through the Bible. A Concordance will serve as an aid to you as you attempt to study and reflect on these aspects of God's character. Record your reflections and life responses for future referencing.

Adopter
Advocate
Alpha and Omega (First & Last)
Amen
Ancient of Days
Anointed One
Apostle and High Priest
Architect and Builder
Arm of the Lord
Atonement
Author of Life
Author and Perfecter of our Faith
Avenger
Awesome

Banner
Beauty of the Lord
Beloved Son
Blotter Out of Sin
Branch
Bread of Life
Bridegroom

Care
Chief Cornerstone
Commander of the Lord's Army
Conqueror
Consolation of Israel
Consuming Fire
Counselor
Covenant Keeper

Defender of Widows
Dependable
Desired of Nations
Dwelling Place

Encourager
Eternal King
Everlasting God
Ever Present Help
Excellence

Faithful Witness
Father of Lights
Favor

Firstborn from among the dead
Fortress
Fragrant Offering

Gardener (Husbandman)
Gate
God of gods
Great High Priest
Guarantee

Head
Hebrew Names of God – see Knowing God Chapter
Heir of all things
Helper
Hiding Place
Holy One of Israel
Holy Spirit
Hope
Humor

I AM
Image of the Invisible God
Immanuel (God with us)
Impartiality
Indignation

Jesus
Justifier

Keeper
Kindness
King of the Ages
King of Glory
King of the Jews
King of Kings

Last Adam
Lawgiver
Life
Lawgiver
Leader
Light of the World
Living God
Living Stone
Lord of the Harvest

Lord of Lords
Lord Most High
Lord of the Sabbath

Majesty
Man of Sorrows
Master
Mediator
Meekness
Mighty God
Miraculous
Morning Star
Most High

Nearness

Omnipotence (all-powerful)
Omnipresence (all-present)
Omniscience (all-knowing)
One to be Feared

Passover
Peace
Perfect
Perfect Man
Personal
Physician
Potter
Precious
Promises
Prophet
Providence
Pure
Purifier

Ransom for all Men
Reconciler
Refiner
Refuge
Rejected (by man)
Reproover
Reward
Rewarder
Righteous Judge
Riser of the Dead
Rising Sun
Rock of Ages
Ruler of Creation
Ruler of the Kings of the Earth

Salvation
Sanctifier
Sanctuary
Satisfier

Searcher of Hearts
Shade
Shelter
Shield
Shiloh
Silence
Son of David
Son of God
Son of Man
Song
Source
Spirit
Splendid
Spring of Living Water
Stone the builders rejected
Strength
Stronghold in Trouble
Sudden
Suffering
Sufficiency
Support
Supreme
Sure Foundation

Teacher
Tenderness
Tester
Transcendent
Trinity
True Light
True Vine
Trustworthy
Truth

Unfailing
Understanding
Unseen
Upright

Vengeance
Very Great Reward
Voice of the Lord
Vulnerability

Way
Ways of God
Will of God
Word of God
Works of God
Worthy of Praise
Wrath of God

Zealous

Akempis, Thomas. *Imitation of Christ*. Nashville: Thomas Nelson Publishers, 1999.

Anderson, Leith. *A Church for the 21st Century*. Minneapolis: Bethany House Publishers, 1992.

Augustine. *Confessions*. Nashville: Thomas Nelson Publishers, 1999.

Bartleman, Frank. *Azuza Street*. Logos International, 1980.

Bennett, William J. *The Broken Hearth*. Doubleday, 2001.

Bickle, Mike, with Michael Sullivant. *Growing in the Prophetic*. Eastbourne: Kingsway Publications, 1995.

Bilheimer, Paul. *Destined for the Throne*. Minneapolis: Bethany House Publishers, 1975.

Blackaby, Henry T., Claude V. King. *Experiencing God*. Nashville: LifeWay Press, 1990.

Bright, Bill. *The Coming Revival*. New Life Publishers, 1995.

Bugbee, Bruce, Don Cousins, Bill Hybels. *Network: Participant's Guide*. Willow Creek Community Church, 1994.

Bunyon, John. *Pilgrim's Progress*. 1678, 1684. Penguin Group, 1965, 1986, 1987.

Campbell, Dr. Ross. *How to Really Love Your Child*. Victor, 1985.

Chambers, Oswald, Jim Reiman (editor). *My Utmost for His Highest*. Discovery House Publishers, 1992.

Clinton, Dr. J. Robert, Dr. Richard W. Clinton. *The Mentor's Handbook*. Barnabas Publishers, 1991.

Clinton, Dr. J. Robert, Dr. Richard W. Clinton. *Unlocking Your Giftedness*. Barnabas Publishers, 1993.

Cloud, Dr. Henry, and Dr. John Townsend. *Boundaries*. Grand Rapids: Zondervan Publishing House, 1992.

Cloud, Dr. Henry. *Changes That Heal*. Grand Rapids: Zondervan Publishing House, 1990, 1992.

Cook, Jerry, with Stanley C. Baldwin. *Love, Acceptance & Forgiveness*. Regal Books, 1979.

Cunningham, Loren, with Janice Rogers. *Is That Really You, God?*. YWAM Publishing, 2001.

Cunningham, Loren, with Janice Rogers. *Winning, God's Way*. Seattle: Frontline Communications, 1988.

Deere, Jack. *Surprised by the Power of the Spirit*. Grand Rapids: Zondervan Publishing House, 1993.

Dawson, John. *Healing America's Wounds*. Regal Books, 1994.

Dawson, John. *Taking Our Cities for God*. Creation House, 1989.

Dawson, Joy. *Intimate Friendship with God*. Grand Rapids: Chosen Books, 1986.

Eastman, Dick. *No Easy Road*. Grand Rapids: Baker Book House, 1971.

Edwards, Gene. *A Tale of Three Kings*. Christian Books, 1980.

Eldredge, John. *Wild at Heart*. Nashville: Thomas Nelson Publishers, 2001.

Elmore, Tim. *Mentoring*. EQUIP and Emerging Young Leaders, 1998.

Erwin, Gayle. *The Jesus Style*. Ronald N. Haynes Publishers, Inc., 1983.

Finney, Charles. *Revivals of Religion*. CBN University Press, 1978.

Foster, Richard J. *Celebration of Discipline*. Harper San Francisco, 1978, 1988.

Fry, Steve. *I AM: The Unveiling of God*. Multnomah Publishers, Inc., 2000.

Grant, George. *Bringing in the Sheaves*. American Vision, 1985.

Guinness, Os. *The Call*. Word Publishing, 1998.

Guyon, Madame. *Union With God*. Christian Books, 1981.

Hayford, Jack. *The Key to Everything*. Orlando: Creation House, 1993.

Hayford, Jack. *Worship His Majesty*. Word Publishing, 1987.

Hegre, T.A. *The Cross & Sanctification*. Minneapolis: Bethany Fellowship, Inc., 1960.

Keller, Phillip. *A Shepherd Looks at Psalm 23*. Grand Rapids: Daybreak Books, 1970.

Lawrence, Brother. *The Practice of the Presence of God*. Spire Books, 1958.

Lovelace, Richard F. *Dynamics of Spiritual Life*. Inter-Varsity Press, 1979.

MacDonald, Gordon. *Ordering Your Private World*. Thomas Nelson Publishers, 1984, 1985.

Marshall, Tom. *Right Relationships*. Sovereign World, 1989.

Mayhall, Jack and Carole. *Marriage Takes More Than Love*. NavPress, 1985.

McAlpine, Campbell. *Alone with God*. Minneapolis: Bethany Fellowship, Inc, 1981.

McAlpine, Campbell. *The Leadership of Jesus*. Sovereign World, 2002.

McClung, Floyd. *The Father Heart of God*. Harvest House Publishers, 1985.

McDowell, Josh. *Evidence That Demands A Verdict*. Campus Crusade for Christ, Inc., 1972.

Murray, Andrew. *Absolute Surrender*. Chicago: Moody Press, 1895.

Murray, Andrew. *Waiting on God*. Minneapolis: Bethany House Publishers, 1986.

Murray, Andrew. *With Christ in the School of Prayer*. Spire Books, 1953.

Nee, Watchman. *Spiritual Authority*. New York: Christian Fellowship Publishers, Inc., 1972.

Nee, Watchman. *The Release of the Spirit*. Sure Foundation Publishers, 1965.

Neighbor, Ralph. *Where Do We Go From Here?* Touch Publications, 1991.

Otis Jr., George. *God's Trademarks*. Chosen Books, 2000.

Packer, J.I. *Knowing God*. InterVarsity Press, 1973.

Pratney, Winkie. *A Handbook for Followers of Jesus*. Minneapolis: Bethany Fellowship, Inc., 1977.

Pratney, Winkie. *Revival – Its Principles & Personalities*. Huntington House Publishers, 1994.

Pratney, Winkie. *Youth Aflame*. Minneapolis: Bethany House Publishers, 1970, 1983.

Sanders, J. Oswald. *Spiritual Leadership*. Chicago: Moody Press, 1967, 1980, 1994.

Schaeffer, Francis. *How Should We Then Live: The Rise and Decline of Western Thought and Culture*. Fleming H. Revell Co., 1976.

Sherman, Dean. *Relationships Workbook*. Crown Ministries International, 1985.

Sherman, Dean, with Bill Payne. *Spiritual Warfare for Every Christian*. Seattle: Frontline Communications, 1990.

Silvoso, Ed. *That None Should Perish*. Regal Books, 1994.

Smalley, Gary, and John Trent. *The Gift of the Blessing*. Nashville: Thomas Nelson Publishers, 1993.

Smith, Ron, and Rob Penner. *Grace...Simply Grace*. JENSCO LTD, 1990.

Sproul, RC. *The Holiness of God*. Wheaton: Tyndale House Publishers, Inc., 1985.

Spurgeon, Charles. *All of Grace*. Chicago: Moody Press, 1984.

Stanley, Paul D. and J. Robert Clinton. *Connecting*. NavPress, 1992.

Synan, Vinson. *The Holiness-Pentecostal Tradition*. William B. Eerdmans Publishing Company, 1971, 1997.

Thompson, Dr. Bruce. *Walls of My Heart*. Crown Ministries International, 1989.

Wagner, C. Peter. *Churches That Pray*. Regal Books, 1993.

Wagner, C. Peter. *Prayer Shield*. Regal Books, 1992.

Williams, Dr. J. Rodman. *Renewal Theology*. Grand Rapids: Zondervan Publishing House, 1996.

Wimber, John, with Kevin Springer. *Power Evangelism*. San Francisco: Harper & Row Publishers, 1986.

Winter, Ralph D., Steven C. Hawthorne. *Perspectives on the World Christian Movement*. William Carey Library, 1981.

9/18/15 { Loving myself. } ✓

- My expectations for God would be for myself to form an actual relationship with the Lord. ✓ Jn 26: Baptized ⚹ Genesis 24 ⚹
(relationship with a young man possibly?) still working on it. - having Godmom me what to look for.
1
3

- Be able to hear what God is saying { how to differentiate between what He is saying as opposed to what I'm thinking. - still working on it.

- For myself to eventually shine as a light to others for God. ✓

- I don't want to be this "lukewarm" person

- I want to be all God all the time for the rest of my life. ✓

- forgiveness of my past mistakes. ✓

- what my life plan is.]

- I am so selfconscious when I speak outloud in group settings, I feel like I never make sense: big insecurity of mine. ✓